BAYREUTH
African Studies Series

Publisher/Editor

Pia Thielmann & Eckhard Breitinger
Bayreuth University
D 95440 BAYREUTH
Germany / R.F.A.
www.breitinger.org

A catalogue record for this book is available from the British Library.

Bibliographic information published by Die Deutsche Bibliothek

Die Deutschen Bibliothek lists this publication in the Deutsche
Nationalbibliografie; detailed bibliographic data is available in the
Internet at http://dnb.ddb.de

Price per copy: EUR 24.95 (plus postage)

ISBN 3-927510-81-5
ISSN 0178-0034

Printed by Rosch Buch, D 96110 Scheßlitz

John Placid Wotsuna Khamalwa

IDENTITY, POWER, AND CULTURE: *IMBALU* INITIATION RITUAL AMONG THE BAMASABA OF UGANDA

Bayreuth African Studies 68

D 703

Dedicated to the memories of my grandmothers, Anna Nabafu and Miliya, my first teachers, who taught me love, and the power of culture. And to my father Athanasius Waburoko, who taught me the meaning of life.

CONTENTS

CHAPTER FOUR: MASABA *IMBALU* – A DESCRIPTION

CHAPTER FIVE: MASABA *IMBALU* – AN INTERPRETATION

CHAPTER SIX: THE QUESTION OF CHANGE

ACKNOWLEDGEMENTS

This work is a result of the interfacing co-operation of the seen and the unseen. I am indebted to the Katholischer Akademischer Ausländer Dienst for the scholarship that enabled me to undertake this study. Special tribute to Dr. Thomas Scheidtweiler and Frau Simone Saure of KAAD, Bonn, for their faith, understanding and encouragement.

I am immensely grateful to my gurus, Profs Ulrich Berner, Thomas Bargatzky, Christoph Bochinger, J.C. Winter, and Till Foerster of Bayreuth University, for their friendship and patient guidance that finally led to the completion of this work. Prof Ogbu Kalu of McCormick University, USA, deserves special thanks for inspiration, friendship, and foresight. Profs Manfred Büttner of Bochum University, and Reinhard Henkel of Heidelberg, thanks for your support. To Profs Suzette Heald and Jean La Fontaine, thanks for pioneering research on the Bamasaba.

To my teachers of the heretofore, Profs Victor Zinkuratire, Laurenti Magesa, Jude Ongong'a, Dismas Masolo, and David Kyeyune, thank you all for being my mentors and friends.

To my friends and colleagues in Bayreuth: Frau Brigitte Menchen and Dr Catherine Agoya, thanks for friendship and selfless assistance; Prof Babila Mutia, Dr Oliver Freiberger, Dr Afe Adogame, Dr Tirop Simatei, Mr Ukah Asonzeh, Mr C.J. Odhiambo, and Mr Tiku Takem, thank you for your friendship.

To Wakoli, Malemo, Walukhaso, Namunyala, Tumwa, Lubango, Mangata, Nelima, Nakhabala, Kharono, Masinde, and Kilande, thank you for your support. Mzee Haajje Gaashegu, Mzee Lawrence Tsemale, Mzee Leo Wawomola, Ludwig Wamono, yaya Augustine Wandende, and yaya Namonywe, thank you for your selfless support and love.

My dear children Karl Mabuka, and Annette Muyama, you deserve special gratitude for your love, sacrifice and understanding when I could not be with you for long periods. Yes, for seeing you only in a new year, a new century, a new millennium.

My special thanks to the best of friends, Dr Catherine Nanjala Agoya, for proof-reading the manuscript several times, and for invaluable support all the way.

CHAPTER ONE: GENERAL INTRODUCTION

The Bamasaba, also known as the Gisu, live on the slopes of Mount Elgon (Mount Masaba) in Eastern Uganda. They circumcise their young males in an elaborate ritual known as *imbalu,* which lasts a whole year. This is a cultural form, which controls the doorway into the community. Its broad range of rich symbolism has a depth of psychological impact on the entire culture, and it is impossible for one to be a full member of the community without undergoing the ritual.

It is as if it occupies the centre of the people's collective life upon which other "superstructures" are built. It weaves the social organisation into a political entity; it defines membership; it serves as a means of sex differentiation and gender construct; and connects maleness and the cult of strength to the defence of land.

The resilience or perseverance of *imbalu* has attracted attention. The depth of loyalty, which the initiation season elicited, stunned a church minister posted to a congregation in one of the Bamasaba communities. He also marvelled at the pensile strength and hold of the ritual on the people, in spite of years of contact with Christianity, modernity, and other change agents.[1]

This raises the problem of the resilience of certain cultural forms in African communities. Why does Christianity fail to eradicate them, and why do education and the insurgence of Western culture all bow at their ritual altars?

The effort here is from an insider's observation aimed at providing fuller data on *imbalu* than already exists with works of non-insiders, yet building on their accumulated knowledge. Three modern ethnographical and anthropological works exist on *imbalu*. Each of the authors had a specific interpretative goal and sought data for an articulated end. It could be possible that new interpretation would emerge from the fuller description and interpretation attempted here, and some old ones discarded.

While the core of the problem is to portray *imbalu* in its full panoply, the backdrop or context is also important. The ecology and economy depict a

---

[1] L. Walakira, "Circumcision Ceremony Among the Bagisu", in *The Second National Theological Week* (August 1983), p. 165.

community in a remote location, with fertile volcanic soils, a cash economy and sufficient food security. Such communities tend to be culturally conservative, bound to land and the ancestors, and endowed with a sense of self-worth and communal pride. *Imbalu* supplies a signifier of these characteristics embedded in the concept of manhood and socially differentiates one from boys. Other gender ideologies follow closely.

1.1.1. What Imbalu Is

Various commentators have attempted to answer this question through the years: missionaries, colonial government officials, anthropologists, and novelists. Their efforts will be reviewed to indicate that none has described the full range of the ritual process, which starts with a dance and ends with a dance in seven phases.

The first goal of this study is to provide a detailed and full description of the structure or ritual process in *imbalu*. Beneath the structure lies meaning, or what is going on underneath the events.

The second goal would be to explain its meaning by exploring the people's perception of the symbols and by applying certain conceptual themes as culture and communalism, identity, power and authority. Theorists of ritual provide other psychological explanations on the depth of meaning behind social and religious rituals.

A third goal recognises that change has, nonetheless, had much impact on this cultural form. A number of theoretical problems follow about the meaning and nature of change. There are different types of change recognised by their character, nature, direction, pace or consequences. Thus, social change differs from cultural change. From such a theoretical framework, it becomes possible to show which aspects of *imbalu* structure may have suffered change and to what extent. As the new generations negotiate with the "guardians of the gourd", changes invade the inner core of its meaning. Such could be traced from the same conceptual scheme applied earlier, as this makes for consistency. It will become possible to show how the symbolism has been modified, and indeed how the issue of identity, community and power have adjusted to "the wind of change".

Explanations of change always run into the complex web of change agents and multivariable causality. Thus it would become necessary to identify the effective change-agents and their relative contributions. This is done in

14

chapter six of this work. Among the religious change-agents, Christianity takes the pride of place since Islam is relatively weak in the context. Christianity, through education, became the instrument through which colonialism inserted modernisation into the Uganda context.

The colonial factor, with its basket of ambiguities, must be carefully assessed.

The role of independent states and their cultural policies explain some of the changes, which have affected *imbalu*. They also explain the resilience, which is the fourth goal of the study.

1.1.2. Significance of Imbalu

Beyond the structure, the meaning of *imbalu* is best captured through themes, which have been articulated in ritual theories. The study will use the conceptual schemes of culture, identity, power and symbolisation to probe the meaning of *imbalu*, and why it possesses such magnetic hold on the people.

In the literature surveyed, the works of Victor Turner and Mircea Eliade stand out. Turner's study of symbolisation has the added importance of a broad comparative perspective between two Bantu speaking communities but with different geographical settings. Its application to *imbalu* has been enlarged.

Mircea Eliade's concentration on sacred agents, their inner experiences and the authenticity of their actions has been criticised by scholars who would rather avoid the uncharted mesh of experience in scientific discourse. They would rather focus on religious expression, on the manifestations at the terrestrial level and from there evaluate the ethics of power play in ritual contexts. Who wins and who loses? Is it the elders who load their authority on the young or is it the initiates who share in that ancestral power? What rational choices do people make in their participation in the rituals? For whom is the resilience of this cultural initiation important? What socio-political and economic roles do the initiation ceremonies play?

The problem arises when it is advocated that the terrestrial, the social function of a religious form should be the focus of the scientific study of religion.[2] It is argued that faith distorts the phenomenon and its interpretation. Therefore, the religious experience or pursuit of the inner layer of the sacred is rejected. Critics of Mircea Eliade aver that he focussed on religious experience and aimed at the transcendent while muting the questions raised in forms of religious practice, context and process.[3] For instance, in every ritual there are winners and losers. In every ritual, some gain legitimacy, wealth, status and power, while others are ritual fodder. Thus, political and class wars are couched in religious rituals. To focus on what priestly agents experience and do may blur the wide range of social analysis.

Both have valid contributions. The effort here skirts between the two warring camps, which dominate the study of religious phenomena. A combination of both an understanding of religious experience and religious expression offers a fuller understanding of *imbalu*. It enables us look at it from inside and from outside; from near and from a distance. To ignore either diminishes the fullness and the rich texture of this complex ritual.

This brings us back to the question of change since cultures are not static. Cultures continually mutate. The key questions of change are the nature, pace, direction and consequences of change. Equally crucial are the change agents. Beyond religious change agents, the modern African state has influenced the survival of cultural forms. It approaches the question from nationalist perspectives. In fact, the colonial government's quest for order produced a culture policy disengaged from that of the missionaries who tended to view it negatively. The former supported existing cultural forms to assist the colonialists in their indirect rule.

Imbalu's structure and its religious depth are important in understanding its socio-political roles, as well as its embeddedness in the mental matrix of the community. When a man is inebriated, he begins to sing circumcision songs, something he would never do when sober. When he has to swear, he swears by his circumcision. *Imbalu* defines both person-hood and community; it is rooted in the land, both as place and as territory, and it

---

2 See especially Bruce Lincoln, "Theses on Method", in *Method and Theory in the Study of Religion* 8-3 (1996), pp. 225-227.

3 See for instance Cristiano Grottanelli and Bruce Lincoln, "A Brief Note on (Future) Research in the History of Religions", in *Method and Theory in the Study of Religion*, 10 (1998), pp. 311-325.

embodies the full profile of the people. Thus, in spite of changes, it has endured and continues to evoke much loyalty. The goal of the study is to convey this through narrative and analysis.

1.1.3. Research Methodology

This study employed a combination of research methodologies. Fieldwork was carried out between August 1998 and November 1999. It concentrated in the Southern part of the district for the simple reason that the ritual of *imbalu* has survived better here due to less exposure to urbanisation. Group interviews were preferred during fieldwork, as these help the interviewees correct one another on certain details. Personal interviews were employed so as to delve into and decipher the meaning and symbolism behind the actions and gestures.

Orientation of the fieldwork was guided by several essential factors including:

- informants who would provide social and historical background to the Bamasaba in general, and to *imbalu* in particular,
- former initiates of circumcision,
- ritual elders,
- circumcisers,
- mothers of initiates.

Some of the respondents did not have much of significance to offer, while others were particularly well informed on many aspects of *imbalu*.

This work consists of seven chapters, the first of which states the problem, and sets out the goals of the study. It also presents a profile of the Masaba people who practise this ritual as their mode of cultural initiation. The second chapter reviews existing literature on the subject of *imbalu*, while the third surveys theories on ritual in general, and initiation ritual in particular, respectively. The fourth chapter describes in detail the ritual as practised by the Bamasaba. The fifth one interprets the data laid out in the description, in view of the theories surveyed in chapter three. It does this by developing the themes of community and culture, identity, power and symbols. By employing the same themes analysed in chapter five, the sixth chapter discusses the question of change in the ritual. It analyses how the change agents, namely colonialism, Christianity, education, modernity and the post-independence state, have affected its individual phases. In view of the fuller description and interpretation, the seventh chapter, which is the general conclusion of the work, briefly reviews earlier interpretations by other authors. It also endeavours to explain the factors under-girding the resilience of *imbalu* in the face of the change agents discussed in chapter six.

Besides fieldwork and personal experience of the rituals, the author carried out library research for a year at the University of Bayreuth. Works on the Bamasaba, on ritual in general, and initiation rituals in particular were studied in depth.

1.2. THE BAMASABA OF UGANDA

1.2.1. Introduction

This chapter sets out to introduce the community of the people who practise *imbalu* as a mode of initiation. A brief profile of the context is certainly germane and may provide the data for connecting particular initiation traditions with ecological and social organisation. The chapter will describe their geographical location, traditions of origin, social and political structure, as well as their religious beliefs.

1.2.2. Geographical Location

Bamasaba literally means the children of Masaba who was their great ancestor after whom the imposing mountain was named. They are a Bantu-speaking community inhabiting the fertile slopes of Mount Elgon (Mount Masaba) in Eastern Uganda, and speak a Bantu language known as *Lumasaba*. The district borders with Kenya on the East, with the district of Tororo to the South, Kumi to the West, Karamoja to the Northwest and Kapchorwa to the North.

Masabaland is very densely populated, numbering 556,900 people according to the National Population Census of 1980. This puts the period average density at 233 people per square kilometre.[4] There are virtually

---

4 H. B. Kabera, *The Population of Uganda by Districts*. Kampala: Department of Geography, Makerere University Press, 1983.

two distinct climatic zones: the higher and wetter slopes of Mount Elgon's foothills and the lower, drier and comparatively less fertile plains at the foot of the mountain. The higher region ranges from 4,000 to 8,000 feet above sealevel, and the upper limit of settlement is the forest line demarcated by the Uganda Government. The lower region comprises the areas below 4,000 feet, which border the drier plains of Tororo stretching westward to the swamps of Pallisa district.

The people are mainly agriculturists though they also keep domestic animals like cattle, goats, sheep and fowls. They practise sedentary agriculture, growing Arabica coffee, which favours the fertile loam soils of the area, as their main cash crop. Cotton, another cash crop, is grown on the lower slopes and the plains. Other crops include tobacco, maize, millet, sorghum, beans, peas, simsim, groundnuts, cassava, sweet potatoes and the staple bananas (*kamatore*), which make the entire countryside look exotically lush green.

The soil is mainly light volcanic loam, which retains its fertility well and is not subject to serious erosion. There are two rainy seasons, the main one from about the middle of March till mid-June and the short spell from September till the end of October. The people practise inter-cropping and there are usually two harvests of maize and beans, while millet has but one harvest around July and August. Cash crops, rich soils, and high level of food security combine to create a society, which is sedentary and attached to traditions. Its remote location protected it from early contact with European change agents, and the sense of pride and sufficiency kept it intact under the onslaught of colonialism. Yet it has not been completely impervious to the phenomenon of change in the long run. On the whole, there is a connection between the ecology, economy, and cultural conservation.

1.2.3. Masaba Myth of Origin

Bamasaba believe that their ancestral parents, *Mundu* and his wife *Seera*, emerged from the great crater on the top of Mount Elgon.[5] These ancestral

---

[5] This is a mythical narrative that has been passed down by word of mouth, and was narrated to the author by Leo Wawomola and Ludwig Wamono on the 6th of November 1999 in Butiru village. Lawrence Tsemale interviewed by the author on 8th November in Bunamboko village confirmed it.

parents had two sons, **Kundu** and **Masaba**, the former was a herdsman while the latter was a hunter. One day while herding his cows, **Kundu** reached the edge of the mountain and saw the vast expanse of country before him, extending as far as he could see. The scenery was too tempting for him to resist, and he consequently decided to venture south, never to come back. The **Basoga** and the **Baganda** who live south of **Masabaland** refer to him as **Kintu** and claim him as their ancestor.

Masaba, on his part, remained with the parents. One day, while going about his hunting, he came across a ravishingly beautiful girl of the **Barwa** tribe *(Elgonyi Maasai)* in the forest. She is referred to as **Nabarwa** in honour of her **Barwa** tribe. He proposed marriage to her but she turned him down because he was as yet uncircumcised! She told him she would only marry him on condition that he agreed to go with her to her people and get circumcised first. Because of his love for her, he agreed to go with her to her people where he was circumcised. Later, he came back with his wife to his father's home, and they had three sons, **Mwambu, Mubuuya** and **Wanale**, and their sister **Nakuti**. Circumcision is therefore traced back to **Masaba**, the remaining son of **Mundu**, and the one after whom the community is named.

Mwambu, the eldest son of Masaba is believed to be the forefather of the clans living in the northern part of the district, Wanale, the forefather of the clans found in the Central parts, and Mubuuya of the Southern clans. Legend has it that one day while Mwambu was herding his father's cattle, the dreaded Elgonyi Maasai attacked and raided them. Mwambu is said to have raised an alarm for help, but while others were rushing to his aid, he single-handedly pursued the raiders and caught up with them. Being warriors themselves, they marvelled at his bravery and surrendered all his cattle to him. They also gave him a bull, known in the Maasai language as *ingisu* as a token of their respect for his bravery. By the time his kinsmen mobilised to pursue the Maasai, they met him coming back driving, not only his father's cows, but an additional bull. When he recounted the episode, his father gave him the nickname **Mugisu** in reference to the Maasai *ingisu*, a name by which he became known.

Though his in-laws circumcised Masaba, it would appear that the practice of circumcision did not catch on until some time later when a man named Fuuya from the Bumutoto clan married a Maasai wife. It is said that their male children were sickly. One day Fuuya's brother-in-law called Aramunyenye came to visit and found his nephews on the brink of death. He informed Fuuya that the spirit of circumcision afflicted the boys. He advised that he should be allowed to circumcise them, after which their illness would cease. With their father's permission Aramunyenye circumcised them. He nursed and fed them well till they were strong and robust young men. It was concluded that there was *kumusambwa kwembalu* (spirit of circumcision) among the Bamasaba. It was also believed that if somebody who had children died in the state of being uncircumcised, this *kumusambwa kwembalu* would afflict not only his offspring, but also his other kin. That is why it became necessary to circumcise all Bamasaba males, alive or dead. Provided one has children and is uncircumcised, he has to be circumcised before burial in order to avert punitive affliction by the spirits upon his kin.

Circumcision, therefore, became a norm with the early circumcisers coming from the Maasai community, as there were as yet no circumcisers among the Bamasaba. *Imbalu* gradually became perhaps the deepest and most pervasive religious tenet among the Bamasaba. In deference to Fuuya, the biennial ritual still begins in the clan of *Bumutoto*, and proceeds to other sub-counties of the district, strictly according to laid down order of seniority. Bumutoto is now claimed as a Masaba sacred site where the circumcision year is inaugurated. An army barracks currently occupies this sacred site, and talks are going on between the central government and the district elders for its reinstatement.

The district acquired the name Bugisu at the beginning of British administration, in the last century. It is said that when the Ganda Chief Semei Kakungulu, sent after the Buganda agreement of 1900 to pacify and administer the Eastern Province of the country, arrived in the district, he met people who spoke a Bantu language resembling his own Luganda. When he asked them who they were, they told him that they were sons of Mugisu their ancestor. He gave them the name Bagisu to differentiate them from their Nilotic neighbours. So though the name primarily referred to the inhabitants of the northern section of the district, it was later used to refer to the whole district. But the name by which the people prefer to be known is *Bamasaba*, children of Masaba, their common ancestor. The language is known as **Lumasaba**.[6] Wherever the Bamasaba find themselves, they call one another by the endearing appellation Masaba, and never Mugisu.

1.2.4. Masaba Traditional Religious Beliefs

To understand Masaba worldview in particular, recourse should be made to the traditional religious beliefs and practices prevalent before the advent of colonialism and Christianity. Though many Bamasaba have embraced foreign faiths such as Christianity and Islam, there are many who still adhere to their traditional religious beliefs. These beliefs and practices pervade the initiation rites and come to the fore during this particular season where the past is brought forward to inform the present.

To understand and try to decipher Masaba culture, one must begin with **imbalu**, as it is at the root of Masaba culture in general, and religion in particular. Cultural initiation is a forum for instructing the initiate and instilling into him cultural norms and values that go into forming the people's worldview.

Masaba traditional religious beliefs posit a hierarchy of divinities thus: **Wele** (Creator God), **ki-wele** (lesser divinities), **kimisimu** (the various spirit forces from which diviners and other religious specialists acquire their powers), and **basambwa** (ancestors). The Creator God *(Wele)*, is believed to reside above the sky. That is why he is referred to as **Wele Wemungaki**, which literally means the God of the Sky or the God who is above. This God is considered to be the creator of all people and all things, giving life and withdrawing it as he wills. He is variously known as **Umubumbi** (Creator or Potter), **Umunyali Byosi** (Able to do everything), **Uwebunyali** (the one who has the power), or **Uwesisa** (the kind one). **Wele** is believed to have a wife called **Nabulondera**, who is the protector of men's possessions against sorcerers and thieves.

Wele cannot be located in a specific place, therefore no shrine is ever built for him, nor are any sacrifices made to him directly. It is, however, believed that he is the ultimate recipient of all prayers and sacrifices made, as it were through the ancestors who are the intermediaries. There is a distinction between **Wele** who is understood as spirit *(imbewo)* and the

---

[6] Leo Wawomola and Ludwig Wamono interviewed by author on 6th November 1999 at Butiru village.

spirits of the dead, (*kimitsimu*). The *Bamasaba* also distinguish between God (*Wele*) and the lesser deities (*ki-wele*). In contra-distinction with *Wele* who is regarded as a benevolent creator and beneficent protector of men and their possessions, the prefix *ki* indicates that these lesser deities are regarded as malevolent actually or potentially, and are better avoided.

The lesser deities are of two kinds: those which are localised and so associated with particular localities like forests, rivers, rocks etc., and those which are not associated with any particular spots yet are believed to be around and about. Notable among the localised deities are *Wele Lufutu* (the rainbow deity) whose visible sign is the rainbow, and is who associated with waterfalls. This deity is believed to suck the blood of its victims, so children and pregnant women are forbidden from venturing near waterfalls, lest they suffer ill fate. Notable among the non-localised deities are *Mayina* and *Nakhalondo*. These two are the ones whom the diviners invoke.

In the event that a deity possesses somebody, sacrifices are offered to both the localised and the non-localised deities, the former at their local abode and the latter at the homestead of the sick person. Below these deities are the ancestral spirits, which are held in high esteem. To the *Bamasaba,* community is understood as comprising the dead ancestors, the living and the unborn. The ancestors are deemed to be the protectors of the living, and the intermediaries between the people and *Wele*.

As a result of the above, respect for ancestors borders on ancestor veneration. The least a person can do to acknowledge the ancestor is to name him or her. As the authors of all the cultural norms and customs including *imbalu*, they are invoked to be present, and to bless the rituals, which are performed at their behest. Shrines are erected in the homestead in honour of the ancestors who are believed to dwell among their offspring.

The ancestors for one reason or another usually interpret barrenness, impotence, madness and others as a result of displeasure. This necessitates consulting *umufumu* (diviner) who is believed to use power derived from an ancestral spirit of divination.

1.2.5. Social Heritage and Organisation

Masaba homesteads are normally scattered within their gardens, surrounded by bananas and coffee. These are grouped in clusters usually focused on a common lineage or clan known as *sikuka.* Before modernity changed habitat structures, a man, his wife or wives, and their unmarried children inhabited a homestead. If a man had more than one wife, each wife would have her own dwelling house, kitchen and fields and kept her own animals. These were hers and her children's to inherit, and the man would not unduly tamper with her estate.

Traditionally, boys and girls of about twelve years of age were not allowed to sleep in their parents' homesteads. Boys had their own common abode called *isimba,* but would move away to establish their own homes after circumcision. The adolescent girls of the same *sikuka* (clan) slept in *isimba* (common hut) under the care of an elderly woman who acted as chaperone.[7] She taught them public decorum and the duties women were expected to carry out as mothers and wives.

The girls would receive visits from young men in the *isimba,* but though sexual intimacy was permitted, full sexual intercourse was strictly forbidden and pre-marital pregnancy was prohibited. Virginity was a premium before marriage and earned the mother and paternal aunts the gift of a goat known as *imbusi iyabwana* from the husband.

Any girl who became pregnant before marriage was a disgrace to the family, and many fathers would chase the daughter away. In some drastic cases, the father of such a shameless girl would spear her to death. To avoid the fury of the father and brothers, such a girl would flee and seek refuge with a distant relative. She would be shunned by young men, and would only end up being married by some old man as an additional wife. Little was paid for such a girl in dowry, just like she was a divorcee or widow. The mother and aunts would not receive the prestigious *imbusi yabwana,* a goat given in appreciation for safeguarding the girl's virginity, as they would have failed in their responsibility. No mother or aunt would want to countenance that type of shame and consequently kept an eagle's eye on their daughters and nieces, to safeguard their virginity. The chaperones would regularly check the girls to see if they had protected themselves. Any man who deflowered a girl was supposed to marry her,

---

7 See J. B. Purvis, *Through Uganda to Mount Elgon.* London: T. Fisher Unwin, 1909, p. 278.

and the brothers would see to it, as sisters were expected to bring home the cows which their brothers would use to pay dowry for their wives.[8]

1.2.6. Traditional Political Organisation

Bamasaba never had a paramount leader but each *sikuka* (lineage) had its own chief called *umukasa*. Elderly men of the lineage concerned elected him on the third day after the burial of the previous head. This office was not hereditary, but a leader was chosen because of certain virtues exhibited by the candidate. These included wealth, sagacity, influence, and social connections. Indeed, "The basis of wealth among the Gisu was land, for which members of a descent group were in competition with one another".[9]

A segment of the lineage is called *inda*, which literally means belly or womb, and refers to the children of one married pair. If a man has more than one wife, one would refer to all the children of one wife as *inda*, but the children of the man from the different wives as *lulwanyi*, which literally means the courtyard of so and so. However, this appellation refers more properly to the sons since as a rule the girls get married and move off to their new clans. The word *lulwanyi* brings home the fact that a man's sons from the different wives always get circumcised on one courtyard. This is normally the courtyard of the eldest wife unless she happens to be barren. This is the man's official place where invocations, sacrifices, libations, and other significant events take place.

Bamasaba are a patrilineal community, and one refers to the children as belonging to the father. After several generations, the *inda* multiplies and becomes a whole lineage *(sikuka)*. In the matter of rites and leadership, the lineage segments are grouped in order of seniority according to the order of birth of their founders. The segment of the eldest son takes precedence in the rituals and supplies the *umukasa* (lineage head).

The *umukasa* wielded considerable power and influence, with each segment having its own leader known as *umukasa umukeekhe* (little

---

[8] Mrs Praxeda Namonywe Wandende interviewed by author on 29th June 1999 in Musiru village emphasised that the old woman chosen as chaperone was charged with the girls' social education. She would enlist the help of other old women known for their good behaviour to train them in bed manners, house management and responsible motherhood.

[9] J. S. La Fontaine, *Initiation*. Manchester: Manchester University Press, 1986, p. 144.

head). These were the first to hear cases and only if they failed to solve them were the cases referred to the *umukasa*. These little heads also acted as the council of elders to advise, but the ruling of the *umukasa* was final.

Currently there are twenty-seven maximal lineages and the rite of circumcision strictly follows the order given here below.

Incidentally, these maximal lineages have become administrative units called *gombolola* or sub-counties. These are:

1. Bungokho-Bumutoto, the sacred historical site of *imbalu*

2. Bungokho/Nambale

3. Wanaale

4. Busoba

5. Busiu

6. Bushiende/Busano

7. Bufumbo/Bukonde

8. Nakaloke

9. Buwagogo

10. Bugobero

11. Butiru

12. Bubutu

13. Bumbo/Bumooni

14. Buwabwala/Bupoto

15. Bududa

16. Bukigai

17. Bulucheke/Bubiita

18. Bukiga

19. Buwalasi/Bukhulo

20. Buyobo/Buteza

21. Busulani

22. Bumasifwa

23. Buhugu/Bukiise

24. Bulago/Simu/Buluganya

25. Buginyanya/Sisiyi/Masiira

26. Muyembe/Bukhalu

27. Bunambutye

CHAPTER TWO: LITERATURE REVIEW

2.1. THE CONTEXT

The study of *imbalu* demands that the context in which it appears should be identified because there are many boyhood initiation rites in Africa, and each tends to emphasise the expression of certain specific cultural norms and values.

In spite of similarities, each ritual system serves as a mark of identity and connects ritual to ecology. This point has adequately demonstrated by Victor Turner in his comparative study of Masaba *imbalu* on the one hand, and Ndembu *mukanda,* on the other.[10]

The first set of literature, therefore, consists of ethnographical materials on the Bamasaba, who are also variously referred to as Bagishu (Purvis 1909), Bagesu (Roscoe 1915), Gisu (La Fontaine 1959; Turner 1969, Heald 1989, 1999), and Bagisu (Walakira 1983). There are about eight published materials which attempt to describe and identify the area in which *imbalu* occurs.

The earliest study was by Church Missionary Society (CMS) missionaries who showed both fascination for the people, and curiosity to gather materials for propaganda and evangelisation. It was quite usual for missionaries at that point in history to report about the people among whom they worked. Pieces of such information would be used in house magazines to raise funds and boost morale. The exotic attracted and left the impression of achievement in far away and hitherto unknown lands. Missionary ethnographical accounts are often uneven, partly because of this motivating and controlling ideology, but they served much use even to Government officials who needed data on these different people for governance. These later commissioned their own anthropological studies to provide information on the "tribes, peoples, and superstitions" of those under colonial rule. In this case, the Government relied upon missionary accounts, especially since in many cases missionaries preceded

---

[10] Victor W. Turner, "Symbolization and Patterning in the Circumcision Rites of Two Bantu-speaking Societies", in Mary Douglas and Phyllis M. Kaberry (eds.), *Man in Africa.* London: Tavistock Publications, 1969, p. 231-237.

Government administration. This was the case with Masaba. Yet missionary accounts sometimes exhibited the prejudice and demonisation of indigenous cultures and religions.

The first ethnographical study of the Bamasaba appeared in 1909, written by J.B. Purvis, an English CMS missionary who arrived in Masaba in 1903.[11] He set out to describe his missionary journey through Buganda, which he calls Uganda, on his way to Masaba, which was to be his missionary station for several years. Out of the seventeen chapters of this book, five of them are specifically about his work among the Bamasaba, whom he describes as,

> A primitive, pastoral, Bantu-speaking people, they are known as Bamasaba or Bagishu, but distinguish themselves as a race apart from others by the name Basani, i.e. men, whilst all men of uncircumcised nations are called Basinde, i.e. boys.[12]

Although he describes *imbalu* only in passing, he certainly captures its central importance to the community when he observes that,

> There is an annual festival of circumcision, when all youths who wish to be recognised as full members of the clan, warriors, and men to be reckoned with, parade, dressed in war dress, and march from village to village to make public their brave decision. They are feted by young and old for days before the actual operation.[13]

His description of the Bamasaba is characterised by such words as "primitive simplicity"[14], "primitive tribes"[15], "native parade"[16], and "cannibals"[17]. The choice of photos points to the same frame of mind as they depict people who are extraordinarily backward.

He lived and worked among the Bamasaba before British administration came to the district through their proxy Chief Semei Kakungulu, who opened up the area under the Buganda Agreement of 1900. He gives a good account of Masaba before Colonialism, and indeed after. As the earliest

---

[11] J. B. Purvis, *Through Uganda to Mount Elgon*. London: T. Fisher Unwin, 1909, p. 294.

[12] Ibid., p. 271.

[13] Ibid. p. 271.

[14] Ibid. p. 21.

[15] Ibid. pp. 64; 271,

[16] Ibid. p. 298.

[17] Ibid. p. 294.

book on the Bamasaba, his contribution to ethnological studies in particular is quite substantial, as he gives us a picture of the community at that point in history.

The next ethnographical description was by John Roscoe, another English CMS missionary. He was stationed at Mengo near Kampala, from where he made visits to several districts, among them Bugisu, which he spells as Bugesu.[18] As he says in the preface to his book,

> Much of the information in this volume concerning the Bahima, the Bagesu, and the Bakene has already appeared in the form of papers contributed by me to the Journal of the Royal Anthropological Institute.[19]

The type of information and choice of photos in this book betray an exotic interest too. The aim of these early missionaries was to write about African communities with an exotic bent so as to attract more interest in their home readers. This helped to show their readers how arduous missionary work was![20]

His central interest in describing the different Bantu communities in Uganda was probably to show their differences with the Baganda, among whom he worked, and whom he described in his earlier volume.[21] The themes which form the refrain of his description of these 'tribes' include *inter alia* the country, their native customs and beliefs, the people, government, clans, totems, terms of relationships, marriage and birth, sickness and death, industries, warfare, hunting, and religious beliefs. Under the theme of religious beliefs, he describes initiation of boys among the "Bagesu", and goes on to claim that there was also circumcision of girls. This however is erroneous as there is no evidence of circumcision of girls among the Bamasaba, though it exists among their Sebei neighbours

---

[18] John Roscoe, *The Northern Bantu: An Account of Some Central African Tribes of the Uganda Protectorate.* London: Frank Cass and Company, 1915, p. v.

[19] Ibid. p. vii.

[20] Ibid. p. 159.

[21] See John Roscoe, *The Baganda, An Account of Their Native Customs and Beliefs.* London: Macmillan and Company, 1911.

to the north.[22] Jean la Fontaine (1959) also found this assertion by Roscoe erroneous.[23] But Roscoe himself admits that,

> I am well aware that the account, which I have given of these tribes, other than the Baganda, is fragmentary and incomplete: the short time which I could devote to the study in my vacations precluded the possibility of a thorough investigation. I feel that I have done little more than scratch the surface of a wide and fruitful field, which will yield an abundant harvest to those who may have the good fortune to cultivate it hereafter.[24]

His contribution to ethnology has been to offer us another early account of the Bantu communities he has written about.

2.2. *IMBALU*

Besides these amateur missionary accounts, trained anthropological reconstructions appeared only after the Second World War. A number of the anthropologists used the ethnographical context as a backdrop to interpret the ritual. Thus, their contributions on ethnography must be discussed within a review of the literature on *imbalu*.

The earliest of these anthropologists was Jean La Fontaine (1959) whose study of the Bamasaba has influenced many modern anthropologists and sociologists. She lived and worked among the Bamasaba from 1953 to 1955.[25] She worked so closely with the people that she was given the endearing Masaba name *Nambozo*. She was honoured further when in 1956 the circumcision season was named after her. In her work, she identified four phases of *imbalu*, namely *isonja* (group dance); *khuwentsa imbalu* (searching for *imbalu*), when individual initiates with their parties' dance and visit far away relatives; *khukhupaka* (thrashing of millet); and

---

[22] This point is most probably erroneous and may have come as a case of generalisation. Nowhere in the oral history of the Bamasaba has it been said that there was female initiation, though it is carried out among the neighbouring Sebei.

[23] J. S. La Fontaine, *The Gisu of Uganda*. London: International African Institute, 1959, p. 41.

[24] Roscoe, *Bantu Tribes*, pp. v-vi.

[25] Jean La Fontaine, "Witchcraft in Bugisu", in John Middleton and E. H. Winter (eds.): *Witchcraft and Sorcery in East Africa*. London: Routledge and Kegan Paul, 1978, p. 188.

khukoya (brewing of ceremonial beer), three days before the circumcision day.[26]

In her study she covered such themes as grouping and demography, economy, social organisation, religious beliefs and initiation. Her contribution has been substantial as the first comprehensive work on the Bamasaba, upon which others have depended in different degrees.

One of those influenced by La Fontaine's work was Victor Turner, who in his article acknowledges his indebtedness to La Fontaine thus,

> I have been fortunate enough to have been permitted by Dr. Jean La Fontaine ... to have access to her unpublished data on the Gisu ... With this excellent background, I was able in the field to focus maximum attention on the symbolic structure and semantics of the circumcision rites themselves.[27]

This does not mean that Victor Turner did not carry out fieldwork. He himself says, "I spent nearly two and a half years in the field among the Ndembu and only two and a half months among the Gisu..."[28] But it also goes to show that though an expert on the Ndembu people of Zambia and their circumcision ritual, he was no expert on Masaba *imbalu* as such. For his comparative study between Masaba *imbalu* and Ndembu *mukanda* and interpretation of the symbolic aspects of Masaba initiation, he was aided by La Fontaine's data where she had delineated four phases. Turner's goal was to compare symbolisation and patterning between the Bamasaba and the Ndembu of Zambia among whom he had worked for a long time. His work has had a definite contribution especially in the rich symbolism and patterning in *imbalu*. Already fine-tuned to the importance of symbolism in his work among the Ndembu, his focus helps to bring out the hidden meanings and nuances behind certain actions, gestures and words in *imbalu*. As he himself has observed elsewhere,

> in ritual context, almost every article used, every gesture employed, every song or prayer, every unit of space and time, by convention

---

[26] La Fontaine, *The Gisu*, pp. 442-43.
[27] Victor Turner, in *Man in Africa*, p. 229.
[28] Ibid., p. 229.

stands for something other than itself. It is more than it seems, and often a good deal more.[29]

Certain things which he observed but which the people involved in the ritual themselves ignored in their discussion about the particular ritual always fascinated Turner. In this particular case, the two societies offered telling contrasts: the Ndembu are matrilineal while the Gisu are patrilineal.[30] His findings are of interest in this present study especially with regard to the interpretation of the symbols used in *imbalu*.

Suzette Heald also followed in the footsteps of La Fontaine for her psychological interpretation of *imbalu* in her article published in 1982, and in her sociological interpretation (1989), respectively. She was attached to the department of Sociology at Makerere University in Uganda from 1968 to 1969, and she did field research among the Bamasaba between 1965 and June 1969.[31] She admits her indebtedness to Jean la Fontaine thus,

> To Jean La Fontaine I owe a special debt. She was remembered in Bugisu with great affection − all knew of Nambozo − and to be credited with a tie of quasi-kinship with her was of immeasurable help during the early period of my work.[32]

She followed in la Fontaine's footsteps, adopting the prefix-less name Gisu (1989:x) for the people, instead of the administrative appellation of Bagisu. But she differed with La Fontaine by identifying three instead of four phases of *imbalu*.[33]

In an article first published in 1982[34], and reprinted in 1999 as part of a collection of her disparate articles, she treats *imbalu* from a psychological point of view. As she herself sums it, the article, "explores issues of male identity among the Gisu of Uganda, within the context of the moral dilemmas faced by men who define themselves in terms of their capacity

---

[29] Victor W. Turner, *The Forest of Symbols: Aspects of Ndembu Ritual.* London: Cornell University Press, 1973, p. 15.

[30] Ibid., p. 231.

[31] Suzette Heald, *Controlling Anger: The Sociology of Gisu Violence.* Manchester: Manchester University Press, 1989, p. 10.

[32] See the acknowledgements in her book.

[33] Ibid., pp. 62-63.

[34] Heald, Suzette, "The Making of Men: the Vernacular Psychology to the Interpretation of a Gisu Ritual", in *Africa* 52.1 (1982), pp. 15-36.

for violence".[35] She discusses the theme of masculinity and how it relates to morality, but hastens to add that 'morality' as a word is suspect as it tends to cover for entrenched privileges. Instead, she sees the debate on gender identity as being "about the distribution of rights and privileges; about the nature of ethical action and the arenas in which that is displayed, judged and reflected upon".[36] She is quick to point out that,

> The morality about which I am talking in these essays is, however, not about issues of laxity or licence. It is about the moral dilemmas faced by men, whose very definition and self-conception is in terms of a capacity for violence. What it is to be a man, a legitimate man, is the burning issue for, like any hegemonic model, it defines in turn its own deviant forms of masculinity.[37]

Her sociological interpretation of **imbalu** (1989) where she identifies **lirima** (anger) as the reason behind the 'reputed' violence of the Bamasaba is questionable. We shall show why **lirima**, which she claims is whipped up during the three days leading to circumcision, could not necessarily be the reason for subsequent violence. This argument will be revisited in the conclusion of this work.

Out of the three phases of circumcision she identifies, she focuses on the phase immediately leading to the day of circumcision to put her case for manhood and morality, arguing that, "In examining the power of masculinity to set the moral agenda, this ethnographic study challenges our preconceptions of manhood, inviting a wider re-evaluation of masculinity".[38]

Her contribution lies in broaching the contentious topic of manhood as it is perceived through patriarchal lenses. Her argument indeed provides food for further debate, especially when she argues that,

> In so far as an upright man can be identified with the privileges exercised within the established patriarchal order ... cannot be seen as 'moral', for their power over women, over resources, symbolic as well as material, runs against the new ideals of gender equality and

---

[35] See the preface to Suzette Heald, *Manhood and Morality: Sex, Violence and Ritual in Gisu Society*. London: Routledge, 1999.

[36] See Heald, *Manhood and Morality*, pp. 2-3.

[37] Ibid., p. 3.

[38] See the preface to the book.

democratic egalitarianism. The *pater familias* ...can no longer stand as a repository of virtue.[39]

She did not set out to describe *imbalu*, but rather to find data for interpreting manhood, and for dealing with new gender issues.

All these works are useful for the present study, but none of them constitutes a full description of the ritual. It will be argued that *imbalu* has seven phases and not three or four. The goal here is to go beyond them to paint a fuller picture of the ritual.

2.3. MEANING AND INTERPRETATION

Suzette Heald's study brings to the fore the problem of interpreting the meaning of rituals. A number of works provide aid for accessing the meaning behind ritual acts. They differ, but each provides a perspective through which we may view and interpret them. When these are joined, the plurality of meanings will provide us with a rich and indeed fuller picture of the phenomenon of ritual. To interpret a ritual needs seeing it from different vantage points. Thus Arnold van Gennep, Mircea Eliade and Victor Turner have, from different perspectives, expressed views, which, in spite of various criticisms by colleagues, enable a reconstruction of the meaning of *imbalu*.

In his book first published in 1909, Arnold van Gennep, a French anthropologist, set out to examine the phenomenon of *rites de passage*, and to identify its defining phases. He brought out the universal characteristics of rites of passage by delineating the three phases of separation, transition and incorporation.[40] As a pioneering work, his contribution to ritual in general, and initiation ritual in particular has been immense. Van Gennep's three phases discerned early last century are still current in discussing rites of passage.

Although Mircea Eliade neither visited nor did any research in Africa, his ideas on initiation ritual in particular have much resonance with what happens in *imbalu*. His understanding and description of initiation ritual in

---

[39] Ibid., p. 2.

[40] Arnold van Gennep, *The Rites of Passage*. Chicago: The University of Chicago Press, 1960, p. 21.

terms of death, sojourn in limbo, and rebirth,[41] is very pertinent to the present study.

Victor Turner set out to study especially symbolism in the rituals of the Ndembu of Zambia, particularly the rite of *mukanda* (circumcision). The contribution of Victor Turner's work rests in his detailed analysis of the different symbols that are found in Ndembu rituals in general, and in *mukanda* in particular.[42] In his 1979 publication, he focussed his attention on liminality, showing it as the decisive and determinant point, not only of transition, but also of transformation. This is precisely because this state defies classification, as the initiates are neither what they were before, nor what they intend to become. As he observes,

> It is as though they are being reduced or ground down to a uniform condition to be fashioned anew and endowed with additional powers to enable them to cope with their new station in life.[43]

Upon this fact, he has built his argument that since these initiates are uniform while sojourning through this classless state where secular distinctions of rank and status have disappeared, they develop an intense comradeship and egalitarianism.[44] His contribution in the understanding of initiation ritual in general, and on symbolism in particular could not be over emphasised.

2.4. LITERARY IMAGINATION

Novels constitute a method of reconstruction, which enable the writer to eschew the limiting rigours of disciplines to recreate a living religion. "Imaginative leaps" assist the novelist to relive the emotions of a ritual "without footnotes". Timothy Wangusa, a Professor of Literature at Makerere University, and himself a Mumasaba, has written a novel, which generates vivid scenes of the *imbalu* ritual during the early years of colonialism, Christianity, and formal education.

---

[41] See especially, Mircea Eliade, *Rites and Symbols of Initiation: The Mysteries of Birth and Rebirth*. London: Harper and Row, 1958.

[42] See Turner, *The Forest of Symbols*.

[43] Ibid., p. 95.

[44] Ibid., p. 95.

This novel (1989) is based on the vicissitudes of village life in his native Masabaland. In it he recounts the impact colonialism, Christianity and modern education had upon the rural folk. In this novel, *imbalu* is the dominant cultural form, which pervades all spheres of life: in the beer drinking parties, the school, the church, etc. The twin ideas of circumcision and manhood come under the microscope as the paradigm shifts. Manhood, which had been hitherto defined within the cultural set-up, had to be redefined within the new and emerging cultural context. As the author quotes a local school headmaster as saying, the enrolment in the schools was low because,

> They were too contented with their mountain spirit. And that spirit, he said was their excessive pride in their manhood! 'How dare you say that to me, a man?' ... But the true manhood of the future, he concluded, was the manhood of the brain, of exchanging the spear for the pen.[45]

Modernity is perceived as having brought the traditional perception of *imbalu* under contestation.

Its contribution consists in being the first novel based on Masaba village life. It is rich on ideas on Masaba culture in general, and *imbalu* in particular. For instance, the circumcision songs and the folk stories he so poignantly narrates, are the songs and stories respectively that were sung and narrated when he was growing up on the ridges of Mount Elgon. In his novel, therefore, he has recounted and preserved the village scenes of Masabaland soon before and after independence. It is of interest to this work in as far as it depicts scenes of *imbalu*, complete with the songs and exhortations that characterise the three days leading to the circumcision day. Indeed, the accuracy of his description could be tested by Lawrence Walakira's brief description in his article on *imbalu*.

In his paper contributed to the Theological Week, the Reverend Lawrence Walakira describes the biennial circumcision ceremony that takes place in the district where he served as a Roman Catholic priest. The focus of this paper is the relationship between culture and Christianity in general, and Masaba culture and Christianity in particular. As an outsider, his thinking is that Christian Bamasaba should be more involved in Church activities,

---

[45] Timothy Wangusa, *Upon this Mountain*. London: Heinemann, 1989, p. 22.

especially the catechumenate and Holy Mass. But in his experience, they remain ambivalent at best, and disinterested at worst. In contrast, they are all actively involved in the cultural ceremony of circumcision. He, therefore, poses the question, "Why do people participate more actively and devotedly in *imbalu* ceremony than in the celebration of Mass?"[46]

Walakira's contribution has injected a new sense of urgency into the question of the relationship between African cultures and Christianity. He has raised a pertinent question concerning the resilience of traditional religious beliefs in spite of the new religious tenets of Christianity and Islam. This paper is of interest to this study in as far as it describes the active and devoted participation of the Bamasaba in their cultural ritual, while exhibiting little interest in Christian activities. It is certainly relevant in our discussion of Christianity as one of the change agents that have affected *imbalu*. We shall come back to this point in the chapter dealing with the impact of the change agents on the ritual.

2.5. AFRICAN PRIMAL RELIGIOUS BACKGROUND

Imbalu is both a cultural and a religious phenomenon. The literature on African Traditional Religion has burgeoned since Parrinder (1949) and Mbiti (1969). A select few are pertinent to this study, namely by Okot p'Bitek (1970) and Robin Horton (1975), Aylward Shorter (1987), David Chidester (1987), Laurenti Magesa (1996), and a section of Ogbu U. Kalu's *Embattled Gods* (1996).

Aylward Shorter, an English missionary, has taught anthropology at Makerere University, Gaba Pastoral Institute for Eastern Africa, Catholic University of Eastern Africa, and now heads the Tangaza Institute in Nairobi. In one of his publications (1987), he argues that what characterises the ethnic traditional religions of Africa is the fact that their religious experiences are expressed in a cultural language which emerges from the interaction of a human society with a given physical environment. He associates songs, proverbs and riddles with the socialisation of the young, a life long learning process, which perpetuates the community's worldview.

---

[46] Lawrence Walakira, "Circumcision Ceremony Among the Bagisu", in *The Second National Theological Week* (August 1983), p. 165.

To him, the riddle is a verbal challenge usually made in the form of a statement with an implied question, to which the initiate must supply the application. The parable, therefore, interrogates the experience of the interlocutor, thus enabling him to appreciate the logic of the symbol, in exactly the same way as the didactic song, proverb or riddle.[47]

He perceives the didactic song as also built around a single symbol, which is repeated again and again as the song is sung. Didactic songs employ a wide range of images taken from the vegetable, animal and human worlds, and the context consists in the ritual or social occasion, which accompanies the song. The didactic song is similar to the sung refrain in the story-song genre.[48] In his opinion, in the various initiation rites the social control of experience and the inculcation of symbolic learning are at their most explicit. The initiate receives learning that conforms to the best theories of pupil-centred or life-centred education today.[49]

He has made an important contribution in writing down these songs and symbols of initiation as he heard them from the Kimbu, before they disappear with the death of the sages who knew them. His explanation of the symbolism used in the initiation ceremonies of the Kimbu applies to other African communities, which practise the rites of initiation.

David Chidester's comparative perspective between religion and ethics is notable especially because of the typology of the features of initiation ritual, which he shows to be *inter alias* authoritative, instructive, physical and corporate. This is certainly germane to our present study of Masaba *imbalu*.

Ogbu Kalu, a Presbyterian Church historian from Nigeria, surveys the nature of the religious landscape prevailing in Igboland prior to the introduction of Christianity. He takes the reader through the type of covenants that the Igbo people had in their search for abundant life, cut with the gods of their fathers. The battle is joined when the Christian God is presented as the only true God. What happens to the gods that had seen

---

[47] Aylward Shorter, *Songs and Symbols of Initiation: A Study from Africa in the Social Control of Perception*. Nairobi: CHIEA Press, 1987, p. 5.

[48] Ibid. p. 2.

[49] Ibid. p. 5.

the people through thick and thin all those centuries? But the Christian God is not necessarily a nemesis to the gods of the heretofore, just as the new covenant with the Christian God does not spell an immediate death and cessation of the earlier covenants. The battle rages on in the minds and hearts of the people who find themselves between two covenants. Though old covenants gradually lose hold and are eventually broken in favour of the new, the spirit remains unconquered. The Igbos were not a clean slate where Christianity wrote its script, and this eventually leads to a position of give-and-take between the two parties.

By taking the reader through the landscape within which Christianity was planted, the author paints a vivid picture of covenant clashes between traditional African religiosity on the one hand, and Christianity on the other. This book is relevant for this study in that it discusses the clash of covenants: cultural and Christian, in the same people. It aptly applies to the Bamasaba who are instructed and initiated into their cultural beliefs and values, many of which have borne opposition from Christianity.

On the other hand, Laurenti Magesa, a Roman Catholic theologian from Tanzania, sets out to discuss African religion from the point of view of its common elements. He has put his finger on the essence of African religion, namely the tradition of abundant life. He elucidates points that many often talk about without a deep understanding of the dynamics behind the issues involved. It is relevant for this study as it links African traditional religion and culture to the Africans' over-ridding goal of abundant life, both here and hereafter. This question influences the beliefs and values that the Bamasaba hold dear.

The author is fully cognisant of the fact that scholars such as Okot p'Bitek and Robin Horton are critical of the approach of Westerners in general, and missionaries in particular towards African religions. The older generation of African Christian scholars such as Mbiti and Idowu were accused of being unduly influenced by Christianity and Western philosophy in their interpretation of African religions. Among the most vociferous critics are Okot p'Bitek[50] and Robin Horton.[51] The former, a poet and anthropologist

---

[50] See Okot P'Bitek, *African Religions in Western Scholarship*. Kampala: Uganda Literature Bureau, 1980.

[51] Robin Horton, "Judaeo-Christian Spectacles: Boon or Bane to the Study of African Religions", *Cahiers d'etudes Africaines* (1986), pp. 391-435.

from Uganda, and the latter a British anthropologist who has researched for long in Nigeria, represent a different approach towards the study of traditional African religions. The above criticisms notwithstanding, the research of these so-called Christian scholars is pertinent to the present study.

2.6. CHANGE IN *IMBALU*

The "anthropological present" tense is used in describing this ritual, yet there is no gainsaying the fact that *imbalu* has changed through time. So far, there is no literature dealing directly with the question of change in *imbalu* as such, so it is incumbent upon the author to provide that. Yet it would not be adequate to discuss the phenomenon of change without talking about what the agents of this change are. This will be done, showing the extent each change agent has affected different aspects of it.

Some literature deals with questions of change, such as works by Malinowski and Geertz. The goal of the study is to illustrate how the meaning of *imbalu* has changed. Concepts of culture, community, identity, and power have been transformed. Similarly, the core ritual structure has also changed. Some phases of it are no longer performed according to customs. This can best be illustrated through examining the pattern of symbolism. Some literature has been useful in doing an anatomy of the change agents. Michael Twaddle (1993) provides a recent study on colonialism and its impact on the people of the eastern region of Uganda including the Bamasaba. Adrian Hastings' work *The Church in Africa, 1450-1950* (1994) discusses the irruption and subsequent influence of Christianity upon the people in terms of education, medical and other developments. Ogbu Kalu's *Embattled Gods* (1996) suggests, albeit from a different context, the dilemma of Christian encounter and the resilient force of primal religions. Similarly, W. B. Anderson's *Christianity in East Africa* (1981) provides a general account of how Christianity has affected the region. The modern state in the task of social control has tapped the bonding force of culture to stem the influence of Western values. Allan Horwitz (1990) emphasises the need to look at change at the level of institutions.

On the theme of change in culture and community, the old anthropological studies are still useful. For instance, Bronislaw Malinowski (1961) writes from the functional theory of culture, with emphasis on external agents of change. The contribution of the book lies in the author's interest in social relationships and, therefore, in institutional change.[52]

On change and identity, the work of Clifford Geertz (1973) is pertinent to the issue. Discussing the questions of culture, its role in social life and how it should be studied, he advocates for religion, ethos and worldview to be brought together to give a set of social values an appearance of objectivity. His contribution on this question consists in his orientation of studying culture as a symbolic system.[53]

Anderson (1981) set out to write an easy-reader history of the introduction and spread of Christianity in East Africa. In my opinion he succeeded in doing that. He characterises the introduction and spread of Christianity as a "revolution" that was typified by the church-school-dispensary model. He has contributed to the understanding of the history of Christianity in this region.

Allan Horwitz's main theme is that "the structure of social relationships shapes the style, form, and effectiveness of social control".[54] This being the case, it would seem to follow that "Fundamental changes in relational structures should, therefore, produce basic shifts in social control systems".[55] This book sets out to synthesise the many findings in the area of social control as contained in ethnographies of tribal societies, archival studies of historical settings, and intensive case studies, as well as large survey research projects of social control systems in modern societies.[56] In doing this he has chosen to use the approach and model of Donald Black on

---

[52] See for instance Lucy Mair, "Malinowski and the Study of Social Change", in Raymond Firth (ed.), *Man and Culture: An Evaluation of the Work of Bronislaw Malinowski*. London: Routledge and Kegan Paul, 1980, p. 233.

[53] Clifford Geertz, *The Interpretation of Cultures*. New York: Basic Books, 1973, p. 131.

[54] Allan V. Horwitz, *The Logic of Social Control*. New York: Plenum Press, 1990, p. 239.

[55] Ibid., p. 239.

[56] Ibid., p. ix.

"how general characteristics of social structure can be used to predict and explain features of social control systems".[57]

Michael Twaddle (1993) narrates the story of Chief Semei Kakungulu whose exploits in the Eastern and Northern Regions of present day Uganda was considerable. As the man responsible for opening up an area which was till then unknown to the outside world, Kakungulu made it possible for the British to introduce their administration over these districts, albeit by proxy. The author contributes to a better understanding of the history of Uganda in general, but especially that of the entire Eastern Region which was then unmapped, and hence considered to be outside Uganda.[58]

---

[57] Ibid., p. x.

[58] See for instance the title of a book like J. B. Purvis, *Through Uganda to Mount Elgon*. London: T. Fisher Unwin, 1909.

CHAPTER THREE: RITUAL THEORIES

3.1. INTRODUCTION

Different scholars approach ritual differently as is evident from their definitions and theories. This chapter looks at some of these diverse theories on ritual, and focuses especially on those which have a bearing upon Masaba *imbalu*. It seeks to answer the question as to what ritual is, and what certain scholars of ritual see it to be.

There are so many and divergent theories on ritual in general, and initiation ritual in particular, that it would not be possible to discuss all of them under this limited space. It has, therefore, been necessary to make a selection of a representative few which are pertinent to this study. These are analysed in two different sections with those on ritual per se being grouped together in a chronological order, and those on initiation ritual also follow chronologically.

3.2. DEFINITION OF RITUAL

In one of his most recent articles on ritual, Ronald Grimes grapples with the problem of defining the notion of ritual, concluding that,

> ritual is not a precisely delineated analytic category as much of the literature on it fails to distinguish between the category and the thing categorised, between the idea of ritual and the enactment of rites.[59]

Both the broad and the narrow definitions of ritual run into problems of inclusion and exclusion respectively, forcing many contemporary definitions to try to steer a middle ground by specifying certain characteristics deemed common to all kinds of ritual. One example of these definitions, which would be pertinent to our study of *imbalu*, is that of Evan Zuesse, who says,

> we shall understand as 'ritual' those conscious and voluntary, repetitious and stylised symbolic bodily actions that are centred on cosmic structures and/or sacred presences.[60]

---

[59] Ronald L Grimes, "Ritual", in Willi Braun and Russell McCutcheon (eds.): *Guide to the Study of Religion.* London: Cassell, 2000, p. 259.

But ritual is more than 'stylised bodily actions' as it also includes words, which accompany these actions, for as Ronald Grimes points out, "Rites are not merely enacted, they are also talked about. And they are talked about by those who perform them".[61] But besides the problem of inclusion and exclusion, there seems to be no agreement whether there is a connection between rite and ritual, or whether the two are synonymous. In *imbalu* for instance, the actions go with words of invocation, blessing, or exhortation.

3.3. PARTICULAR THEORIES ON RITUAL IN GENERAL

3.3.1. Hans J. Mol

Hans Mol compares van Gennep's three stages of separation, transition and incorporation with three of his own, which he gives as,

(1)   emotional detachment

(2)   phase of meaninglessness

(3)   emotional attachment to a new focus of identity.

For Mol, rites are important ingredients in social order, giving it meaning and identity since they,

> articulate and reiterate a system of meaning and prevent it being lost from sight. They act out and sacralise sameness. They restore, reinforce, or redirect identity. They maximise order by strengthening the place of the individual in the group, or society, and vice versa by strengthening the bonds of a society *vis a vis* the individual. They unify, integrate, and sacralise.[62]

In other words, ritual contributes to the cohesion of society and therefore to the survival capacity. Ritual diverts energies or libido from potentially group-weakening activities to group-strengthening ones. In so doing rites cleanse society and in the process, reinforce social expectations and superimpose constraint.[63]

---

[60] Evan M. Zuesse, "Ritual", in Mircea Eliade (ed.), *The Encyclopedia of Religion*, vol. 12, New York: Macmillan, 1987, p. 405.

[61] Grimes, "Ritual", in *Study of Religion*, p. 262.

[62] Hans J. Mol, *Identity and the Sacred.* New York: The Free Press, 1977, p. 223.

[63] Ibid., p. 223.

He, therefore, sees initiation ritual in terms of identity rather than mere status change. In a nutshell, he sees it as but the desacralisation of the old identity and the sacralisation of the new. The novice aspires to the acquisition of what is posited as a higher status, and wants to identify him with men instead of boys. The individual initiate is willing to be absorbed into the common cultural fabric, where the community fills the emotional void of his rational existence by surrounding him with emotional support from peers. By linking the past with the present, the community extends itself to include the ancestors.[64] To him, then,

> Rituals articulate and reiterate a system of meaning, and prevent it being lost from sight. They act out and sacralize sameness. They restore, reinforce, or redirect identity. They maximize order by strengthening the place of the individual in the group, or society, and vice versa by strengthening the bonds of a society vis-à-vis the individual. They unify, integrate, and sacralize.[65]

He perceives the sameness in action represented by rites as meant to consolidate the sameness of a system of meaning, thereby restoring, reinforcing, or redirecting identity. This is done through recommitting to memory, a system of meaning, through re-absorbing individuals in the common fabric of society.

In summary, Hans Mol emphasises identity as resulting from the destruction of an earlier identity that was less than desirable. The new identity comes about when the community absorbs an individual unto itself. Through linking the past to the present, rites reinforce identity by filling the emotional voids of instrumental rational existence. They redirect through surrounding stressful situations with emotional support, through desacralising an old identity, and through sacralising a new one.[66]

3.3.2. Frits Staal

Frits Staal looks at why people engage in ritual, which is said to be the language of religion. It is believed that in it something is being said and done, something of importance is being symbolically asserted.

His main argument is that,

---

[64] Ibid., p. 239.
[65] Ibid., p. 223.
[66] Ibid., pp. 244-245.

The performers are totally immersed in the proper execution of their complex tasks... they concentrate on the correctness of an act, recitation and chant. Their primary concern, if not obsession, is with rules. There are no symbolic meanings going through their minds when they are engaged in performing ritual.[67]

Secondly, that when the performer is asked explicitly as to why the rituals are performed, his answer does not refer to symbolic activity. Instead it will be varied, e.g. because it is good for the society; it is good; it is a duty; etc.

This is precisely because in many cultures there are no traditions of exegesis or discussion. The interpretations offered for these objects and gestures of ritual will vary according to variables such as age, social position, personal knowledge of ritual, education etc. Knowledge may be reserved for specialists or a few senior people, and questions about certain things may be frowned upon.[68] It follows then that people will know what to do and how to do it but may lack the explanation.

Staal seems to confuse symbolic activity with the intended goal behind the activities. Rituals are not mere symbolic activities, as they are aimed at achieving tangible results. The symbolic activities are used as outward signs of inward meaning. So when the performer is asked about what he is doing, it is only logical that he will not refer to the symbolic activity but rather to the meaning behind the activity. For instance if a rain-maker was asked why he was burning green leaves which produce thick dark smoke, he will not refer to the activity but to the intended goal, namely the rain. He may not even realise that there is similarity between the dark smoke with the dark rain-bearing cumulus clouds. What he knows is that this action if performed correctly brings about rain, and that is what his answer will be about. Staal's conclusion that,

> Ritual then is primarily activity. It is an activity governed by explicit rules. The important thing is what you do, not what you think, believe or say. In India this has become a basic feature of religion,[69]

seems to be misguided! There is a relationship between right acting and efficacy. The important thing is not mere activity but right acting so as to

---

[67] Frits Staal, "The Meaninglessness of Ritual", in *Numen*, Vol. xxvi, Fasc.1 (1979), p. 3.

[68] J. S. La Fontaine, *Initiation*. Manchester: Manchester University Press, 1986, p. 12.

[69] Staal, p. 4.

effect efficacy. It is the efficacy that is important hence the need to act rightly, and not the activity *per se*. I certainly agree with the sentiment expressed by La Fontaine when she says that,

> Ritual action is not irrational, it is purposive, but its success or failure cannot be measured in Western scientific terms. Some confusion has been added to the discussion by attempting to substitute the social effects of rituals (as perceived by the observer) for the purposes, as expressed by those who perform them, and writing as though the symbolic means used in ritual constituted its sole purpose.[70]

In his pursuit of the thesis that rituals are meaningless, Staal questions the theory that rituals are used in preliterate societies to transmit cultural and social values to the younger generations. He correctly argues that rituals are not confined to preliterate communities. Instead it is the anthropologists who tend to confine themselves to preliterate societies. His conclusion that, "In ritual activity, the rules count, but not the result"[71], is not correct either. For Staal, the meaninglessness of ritual explains why there are many meanings attached to it.

> Ritual became deeply involved with religion, which always stands in need of the mysterious and unexplained. Rites were attached to all important events. In the course of time, rituals, instead of remaining useless and pure, became useful and meritorious.[72]

In summary, Staal's problem lies in his failure to delineate meaning from symbolic activity, and in failing to see ritual as religious language. La Fontaine cautions that "objects and gestures of ritual cannot be dismissed as meaningless and irrational".[73] Instead, what is usually problematic is "the repetition of traditional behaviour whose origins lie beyond recovery".[74]

---

[70] La Fontaine, *Initiation*, p. 12.

[71] Staal, p. 9.

[72] Ibid., p. 14.

[73] La Fontaine, *Initiation*, p. 12.

[74] Ibid., p. 12

3.3.3. Catherine Bell

Catherine Bell was influenced by Emile Durkheim's *Elementary Forms of the Religious Life*, or what she refers to as "Durkheim's pragmatic formulation of religion as a matter of primary beliefs and secondary rites".[75] She takes earlier theories to task for not avoiding what she sees as a predetermined circularity which "functions to constitute ritual as an object of analysis in such a way as to mandate a particular method, expertise, and way of knowing".[76] Instead she abandons this circularity model, which perceives,

> the focus on ritual as a set of special practices in favour of a focus on some of the more common strategies of 'ritualisation' initially defined as a way of acting that differentiates some acts from others. To approach ritual within the framework of practical activity raises ... potentially more fruitful questions about the origins, purposes, and efficacy of 'ritualised actions' than are accessible through current models.[77]

In her aim to reconcile theory with practice, she questions theoretical descriptions of ritual, which regard it as action thus unfortunately separating ritual from beliefs, symbols, and myths, which are taken as merely conceptual aspects of religion.[78] She sees this as one of the reasons why,

> Ritual is ... described as particularly thoughtless action-routinised, habitual, obsessive, or mimetic-and therefore the purely formal, secondary, and mere physical expression of logically prior ideas. Just as the differentiation of ritual and belief in terms of thought and action is usually taken for granted, so too is the priority this differentiation accords to thought.[79]

She argues that ritual enacts, performs or objectifies religious beliefs, where action gives expression to thought, and in so doing fuses the

---

75 Catherine Bell, *Ritual Theory, Ritual Practice.* Oxford: Oxford University Press, 1992, p. vii.

76 Ibid., pp. viii-ix.

77 Ibid., pp. viii-ix.

78 Ibid., p. 19.

79 Ibid., p. 19.

conceptual and the dispositional aspects of religious symbols. Ritual then, integrates thought and action.[80]

In her later work, which is mostly dedicated to different perspectives and dimensions of ritual, she is of the opinion that,

> life cycle rituals seem to proclaim that the biological order is less determinative than the social. Physical birth is one thing; being properly identified and accepted as a member of the social group is another. Likewise, the appearance of facial hair or menses does not make someone an adult; only the community confers that recognition, and it does so in its own time.[81]

This is very pertinent to the present study where it is *imbalu* which makes a Masaba male a man, and not his physical age.

3.3.4. Ronald L Grimes

Ronald Grimes has contributed much to the study of ritual, especially with his discussion of ritual space, ritual objects and ritual time. Ritual space has been given prominence, as he argues that all the items which have to do with the ritual are symbolically important. This includes the site, whether natural or constructed, temporal or permanent, the ritual qualifications of the builders, and its surroundings.[82]

Ritual objects are also singled out for special attention in terms of their physical dimensions, shape, weight, colour, age, and other features. Whether these objects are considered sacred or profane, where who keeps them, and the stories connected with them, are all important.[83]

Ritual time covers questions of when the ritual should be performed, daytime, night, dawn, dusk, year, month, season, etc. Ritual time also covers the idea of how the community organises their calendar, and if life-cycle rhythms are significant in the rituals. As he says, in ritual certain questions become important. For instance,

---

[80] Ibid., p. 27.

[81] Catherine Bell, *Ritual: Perspectives and Dimensions.* Oxford: Oxford University Press, 1997, p. 94.

[82] Ronald L. Grimes, *Beginnings in Ritual Studies.* New York: University Press of America, 1982, p. 21.

[83] Ibid., pp. 23-24.

Does the ritual commemorate historical eras or recall paradigmatic events ... Is it essential to remember things, events, or persons of the past ... Does the ritual anticipate a particular future ... Does it have phases, interludes or breaks...Does the ritual taper off or end abruptly ... Are ancestors felt to be present during the rite ... Was there a past or mythical time which is a model for the present enactment?[84]

The three aspects of ritual, namely ritual space, objects and time, are very important in discussing *imbalu*, since they entail special symbolic meaning and determine whether the ritual is validly conducted or not. Our description and interpretation of the ritual will bring out the importance of these aspects and show their indispensability. They will be described and duly explained in the relevant stages. In one of his latest writings, Grimes is of the view that since ritual is different from, yet implicit in daily interactions, it is both special and ordinary. He argues that both the broad and the narrow definitions of ritual run into problems, so most contemporary definitions avoid that pitfall by specifying certain characteristics common to all kinds of ritual. "In these middle-range definitions ritual is a style of action, one that is formal, stylised, prescribed, symbolic, non-technological, repetitive, traditional and so on."[85] He contends that

Rites are among the most visible aspects of a religion or culture ... taken to be enactments of religious beliefs and myths, become a privileged object of study, because they are thought to condense a society's values. In effect, ethnographers documenting rites become a second class of ritual interpreters. Unlike ritual specialists, ethnographers stand outside the sacred circle with no obvious vested interest in either the outcome or meaning of the rite.[86]

In summary, Grimes emphasises that ritual is closely connected with a people's religion and culture. Ritual space, ritual time and ritual objects all contribute in bringing about the efficacy that is intended.

---

[84] Ibid., p. 25.
[85] Grimes, "Ritual", in *Study of Religion,* pp. 261-262.
[86] Ibid., p. 263.

3.4. PARTICULAR THEORIES ON INITIATION RITUAL

3.4.1. Arnold van Gennep

Using the example of a territorial frontier, which is "an imaginary line connecting milestones or stakes", van Gennep's work brings out initiation in terms of territorial passage. He divides the rites of passage into three major phases:

1. Separation (Pre-liminal),
2. Transition (Liminal), and
3. Incorporation (Post-liminal/Integration).

Van Gennep sees initiation as serving a magico-religious role since in almost all spheres of man's life: from giving birth and being born to hunting, there is an irruption of the sacred.[87] According to him, initiation has to do with magico-religious crossing of borders, comparable to territorial ones.[88] The passage from one frontier to the other, from the profane to the sacred, is so great that one needs an intermediate stage, which in conventional terms would be a "no man's land". This is the purpose of the transition stage when the initiate is neither what he has been hitherto, nor the new being that he intends to become. This passage from one territory to another, from the profane to the sacred, is so great that this intermediate ground is absolutely necessary.[89]

> We see that in the least advanced cultures the holy enters nearly every phase of a man's life. Being born, giving birth, and hunting ... are all acts whose major aspects fall within the sacred sphere. Social groups in such societies likewise have magico-religious foundations, and passage from group to group takes on that special quality found in our rites of baptism and ordination.[90]

Ritual, therefore, exists in many spheres of life, in both less developed and highly developed communities. In as far as initiation is a crossing of

---

[87] Arnold van Gennep, *The Rites of Passage.* Chicago: University of Chicago Press, 1960, p. 2.
[88] Ibid., p. 15.
[89] Ibid., p. 1.
[90] Ibid., p. 2.

thresholds, modern life in both its private and public spheres is full of initiation rites too. Every civilisation has its baptisms, initiation in public schools, marriage ceremonies, sports teams, clubs, and others where the crossing of threshold is celebrated with rites. For instance the bachelor's party on the eve of a wedding is to de-initiate the groom from bachelorhood and usher him into marital life. Boarding schools, sports and other clubs too have some sort of initiation for new members to establish loyalty and trust among the members. As he himself shows in his discussion of the sacred, the presence of the sacred is variable and not absolute, brought into play by the nature of a particular situation. What makes an act sacred or secular is the particular worldview. Sacrality, therefore, resides not in the thing but rather in the people who ascribe it to a thing. In religious cosmology, passage through life is celebrated with rites of passage.[91] The rites are ascribed to a deity for the purpose of giving them supernatural sanction. Consequently, human values and practices are given sacral power and come across as being sanctioned by the supernatural, thereby compelling and facilitating observance and acquiescence from members of the community.

Van Gennep sees mutilation as a separation too, since that physical mark separates the initiate from others. In his own words,

> The mutilated individual is removed from the common mass of humanity by a rite of separation ... which automatically incorporates him into a defined group, since the operation leaves ineradicable traces, the incorporation is permanent ... it is clearly a 'sign of union' with a particular deity and a mark of membership in a single community of the faithful.[92]

In summary, through his three phases, van Gennep portrays initiation as a drama, a structured movement all the way from pre-liminal activities through a transition to a denouement and incorporation into the community.

3.4.2. Mircea Eliade

Mircea Eliade's approach of initiation is that of birth, death and rebirth. In initiation the initiate symbolically dies, and is later reborn as a different

---

[91] Ibid., p. 2.
[92] Ibid., p. 72.

person altogether. In the introduction of his book on *Rites and Symbols of Initiation* he defines initiation thus,

> The term initiation in the most general sense denotes a body of rites and oral teachings whose purpose is to produce a decisive alteration in the religious and social status of the person to be initiated. In philosophical terms, initiation is equivalent to a basic change in existential condition, the novice emerges from his ordeal endowed with a different being from that which he possessed before his initiation; he has become another.[93]

According to him initiation has the important role of inserting the initiate into the inner life of his community, for he has to learn and absorb the values and norms of therein. It, however, goes beyond the human sphere by introducing the initiate to the sphere of the supernatural.

To him the myths and traditions of the community are important, for it is these which open the history of the community to the initiate, establish a past upon which the present hinges and gets continuity, and hence give him meaning. In other words,

> Initiation introduces the candidate into the human community and the world of spiritual and cultural values. He learns not only the behaviour patterns, the techniques, and the institutions of adults but also the sacred myths and traditions of the tribe, the names of the gods and the history of their works; above all, he learns the mystical relations between the tribe and the Supernatural Beings as those relations were established at the beginning of Time.[94]

That is to say that initiation transcends the social function to assume a religious role, where the initiate is introduced to the gods of his community. So there is need for him to know them and the history of their works within the history of that community. And the medium of effecting the ritual death in the initiate is the ritual ordeal, which he puts forward as the encounter with the sacred.

This ritual death to the earlier mode of existence "provides the clean slate on which will be written the successive revelations whose end is the formation of a new man".[95] The fact that the dead are regarded as an

---

[93] Mircea Eliade, *Rites and Symbols of Initiation: The Mysteries of Death and Rebirth.* New York: Harper and Row, 1958, p. x of the introduction to his book.

[94] Ibid., p. x.

[95] Ibid., p. xiii.

integral part of the community, who come back as ancestors to take part in the initiation ceremonies, shows that death is not final but rather a transition from this life to the next. In his opinion, rubbing the initiates with a white powder is meant to make them resemble ghosts. In his words,

> Ritual death tends to be valuated not only as an initiatory ordeal necessary for a new birth but also as a privileged situation in itself, for it allows the novices to live in the company of the ancestors.[96]

In a nutshell, Eliade perceives ordeals as meant to "provide the experience of ritual death" and initiation in general as being "equivalent to introducing the novice to the mythical history of the tribe".[97]

Symbols and myths of existence play an important role in this transformative process. Mircea Eliade's emphasis lies in his psychological approach to understanding initiation ritual, where he perceives change as occurring in the existential condition of the initiate. He also sees a connection between initiation and cosmology, since the transformation instituted by mythic beings is facilitated by the dramatic nature of the myths and symbols.

The author is fully aware of the criticisms levelled against Mircea Eliade by different authors. Perhaps the most severe and even polemical attack is by Edmund Leach.[98] Eliade was, however, defended by among others Mac Linscott Ricketts who tried to "bridge the communications gap between Anthropology and the History of Religions".[99] The line of debate continued with Russell McCutcheon,[100] but Eliade was again defended, this time by Bryan Rennie. It is interesting that the same Mac Linscott Ricketts who had defended Eliade twenty years earlier wrote the foreword of his book.[101]

---

[96] Ibid., p. 37.

[97] Ibid., p. 38.

[98] Edmund Leach, "Sermons By a Man on a Ladder", in *The New York Review* (October 20th 1966), pp. 28-31.

[99] Mac Linscott Ricketts, "In Defence of Eliade: Toward Bridging the Communication Gap Between Anthropology and the History of Religions", in *Religion, Journal of Religion and Religions 3* (1973), pp. 13-34.

[100] See Russell T. McCutcheon, *Manufacturing Religion: The Discourse on Sui Generis Religion and the Politics of Nostalgia*. Oxford: Oxford University Press, 1997, pp. 74-100.

[101] Bryan S. Rennie, *Reconstructing Eliade: Making Sense of Religion*. New York: State University of New York Press, 1996, pp. vi-ix.

Bruce Lincoln was again back criticising the Eliadean approach recently,[102] and the debate is certainly continuing.[103] But all the foregoing criticism notwithstanding, Eliade's theory on initiation ritual is found to be pertinent to this study. It sits well with that of *imbalu* perceived by the Bamasaba as consisting in the symbolic death of the child and his being reborn as an adult, after sojourning in ritual limbo.

3.4.3. Victor Turner

Victor Turner in particular shows how social bonds, what he terms *communitas,* are engendered out of the spontaneous sense of unity and solidarity especially during the transition phase of a ritual.

Societies attach a lot of significance to ritual because of its expressive value, whether or not it brings out the desired state. In ritual, something is being said and done, something of importance is being symbolically asserted. It has been described as religious aspiration which has been given the form of corporate art, a special language for speaking about God and men. It is, from that standpoint, able to be explicit about religion, about the difference between men and the gods they worship. The same honesty that marks the ritual approach allows people to be themselves in the presence of one another, acting out with their bodies what they think with their brains.[104]

Ritual is important too, because of its extra degree of intensity, normally brought about by the fact that its behaviour pattern is a contact between the secular and the sacred. It is, therefore, able to affect the bodily posture, the

---

[102] Cristiano Grottanelli and Bruce Lincoln, "A Brief Note on (Future) Research in the History of Religions", in *Method and Theory in the Study of Religion,* 10 (1989), pp. 311-325.

[103] See for instance Wayne Elzey, "Mircea Eliade and the Battle against Reductionism", in Thomas A. Idinopulos and Edward A. Yonan (eds.), *Religion and Reductionism: Essays on Eliade, Segal, and the Challenge of the Social Sciences for the Study of Religion.* Leiden: E. J. Brill, 1994, pp. 83-94; and Brian Rennie (ed.), *Changing Religious Worlds: The Meaning and End of Mircea Eliade.* New York: State University of New York Press, 2000.

[104] Roger Grainger, *The Language of the Rite.* London: Longman and Todd, 1974, p. xi.

gait, indeed the whole disposition of the general demeanour of the participants.[105]

In his account of **Mukanda**, the rite of circumcision among the Ndembu, Turner posits three phases identical to the ones given by van Gennep, namely,

(1) *kwing'ija*, "causing to enter"; (2) *kungu'la*, "at the circumcision lodge"; and (3) *kwidisha*, "to take outside", a verb that has the additional sense of "to approve publicly". These rites are orientated towards the lodge and are regarded as preparation to enter it, sojourn within it, and the subsequent removal from it.[106]

According to him, "in all life-crisis rituals changes take place in the relationships of all those people closely connected with the subject of the ritual".[107]

In *The Ritual Process: Structure and Anti-Structure,* Turner makes rites of passage the model for understanding how ritual in general works. He identifies the transition phase of initiation and puts special emphasis on it as being definitive of ritual. Noting the importance of the individual initiate's insertion into the community, Turner argues that liminality is the creative space, and it is liminality, which allows ritual to do the work of transformation. He asserts that

> Liminal entities, such as neophytes in initiation or puberty rites, may be represented as possessing nothing. They may be disguised as monsters, wear only a strip of clothing, or even go naked, to demonstrate that as liminal beings they have no status, property, insignia...[108]

Liminality also leads to deep communality because finding themselves in this unenviable indeterminate uniform state, the initiates develop a strong sense of identity with one another. These bonds will be maintained throughout their lives, creating social cohesion. Ronald Grimes has a point, therefore, when he observes that,

---

[105] Margaret Mead, "Ritual and Social Crisis", in J. D. Shaughnessy (ed.), *The Roots of Ritual*. Grand Rapids: W. B. Ferdmans Publications, 1973, p. 87.

[106] Turner, p. 187.

[107] Ibid., p. 9

[108] Turner, *The Ritual Process*, p. 95.

For Turner, the whole of ritual theory, not just rites of passage, was determined by the image of passing across a threshold or a frontier ... real ritual effects transformation, creating a major 'before' and 'after' difference ... the limen, or threshold, is not just a phase in a rite but a creative 'space' resulting in a temporary state known as liminality.[109]

Turner lays a great deal of emphasis on symbolism, body movement, colour, magical words, community and family involvement. Symbolism is central to an integrated and balanced view of reality. It is an appeal to experience, and at the same time an appeal to the meaning, which underlies the experience. It is a means by which the sphere of sacred and secular is bridged, by which the sacred is spoken of in secular terms. This is precisely because symbols tend to bring the external world of religion into our physical world, so they are a medium between the two worlds.

For Turner, the whole ritual process, and rites of passage in particular, is determined by the fact of crossing of the *limen* (threshold), and to him real ritual necessarily effects a transformation.[110]

3.4.4. Jean La Fontaine

La Fontaine carried out some of her research among the Bamasaba before going on to study male initiation among the Wogeo of Papua New Guinea. Her ideas about initiation ritual accrue from her understanding of ritual in general. To do justice to her, it is imperative to present a glimpse of her theory on ritual before focussing on her description of initiation ritual in particular. According to her, ritual is concerned with,

> religious behaviour, with the details of the persons involved, the objects used and the acts performed in an ordered sequence which has purpose and meaning for the people concerned.[111]

She points out that in order to successfully analyse ritual, a number of different dimensions should be considered, kept distinct, yet their relationship with one another should be shown. One of these is ritual action, comprising a sequence which accomplishes a purpose, or what it aims to do. The other dimension is that of meaning, both to the action in

---

[109] Grimes, "Ritual", in *Study of Religion*, p. 264.
[110] See Grimes, "Ritual", in *Study of Religion*, p. 264.
[111] La Fontaine, *Initiation*, p. 11

ritual, and the nature of society, whether this is made explicit, or whether it consists of overlapping metaphors.[112]

After all, ritual is but,

> social action, its performance requires the organised co-operation of individuals, directed by a leader or leaders. There are rules indicating what persons should participate and on what occasions; often the rules excluding certain categories of people are of as much significance as those which permit or require others to take part.[113]

Since the actions are expected to make meaning for the people who practise the ritual, it would follow that one has to understand the performing community before grasping the meaning behind the actions and gestures. Something about the social organisation of the people would seem necessary for understanding their ritual. Indeed she asserts that,

> Social relationships are represented in the organisation of ritual; the constitution of the congregation, the allocation of roles in the performance, and the identity of those directing it, are modelled on the structure of the society concerned.[114]

Ritual is intimately connected with the performing community because it is concerned with legitimating and affirming the divisions and hierarchies, which are indispensable to their system of authority. This is in keeping with the fact that in the ritual there are officiates whose legitimacy must depend upon their knowledge of traditions. They must have information and experience needed for the successful and correct performance of the ritual.[115] This knowledge is what lends legitimacy to their positions and roles. There is a distinction between the elders who have knowledge, and the initiates who do not, creating a need for the latter to aspire to the higher and knowledgeable status of the elders. In her words,

> Knowledge often appears to be equated with power, power based on the control of mystical rather than material resources ... The first of them is power which can be defined as coercive force, whether as the result of physical or economic pressure. The other is authority which

---

112 Ibid., p. 15.
113 Ibid., p. 11.
114 Ibid., p. 11.
115 Ibid., p. 17.

is the recognised right to command, legitimised by appeal to principles which are part of the moral order.[116]

She avers that initiation ritual in particular is aimed at sexual identity, which is an important aspect of adult status. She argues that in initiation boundaries are defined between members and outsiders. Even among the insiders, boundaries are also defined between people with different statuses. In a nutshell, initiation ritual is about hierarchical order in a society.[117] One of these demarcations is between male and female gender in society. As she puts it,

> All maturity rites proclaim a fundamental distinction between male and female, which is imbued with social significance ... the concepts of 'man' and 'woman' are constructed and justified by references to what is selected for emphasis by the society in question.[118]

She sees initiation as overtly aimed at testing and enhancing male powers, which though already developed have to be intensified by the ritual.

It is her contention that society dramatises sexual distinctions designed to reinforce and underline separation between genders. This explains why the initiation of boys and that of girls are normally exclusive. Each gender is usually initiated separately from the other to emphasise this difference. She compares this with the ritual division between outsiders and insiders in secret societies. The difference between maturity rituals and those of secret societies is that the former is public while the latter is not.[119]

The separation between the sexes in ritual helps to sustain social role division, in such a way that the two are socially indispensable to one another. This is yet another difference between maturity rituals and those of secret societies. According to her, in spite of men's opposition to women because of the formers exclusive secret knowledge, they are intimately associated with women in joint domestic enterprises. This means that,

> The social division by gender may imply complementarity but it usually implies asymmetry as well. The ideas associated with maleness are represented as superior. Thus the ritual which marks the division of the sexes also produces the justification for male

---

116 Ibid., p. 17.
117 Ibid., p. 16.
118 Ibid., p. 117.
119 Ibid., p. 118.

domination of society, even in societies where descent is reckoned through women and only women are initiated.[120]

She sees oaths as an important element in initiation rituals where some sort of secret information has to be protected, for fear that it might be revealed. Where oaths may be absent in initiation, other mechanisms compel the initiate to recognise his or her changed state and new obligations, which is essentially what an oath does.[121]

She has no doubt that in all initiation rituals there are highly dramatic moments, of excitement and tension, of solemnity and grandeur, and also of comedy.[122] I find her theory on initiation pertinent to Masaba cultural initiation, which after all informs some of her theory on ritual in general, and initiation ritual in particular.

3.5. THE SIGNIFICANCE OF RITUALS IN SOCIETY

Rituals dramatise an anticipated crisis or event, thereby generating a sense of familiarity and confidence in the people who participate in them. Having gone through a ritual people tend to have the confidence that they can do that which was being acted out. They tend to think that it is familiar and that they already know it.

What is acted out tends to be confused or identified with the reality, the hoped for with its achievement. They feel that they can do actually what they have already done ritually. It could be explained by recourse to the fact that rituals are normally potent and fundamentally expressive. This is easily confused with being instrumentally effective, just like the symbol often gets mistaken for that which is symbolised, or a statue with the real. Having undergone death and resurrection symbolically, one has the sense of being familiar with death.

Rituals create a sense of unity among the participants who now identify with one another, giving them a sense of solidarity and comradeship. This is in contradistinction to parochial kinship identity, and opens up new avenues for ever more relationships.

---

[120] Ibid., p. 118.
[121] Ibid., p. 16.
[122] Ibid., p. 181.

Rituals also provide renewal for the community. Whenever the initiated members participate in subsequent initiations they are reminded of their own initiation. These are opportunities for renewal and re-dedication to uphold the beliefs and values of the community. It could be argued that by successive initiation of the youth, the community at large is re-initiated, renewed and newly imbued with life and hope. By witnessing the initiation of young members the older folk relive their own initiation and realise the passage of time, as they will now have become a generation of elders with new and specified roles in the community.

Successive initiation ceremonies avail the older generation the opportunity of ongoing formation. As they now mete out instructions and exhortations, they are challenged to re-examine their own lives to see as to whether they have internalised and experientially lived these values. That is why the community will only allow people who have internalised the values they preach to officiate at such rites. The candidate only has to look at the personal life of the preaching elder to understand his admonitions. This is experiential teaching.

Rituals bring change of status, not only for the newly initiated but also for their parents and the entire community through the network of kinships. They provide an opportunity for blessings in terms of sprinkling, invocations, blowing upon with beer, smearing with chime and yeast. They avail protection to the initiates by way of the blessings and incantations, and provide separation from the others who have not undergone initiation. They relieve tension in the community by bringing the excess energy of the young under the control and guidance of the elders who have experience in life.

There is implementation of the community's values and beliefs, without which the ritual would be but a mere feast or play. The faith of the performing community comes into play and pivots the sacred by attributing sacrality to particular situations. Without the faith of the religious community, the objects they regard as sacred would be but ordinary objects. As van Gennep puts it,

> Characteristically, the presence of the sacred (and the performance of appropriate rites) is variable. Sacredness as an attribute is not

absolute; it is brought into play by the nature of particular situations.[123]

Without inner eyes to behold their sacred nature, these rites would be but secular activities: the procession but a mere dance, the sacrifices but a feast to be partaken of by all and sundry.

Sacrality, therefore, is extrinsic, found in the believers and not in the objects regarded as sacred. The community of believers bring the sacredness to the object, but sacredness is not found in the object by its very nature. It is the religious beliefs of the performing community which give meaning to what is happening.

3.6. RITUAL AS EXPRESSION OF RELIGIOUS BELIEF

Religious behaviour has to do with reciprocity between the human and that which he considers to be the recipient of his prayers and worship. This interaction takes the form of prayer, invocation, sacrifice, praise and so on. Rituals are normally associated with so-called preliterate societies to transmit cultural and social values to the younger generations.

Yet the central interest of religion appears to concern something which is comparatively vague and intangible, something whose empirical reality is not at all clear. It is concerned with a beyond, with man's relation towards that beyond, and with what these particular people consider to be the practical implications of that beyond for their life.[124]

One important reason behind the power of ritual is its rich symbolism. Symbols are themselves rich in expression as they are flexible, having power to push forward the frontiers of knowledge beyond the empirical in their pursuit of ultimate reality. Rituals are, therefore, used to communicate something of a religious value to other members of the community, through word, symbol, or action. The people involved in ritual are saying something and doing something they value and believe, something they desire and hope to achieve, for as Beattie observes,

---

[123] Van Gennep, *Rites of Passage*, p. 12.

[124] Thomas F. O'Dea and Janet O'Dea Aviad, *The Sociology of Religion*. Englewood-Cliffs: Prentice-Hall, 1983, pp. 1-2.

Rituals almost always embody beliefs, and these beliefs may provide acceptable explanations for events which would otherwise be inexplicable ... they provide an antidote to ignorance and doubt. For most people, in all times and cultures it is important to know, even know wrongly, rather than not to know at all.[125]

3.7. MYTHS AS BASIS FOR RITUAL

Hans Mol sees a close connection between rites and myths, and he observes that,

> ... irrespective of whether a particular myth is primarily a narrative, an iterative tale, or a speculation about existence, it is always an implicit or explicit statement about man's place in his environment. And this universal function of making statements about man's place is the common character of myths.[126]

He sees the iterative nature of myths as playing the important role of sacralising, and paradoxically, the farther one goes into history the more powerful the myth tends to become. Even in primitive cultures, behind these myths are fundamental notions of integration and instrumentality. He asserts that,

> Myths socialize through the emotional anchorage of integrative reconciliations, but they can do so only through the presentation of the binary opposition with instrumental symbolism. It is in the repetitive presentations and representations that the reconciling function of myth resides.[127]

Myths are important in ritual for the simple reason that they embody claims to divine or miraculous origin and sanction, thereby sacralising human norms and beliefs. For Monica Wilson, the force of ritual comes partly from this connection with antiquity, whether real or supposed. And she sees as a problem facing all who celebrate rituals in this fast changing society, as how to combine relevance to changing circumstances with the sanctity of tradition.[128]

---

[125] John Beattie, *Other Cultures*. London: Routledge and Kegan Paul, 1977, p. 206.

[126] Hans Mol, *Identity*, p. 246.

[127] Hans Mol, *Identity*, p. 261.

[128] Monica Wilson, "The Wedding Cakes: A Study of Ritual Change", in J. S. La Fontaine (ed.), *The Interpretation of Ritual*. London: Tavistock, 1972, p. 188.

Myths bring to the present something from the past, and convey a message to the performing community concerning the importance of the ritual. Myths, therefore, play the central role of trying to explain the origin and hence importance of the ritual, by recourse to the ancestors, thereby situating it within the sacred history of the community. It is an essential element in the rituals because it is myth that bridges the historical gap and relates the initiates to a past.

It is indeed evident that,

> Myth treats of origins but derives from transitions ... Myths relate how one state of affairs became another, how an unpeopled world became populated; how chaos became cosmos; how immortals became mortal; how the seasons came to replace climate without seasons ... and so on. Myths are liminal phenomena: frequently told at a time or in a site that is betwixt and between.[129]

John Beattie who sees as a major function of ritual the expression and reinforcement of certain sentiments or values, to which the smooth running of the performing society depends, shares this same viewpoint. This is achieved especially through indoctrination.[130]

Among the basic functions of myth then is that of evoking the community's memory as a way of reminding the members of their deepest identity. It achieves this by recourse to their collective evolutionary history, thereby forging and integrating the corporate identity of the community.[131]

---

[129] Victor Turner, "Myth and Symbol", in D. Sills (ed.), *The International Encyclopedia of the Social Sciences*. New York: Macmillan Publishers, 1968, p. 576.

[130] John Beattie, *Other Cultures*, p. 217.

[131] Dan Sperber, *Rethinking Symbolism*. Trans. A. L. Morton, Cambridge: Cambridge University Press, 1975, p. 145.

CHAPTER FOUR: MASABA *IMBALU* – A DESCRIPTION

4.1. INTRODUCTION

Gisu initiation ... defines unequivocally for any Gisu the widest group with which he can identify himself. This community can be described as 'we', as against its opposite, 'they', the non-initiate aliens. This common identification indicates the acceptance of common values and a common code of ethical norms, so that what is defined is a moral community, i.e. a category of people whose guiding values are known and accepted by all members.[132]

The origin of the word *imbalu* has been traced to the double-edged knife used in the past for circumcision. This knife was forged out of flint stone, which was put in the fireplace till it turned red-hot before it was beaten flat and sharpened on both sides.[133] The *Lumasaba* (language of the Bamasaba) word for circumcision is *khukhwingila imbalu*, which literally means, "to enter". This is in reference to the fact that the novice formally enters the community as a full member, with full rights and duties therein. Having accomplished this public requirement which leaves an indelible physical mark, he is now fit to be trusted with the secrets and burdens of the community.

Imbalu is the initiation ritual through which manhood is conferred upon Bamasaba male youth. In the past it was the prelude to marriage and the novices would be anywhere between 18 and 25 years of age, though some were older. It is regarded as *likobi lye Bamasaba*, a cultural debt, which ought to be paid voluntarily or otherwise, alive or dead. Defaulters who manage to escape are required to be circumcised before burial, normally at a very high price to the family. This is because the *umukhebi* (circumciser) who carries out this operation has to be paid heavily as he must proceed into retirement henceforth. His knife is considered as permanently and irreparably ritually defiled, so he would not be allowed to circumcise the living anymore. *Imbalu* is, therefore, the gateway through which a male

---

[132] J. S. La Fontaine, "Tribalism Among the Gisu", in *Tradition and Transition in East Africa*. London: Routledge and Kegan Paul, 1972, p. 187.

[133] L. W. Wawomola and L. Wamono interviewed by author on 6th November 1999 at Butiru village.

child acquires full membership and identity in the community, where he is gradually ushered into positions of power and responsibility. This ritual, which defines both self and communal identity, is a covenant with the community comprising the departed, the living and the yet-to-be-born members. The initiate becomes the *tabula rasa* on which society inscribes its accrued indigenous knowledge and mores, and he is taught to think with the community and to see the world as it sees it.[134]

Through it an initiate enters the interior of the community life, which is the exclusive preserve of adults, and by extension, of full members. This ritual emphasises *communitas,* for community is life and through *imbalu* community stamps the seal of belonging upon an individual. It is the beginning of the journey, through rites of passage, towards marriage and parenthood, elderhood, and finally ancestor-hood. The human and the spirit world are after all linked as the ancestors were only recently here before passing on to yet another plane. Death is itself but a rite of passage in the graduation of roles.

This chapter describes the ritual of *imbalu*, as it was traditionally practised by the Bamasaba before the changes brought about by European rule, missionary Christianity and the post independence nation state set in. For purposes of easier reading, and indeed to show continuity, the historical present is preferred to the past tense in the description of *imbalu*.

4.2. THE CANDIDATE AND THE CLAN

Before the coming of European rule, Christianity and modern way of education, circumcision was regarded as a test and stamp of maturity and preceded marriage. The candidate would be anywhere between the ages of 18 and 25 years, though some would be even older. A boy who felt he had reached maturity and wanted to be circumcised would inform his father or another relative with whom he had a cordial relationship about his intended initiation. This relative in turn would speak to the father on the boy's behalf. The father, for his part, informed the elders of the clan about the boy's intentions.

---

[134] For more see especially Aylward Shorter, *Songs and Symbols of Initiation: A Study from Africa in the Social Control of Perception.* Nairobi: CHIEA Press, 1987, pp. 3-5.

The elders would choose a day when to meet on the village green to ascertain the boy's claim to maturity. On this day an elder would give a stick and shield to the boy, and the father would take up his own weapons. Father and son began fighting while the elders watched as they drank *kamalwa* (traditional beer). If they judged that the son was stronger than the father, or at least as strong as the father, an elder would rise and put his own stick between the two combatants to stop the mock fight. The elders would then give the boy the go-ahead knowing that he was old enough to defend himself, his family and indeed the clan in case of attack. It was only after receiving permission from the clan elders that the boy would begin to acquire the appropriate items of *imbalu*, in preparation for the time of *isonja* (communal dancing).[135]

4.3. THE MAIN ACTORS IN *IMBALU*

The main actors in the rites are the following:

Umusinde (the novice) himself: He is the main focus of the entire community and the most important, for without him the festivities of initiation would not be possible. Though he is in focus, he needs the community and other specialised persons to make his desire for circumcision a reality. There is a saying that *akhaba umurafu sekheba taa*[136] (even a brave one does not circumcise himself). This underlines dependence upon others for many things, as nobody is self-sufficient.

Umukhebi (the surgeon or circumciser) is an important personage as he is the efficient cause, as is *umunutsi* (his assistant). These are professionals in their field, charged with the actual act of circumcising. They receive their profession as a calling, usually through spirit possession or dreams, and the profession runs in particular clans known for *kumusambwa kwebukhebi* (the spirit of circumcision). But apart from being surgeons, they are believed to possess certain spiritual and magical powers, including herbal knowledge. As such they are treated with care and awe by the community, but especially by the young who are prospective candidates for

---

135 L. W. Wawomola and L. Wamono interviewed by author on 6th November 1999 at Butiru village.

136 This common saying among the Bamasaba underscores human limitation and the absolute need of belonging to and being assisted by a community.

circumcision. The surgeon maintains a unique relationship with the people he circumcises, and these address him by the endearing title of *kuka* (grandfather).

Namyenya (song-leader) is the one charged with the organisation and discipline of the group during *isonja* (collective dancing) and later takes charge of an individual initiate or group of initiates during the phase of visiting relatives.

Uwetyanyi (medicine-man) is a person believed to possess knowledge of how to fortify the candidate with certain potent herbs in food and/or drink. Sometimes, he hides the medicine where the candidate can stride over it. He also has the power of rendering medicines and spells cast against the novice by evil-minded people useless.

Uwesanda (gourd-bearer) is an elder of exemplary behaviour, wealthy, generous, kind, slow to anger and one who has sired many sons. He should not be a widower, as losing a spouse is a misfortune usually attributed to some personal fault, broken taboo or displeasure by the ancestors. The duty of the gourd-bearer is to carry the gourd containing the ritual beer with which the initiates are blessed, to invoke the ancestors and ward off evil spirits. This he does by drinking the beer, holding it in the mouth and spewing it upon the initiate and the escorts, as he recites a litany of ancestors, beseeching them to be present and to shower blessings upon the rituals. This is believed to undo or render ineffective any spells cast upon the novice, and to exorcise him of any evil.

Umuakhi (yeast-man) is an elderly man possessing the qualities required of the gourd-bearer above. On the other hand, the duty of the *umuakhi* is to smear the candidates and their near of kin with the ritual yeast paste. Yeast is made from sprouted millet, which is ground and mixed with water to form the paste.

Umulongi is the ritual elder whose job it is to smear the candidates with sacred clay on the day of circumcision. He must possess the same qualities as those required of the *uwesanda* and *umuakhi* .

Umutiliini (attendant) is the person charged with the well being of the *umufulu* (newly circumcised initiate). This is usually a young boy of exceptionally good behaviour. His duties include cooking for the newly initiated, and running errands for him. He is also the one to enforce the restrictions that regulate life during convalescence. For instance the *umufulu* should not be rained on, may not shelter in a house other than *likombe* (convalescence hut), either his own or a friend's. He is not supposed to come home late from a walk, etc. In the event that this happens he must pay his *umutiliini* an egg or a chick given him by friends during his walks, before being let into the hut.

Basaali (the parents) occupy an important and special role in the rituals. They are the hosts and if anything goes wrong during the rite of circumcision, it is they who bear the brunt of the embarrassment, not to mention the material penalties some of these may imply.

Baakhootsa (the maternal uncles) are of very special importance too. Although the Bamasaba are patrilineal, the maternal uncles come second only to the mother in caring for the children of their sister. If a boy falls out with the father and the clan, he normally seeks refuge with his maternal uncles and will feel safe. Maternal uncles' express permission is, therefore, required before a boy can be circumcised. This permission is given in the form of *isoso* (twigs) bunched together or singly, given to the novice to hold in the hands as he goes for the circumcision ritual. The permission of the maternal uncles is also required for the practical purpose that they must prepare themselves to receive and send him away with honour. Normally the maternal uncles are expected to give to their nephew a gift of a cow, either live or slaughtered. They therefore need ample notice to prepare themselves.

Baraara (paternal uncles) are also important for they constitute the clan as Bamasaba are a patrilineal and virilocal community. The paternal uncles are the immediate community upon whom the duty of ensuring that the rites are carried through successfully is incumbent. They contribute in giving moral and material support to the family, and are always present all the way. The ritual elders who are central to the ritual, namely *umuakhi*, *uwesanda* and *umulongi*, are normally taken from among the paternal uncles. Whatever differences may have existed between them hitherto are supposed to dissolve and are forgotten during this most important of the clan's festivals. If anything goes wrong the whole clan comes under ridicule especially from their *bakulo* (people with whom they have a joking relationship). Allowing differences to prevail during such a time would be tantamount to injuring oneself in the process.

Bakulo (joking partners) are members of nearby clans with whom a clan has an historical joking relationship. They are neither strangers nor blood relatives, but are a special and privileged group with unique freedom of action and speech towards their counterparts. This institution is strictly sanctioned by taboo, and invested with unique roles.

These were once enemies of the clan, because of inter-clan killings. This may have occurred during a fight over land demarcation disputes, or perhaps when a member of one clan was caught *flagrante delicto* with a wife of a member of the opposite clan. The bereaved clan would seek revenge, and this became a vicious circle with each clan killing a member of the opposite clan at the earliest opportunity, and at the slightest provocation. To stop these killings and end the state of war, the elders from both clans met to resolve the matter. They made a covenant of friendship by cutting a dog into two. All the members passed between the halves and they took an oath to end their mutual hostility. They called down a curse upon whoever would contravene the covenant, saying, "May what has happened to the dog befall whoever contravenes our covenant".[137]

This covenant was known as **khukhala imbwa** (cutting a dog). Then each clan buried their half of the dog on their side of the boundary, and declared a cessation of hostilities henceforth. But the members would still harbour painful memories of the loss of their loved ones. If these painful memories were left unattended to, it would be simply a matter of time before they were given vent when the opportunity arose. To get rid of these hard feelings and take care of this spectre of renewed hostilities, the elders instituted **bukulo**, a joking relationship where members of these clans would barter insults without either party taking offence. Instead of fighting which would ignite more hostilities, the insulted party simply goes to the home of his tormentor and takes away a hen, a goat, a cow, or even a girl for marriage. But this has to be done during broad daylight for all to see, and has to leave a trail or a message so that the owner knows who has done this to him.

After some months or even years, the other person may reciprocate and the relationship continues. The highest prize is when the parties take away girls

---

[137] J. B. Purvis, *Through Uganda to Mount Elgon*. London: T. Fisher Unwin, 1909, pp. 292-293.

from each other's clans for wives: No bride price is demanded, but the other clan bides time before they too takes away a girl from the opposite clan as revenge. Inter-marriage marks a turning point in the joking relationship, which continues down the line through their offspring. Referring to the importance of joking relations, Laurenti Magesa notes that,

> ... joking relationships ... provide assistance for such activities as burials (where dealing with them might be forbidden within the family) ... and handling medical or religious functions for one another.[138]

Because of this special relationship, members of such clans are bold enough to disclose to one another things nobody else would dare mention. If a member of one clan is seriously erring, a *mukulo* (joking partner) is tipped off and detailed to advise him. He does this in a joking manner but the culprit certainly gets the message without the possibility of taking offence or resorting to legal redress.[139] These neighbours come to witness the circumcision ritual and throw challenges at the initiates by alluding to them as cowards. If the initiate exhibits fear and cries out during the circumcision rite, it is perceived as a curse. It is the duty of the *bakulo* (joking partners) to seize the cowardly initiate, pin him down and to forcefully circumcise him. Then they reward themselves by looting homes of the parents and other clansmen.

Besikuuka (kinsmen and women), are actively involved, as the novice is theirs as opposed to those of other clans. Commensality is a key issue, and the idea of belonging strongly comes into play especially during this time, as the novice is presented as belonging to a particular clan. In the event that he exhibits fear and thereby defiles the ritual, it would be perceived as a curse to the said clan. It would, consequently, be very hard for people from that clan to get marriage partners, as they would be seen as a clan of cowards, and as people with a curse.[140]

Balebe (relatives) individually and collectively are actively involved. It is especially during this time that the spirit of collective responsibility comes

---

138 Laurenti Magesa, *African Religion: The Moral Traditions of Abundant Life*. Maryknoll, New York: Orbis Books 1997, pp. 112-113.

139 L. W. Wawomola and L. Wamono, interviewed by author on 6th November 1999 at Butiru village.

140 L. W. Wawomola, and L. Wamono, interviewed by author on 6th November 1999 at Butiru village.

alive, just as it does during marriage and funerals. If one is known to be selfish, one is told to one's face by the *bakulo* (joking partners) and if one does not reform, then one faces social sanctions like public ridicule and/or by being ostracised.

Basambwa (ancestral spirits), both paternal and maternal, are a very important and integral component of the clan in the rituals. *Imbalu* is said to have been instituted by them, so they are invoked to be present and to see them successfully through to their logical conclusion. As Charles Nyamiti has noted, "The present world is closely connected with the world after death, and one lives in close contact with one's ancestors...".[141]

Most importantly, *Wele* (God Himself) is believed to be present in a special way during the initiation festivities.[142]

4.4. WAY OF DRESSING

According to their ability to collect from relatives and friends or hiring from those who possess them, some novices wear more items and others less, but the very basic ones are the following:

Bitzentze (iron thigh-bells), worn three or four on each thigh. The thigh-bells make a jingling musical rhythm to the accompaniment of song and dance.

Bibyuma (strings of beads), worn over one shoulder and passed under the other armpit. Upon these are hung handkerchiefs donated to the individual by sisters and girlfriends. Some of these beads are given to the novice by the aunts. Traditionally women wore beads round their waists, believed to increase erotic stimulation by their smooth feel. Beads, therefore, are associated with virility and fecundity.

Tzinyimba (hand bells) are a substitute for thigh bells for those initiates who would rather use the upper part of their bodies. It is an option which some initiates and/or parents prefer. The focus is the same: the production of music.

---

141 Charles Nyamiti, *The Scope of African Theology*. Kampala: Gaba Publications, 1973, p. 21.

142 Lawrence Tsemale, Antony Matanda and Fab Ronald Walukhaso interviewed by author on 11th September 1999 at Bukhaweka village.

Ikwena, a circlet of wood or ivory worn on the forehead for decoration, but which makes the initiate look as if he has horns.

Lilubisi, a headdress made from colobus monkey skin.

Likhalala, a skin belt decorated with cowry shells.

Kamakayi, strips of hide also decorated with cowry shells worn hanging down the back, and swirl like tails as the novice dances or jumps in the air.

Ikutusi, a leopard skin worn hanging down the back. A leopard is a taboo animal among the Bamasaba.

Copper or iron bracelets worn on the wrists. These were traditionally only worn by *bakasa* (chiefs) as an insignia of authority and elevation in society.

The novice is at this time set apart in society for a space of time, and for a special function in which the whole community has a stake. He is the centre of attention and attraction of the whole community, so he actually shares in the importance of the chief. The community invests their hope and future in the young persons as the future well being of the community depend upon them. The memory of the dead can only be kept alive through procreation and successive naming by the younger generations, thereby ensuring their immortality. The future of the older generation, therefore, depends on the fecundity of these novices.

The animal skins and other paraphernalia have the overall effect of making the candidate look spectacular and "less-than-human". They make him feel no longer, or rather not yet, a human being, and are meant to leave a lingering sense of revulsion whenever he remembers how he looked and was treated. He would then ascribe this to the condition of *businde* (childhood), thereby making the acquisition of manhood something of a hard-won achievement to be proudly treasured, while *businde* and all its concomitants are seen as undignified. It is society's way of perception control where this feeling helps to associate boyhood with a lower status, and presents *busani* (manhood) as the coveted target for it is more dignified.

The candidate for *imbalu* becomes the medium through whom the life of the ancestors continues to flow. He is the link with the past represented by the ancestors whose names he bears, the present whose blood he carries in his veins, and the future generation whom he holds in his loins. He, therefore, gives meaning to the life of the ancestors, to that of his parents, and hope to the clan as a whole that their death will not be the end of the stream of life. It is this realisation that makes the community come alive for indeed they all have a stake in the initiate's manhood.

4.5. MAIN PHASES OF *IMBALU*

Imbalu is carried out every two years in the months of August and December, for village based and school going initiates, respectively. August is suitable because it is after the main harvest of millet, maize, sorghum, beans and peas, to feed the novices and their parties of participants. December became necessary because it is the time of the long school holidays, and it is also after the second harvest.

Imbalu begins and ends with a dance, and the entire season is a festival characterised by music and dance. The initiates wear thigh bells and jingles, while others carry hand bells, as their main instruments of producing music. There is also the added introduction of *tzing'oma* (drums) accompanied by songs where the *namyenya* (song leader) or the initiate himself sings the stanzas while the congregation sing the chorus. The first and concluding dances, namely *isonja* and *ineemba*, are collective in nature and have a special symbolic aspect. The main phases of *imbalu* are the following:

4.5.1. *Phase One:* Isonja, *Initial Group Dance*

Isonja (group dance) marks the first serious phase, and takes place between March and May during the weeding season. This is when the novices from one ridge meet on the playground and choose their own *namyenya* (tutor cum song leader) to lead them in song and dance. It is a group dance where the prospective candidates come out for a drill in the art of singing and dancing, and is used for acclimatising them to wearing *bitzentze* (thigh bells) and other items of dress worn by novices. *Namyenya* is a local poet and historian, adept at composing didactic songs, knowledgeable in the history of the tribe in general, knows the myths and genealogies of different clans, as well as the legends associated with the different heroes. *Namyenya* also acts as the chief soloist, instructor and master of ceremonies all in one.

All meet in the evenings to sing and dance until dusk before retiring to their respective homes. At this early stage the candidates for *imbalu* are not taken seriously, and only a few relatives accompany them to the *isonja* ground. The candidates are at this time testing their own resolve, and many quietly withdraw, waiting for the next circumcision period.

During *isonja* different *namyenya* (composers) vie with one another in composing danceable tunes and invent different dancing styles. People turn out to watch and to be entertained by the music and dance. The novices also compete to see who will dance better than the others, to impress the spectators and win the hearts of girls. It is a show of strength and style, as those who are not strong enough are elbowed away to dance on the fringes, or wait for the next season.

The strength and enthusiasm exhibited during *isonja* is a pointer to both the physical preparedness of the novice, and indeed of his inner resolve to go through with the exercise. Normally those who are unable to cope with *isonja* are pronounced immature and are advised to lay off and wait for the next season while they grow stronger. *Isonja* is also the time when the candidates learn the art of composition that comes handy later on when they are on their own. The novice with the best array of danceable songs also attracts more followers who have to sing and dance to the chorus.

Novices and their parties travel long distances visiting relatives, and the strength to cope with the performance and distance depends much on the type of inspiring songs led by the novice and chorused by the group. The terrain determines the tempo of the music: quick tempo is for trotting downhill while a slower tempo is for climbing hills.[143]

Below are two samples of songs sung during the *isonja* dance, with the soloist singing the stanzas and the whole group responding with the chorus.

---

[143] L. W. Wawomola and L. Wamono, interviewed by author on 6th November 1999 at Butiru village. Lawrence Tsemale interviewed by the author on 9th November 1999 at Bukhaweka village corroborated this information about *isonja*, and saw it especially as a way of building stamina for the ordeal.

1. Imbalu Mulilo   *Imbalu* is Fire

Mulembe,	Salutations,
Eeh!	Eeh!
Mulembe wamuna	Salutations to you Wamuna
Imbalu mulilo	*Imbalu* is fire
Musinde	Initiate
Eee!	Eee!
Musinde Wamuna	Initiate Wamuna
Imbalu mulilo	*Imbalu* is fire
Musinde	Initiate
Eeh!	Eeh!
Wamwene Wakikanile	You yourself wanted it
Imbalu mulilo	*Imbalu* is fire
Wamwene	You yourself
Eeh!	Eeh!
Wamwene Wakikanile	You wanted it yourself
Imbalu mulilo[144]	*Imbalu* is fire

---

[144] John Bukuna and Steven Namunyala interviewed by author on 28th September 1999 at Buketera village.

2. Bari-Nasyombe   That You are Mature

Bari Nasyombe!	That you are mature!
Rera *imbalu* Nasyombe kawazowa	Exhibit *imbalu* to us, as you are now mature
Rera mbola musani kawazowa	Exhibit *imbalu* gently, you are mature
Rera mbola wandayese kano bone	Exhibit *imbalu*, my brother you are mature
Rera mbola *imbalu* kano male	Exhibit *imbalu* gently, you will make it
Sanyisa *imbalu* wandayese kanomale	Dance *imbalu* my brother, you will make it
Bari Nasyombe kanomale [145]	You great one will make it

4.5.2. Phase Two: Khuwentza *(searching for)* Imbalu

From May to July after the *isonja* is over, the novices with their own parties of participants visit far away relatives to inform them about their intention and ask for blessings. Coming to dance in a relative's homestead is known as *khuyila kumukheti*. The novice carries a long stick whose bark has been peeled off. This stick known as *kumukheti* is what waves in the air as he dances. Hens or even a goat are slaughtered and food cooked for the novice and his party, and sometimes a gift of a goat is given to the novice to take home. Such gifts are either repayment for those given by the novice's father, or are expected to be reciprocated when the giver's own son also dances *imbalu*.

4.5.3. Phase Three: Khukhupaka *(thrashing millet)*

Two weeks before the date of circumcision the novice thrashes millet for brewing beer that will be drunk on his initiation day. On this day the novice

---

[145] Ibid.

invites his fellow novices from the neighbourhood to help him perform this rite. They thrash millet at his grandfather's home first, but if the grandfather is already dead, they do it at the home of the elder where he will be circumcised. Then they come back to thrash more millet in his father's homestead. Millet used for this ceremony is normally from previous harvests, and must not be from the harvest of the particular year. The symbolism for the preference of old items to new ones is discussed under the interpretation of *imbalu*.

A hen is held by its legs and passed over this millet, with some feathers being plucked and scattered among the millet before thrashing. The novices leave the thrashing process halfway, to be completed by the family. He and his friends go to the bush to roast and eat the chicken with roasted bananas. As a rule this millet is ground and fermented on the very day.[146]

4.5.4. *Phase Four:* Khukoya *(brewing of beer)*

The brewing of beer, two days before the circumcision day, ushers this phase in. It is the most intense of all the phases as it immediately builds towards the climax of the whole exercise, which is *khukhwingila imbalu* (circumcision). Consequently, most rituals are concentrated into these three days, which mark the countdown to success or failure, for both the family and clan in general, and for the novice in particular. This period is the heart of the circumcision festivities, and is pervaded with invocations, sacrifices, divinations, purification, and other rituals. It is the sacred time, which determines the fate of all parties concerned in the final ritual.

Two days prior to the actual day of circumcision, the scene undergoes a dramatic change as the dancing builds momentum towards the climax. Candidates from the same ridge or village gather on the common playground before proceeding to the home of the *umukasa* (chief). They dance on his courtyard as a sign of respect and as a humble request for permission to brew the beer, which will act as the countdown to their circumcision. The *umukasa* formally asks them if they have actually resolved to become men, to which all the novices shake their thigh bells in unison. He then proceeds to exhort and admonish them to be brave, and to

---

[146] Augustine Wandende and Ludwig Wamono interviewed by author on 22nd August 1999 in Nakaloke village.

do the clan proud by living up to the expectations of the community. The following is a sample of such exhortation:

Inywe mwabene kamwerusa ibulafu	You yourselves have come out
Bari nanywe mukan *imbalu*.	That you want to be circumcised
Uli khukana bamukhebe ali?	Who among you wants *imbalu*?

(They all shake the thigh bells in unison).

Imbalu isimuli khukana, iyebakuka	The circumcision you aspire to belongs to the ancestors
Iya Nabarwa	It belongs to *Nabarwa*
Ne *Imbalu* yarafua! *Imbalu* kumulilo!	But *imbalu* is not a joke. It is fire.
N'enywe basani mwaangala.	But you are mature.
Imbalu urakho kumwoyo nawengila	You need to put your heart in it.
Ife Banambogo sikhuriatsyaka taa	We Banambogo do not fear it.
Nga nimwirerekho khumbalu,	Since you yourselves will it.
Mwitsa *imbalu* iyefe ing'ene.	Imitate our example,
Musangase bakeni,	Delight the visitors,
Mufumise sikuka sye Banamboko.	Do the Banamboko proud.
Ari khina kamabeka khubone .[147]	Now let us see you dance.

The candidates then dance and thank him in song and dance. The **umukasa** performs the ritual brewing of beer himself pouring water in a small pot containing **tsimuma** (roasted dough). He proceeds to bless them by blowing beer upon them while invoking the blessings of the ancestors upon the festivities. This is a formal permission for them to go back and brew beer in their respective homes. They all return, each to the homestead where they will be circumcised, to start the brewing exercise.

---

[147] Abdul Matanda, interviewed by author on 1st October 1999 at Bukhaweka village.

4.5.4.1. Iluutzi, *Journey to the Stream*

The candidate takes an old pot and goes running to the stream to fetch water. He scoops water with his bare hands to fill the pot, which he then carries on his bare head without anything to cushion it, and goes back home at a trot. He pours the water into a small pot containing *tsimuma* (roasted dough), placed beneath the *lukangu* (ritual pole). It is at this particular spot that all subsequent sacrifices will be offered to the ancestors. It is also the spot where the initiate will stand, both to be smeared with yeast and later to be circumcised.

The beer that the novice himself brews is what the circumciser's drink; while the rest of the guests drink that which does his father brew. His mother later adds yeast to this hitherto insipid and dormant mixture of water and dough, thereby setting the fermentation process into motion.

4.5.4.2. Khuuakha, *Rite Of Smearing*

After the brewing of beer the candidate, dressed in the traditional regalia, stands erect under the ritual pole, waiting for the rite of *khuuakha limela* (smearing with yeast). This is a loose paste of sprouted millet that has been dried and ground into fine flour mixed with water.

An exemplary elder noted for his benevolence, generosity and forbearance, one who is wealthy and productive, is asked by the presiding elder to perform the rite of smearing the novice. The boy's unmarried sister stands beside the novice and is smeared together with him. Smearing is done amidst exhortation to the candidate to be of good conduct, obedient, respectful to old and young, responsible and upright in his dealings with all and sundry. The elder addresses the candidate as grandfather, and again as father before he proceeds with the following exhortation, saying:

Aa kukaa; aa papaa!	Aah grandfather, aah father
Umusani nga wimil'orio wamalile	The way you are standing is enough
Niwima wewoleles'oryo, uba wamalile	You stand firm and unflinching
Sindi khukhuakha kamamela kano	I am not smearing you

Ndi utsye bukhwale tawe	To get married.
Ndi khukhua kumusambwa kwembalu.	I am giving you the rite of *imbalu*
Umusani usindikha kumwena	As a man you push the navel forward
Kumubano kwakendakho newewolelesile	Let the knife do the rounds
Kumuya uela mbola	Release the breath gradually
Ulinda kumurundula	Beware of the lower incision
Umusani ulinda *imbalu* iyefwe inyene	As a man emulate our bravery
Imbalu yarafua, *imbalu* kumulilo	Circumcision is painful, it is fire
Ne umusani watsoa, itsa iyefwe inyene	But you are mature, emulate us
Uone bakeni, usangase sikuka.[148]	Dismiss the guests, delight the clan.

The candidate stands erect, his eyes fixed ahead and unblinking, and his body motionless. The elder takes his time to do his duty, and whoever among the congregated elders has an observation to make, or just to lend weight to the words of others throwing in his own words of wisdom. They all chorus their approval of his words to lend weight to them, as they roundly condemn any trait in the initiate's behaviour which is unbecoming of a man and exhort him to abandon it forthwith.

He is absolutely at the mercy of the elders who are believed to possess knowledge and power to punish him by causing him to fear circumcision or to bleed profusely if they are displeased. He remains silent through this harangue, impassively staring into space and his face deadpan. The elders will be keenly scrutinising his face for any signs of rebellion, anger, defiance or amusement in his eyes. It is the only time they will ever have him so helplessly under their power and at their mercy, so they take their

---

[148] Abdul Matanda and Damascus Wandende interviewed by author on 1st October 1999 at Musiru village.

sweet time about it. Any inkling of defiance will call down a barrage of condemnation upon him.

When they are eventually through with him he leaps into the air three times, then he thanks them in song, pledging that he has taken to heart all that the elders have said. It should be noted that from the time beer is brewed, the novice does not say anything in his normal voice but has to intone it while the participants answered. He does not use the singular "I" but the plural "we". The following is a sample of what the candidate says in response.

Basakhulu balomile khwawulile	The elders have spoken and we have heard
Tsingano ni tsindikha khwawulile	We have understood the myths and proverbs
Khukambila ni bibindi khwahambile	We have heard the exhortation and the riddles
Ibyo byosi khufukilila khubilinda	We pledge to observe all the exhortations
Basambwa ni bakuka bakhuyete	We implore the ancestors to assist us
Kumusambwa kwembalu khukumale[149]	To successfully finalise the rite of *imbalu*

This is the beginning of the countdown to the actual operation. From then till his circumcision on the third day, he is not allowed to speak in his normal voice but must chant whatever he wishes to say. The air becomes festive and the code of conduct is temporarily suspended as words and actions normally deemed socially offensive, obscene or sexually explicit are allowed for the period of three days. Relationships, which are normally defined by mutual avoidance, for instance those between children and parents in law, are relaxed. The boundary between humans and spirits is transgressed by the wearing of masquerades to scare women and children.

---

[149] Ibid.

The demarcation between the sexes is blurred too as men turn out with plaited hair wearing women's dresses and answering to feminine names, as women too wear men's clothes and answer to male names and titles.

The *imbalu* procession may pass through people's homesteads or gardens as the escorts circumvent any cross-roads where evil-minded persons may have planted medicines to make the novice fearful or to harm him in any way. At this time the individual good and personal rights are held in abeyance in deference to the higher common good. Nothing is more important at this time than the job of successfully bringing the novices safely through this exercise. The atmosphere is highly charged, and whoever does not move away fast enough from the path of the procession risks strokes of the sticks the people carry. The everyday running of the show like guiding, escorting the novice, protecting him from the spectre of witchcraft and sorcery and related issues are left to the younger generation of his initiated brethren.

The elders do not accompany the dancing party to the different relatives, for they lack the physical stamina required for such long journeys. Instead they remain home planning which relatives the novice should visit next. They are also concerned with the technical side of the ritual, an area which needs knowledge and wisdom, not to mention experience and expertise. By virtue of their age, they are closer to the ancestors who are the lawgivers and guardians of *imbalu.*

4.5.4.3. Kumululilo, *Day Of Circumcision*

The third day after the brewing of the beer is the climax of the festivities and is also the most memorable day in the life of a *Mumasaba* man. Much is at stake on this day for better or for worse, as good reputation or embarrassment and stigma are all distinct possibilities.

The ceremony is one, which has a lasting impression upon the novice, the determinant factor as to how his subsequent life will be. The day begins with a visit to the ancestral burial place where the elders charged with its custody will have cleared and re-marked them earlier that same morning. A man must know where his ancestors were buried, and it is considered negligent for one not to know the persons whose bones lie under the different graves, or whose skulls rest between the forked branches of trees behind the homestead. For how can he identify with people he does not know?

This has something to do with the central issue of land ownership. Where the graves of one's ancestors are located is powerful proof that they owned the land where they were buried. Traditionally all land belonged to the clan and nobody allocated ancestral land was allowed to sell it for whatever reason. Even if he wanted to move away to another place he would negotiate with members of the clan for some sort of compensation. One of the reasons behind this stipulation was fear of desecration of the resting places of the ancestors by strangers. Even those who were unfortunate enough not to have sons to inherit their land were required to pass it on to one of their "sons" in the clan.

The sacred grove is out of bounds to women and uncircumcised boys, so only the elders and the initiates are allowed into it. The elder in charge of the grove pours libation to the ancestors amid invocation for them to bless their offspring. A fowl is slaughtered as propitiation and communion sacrifice to the ancestors in the presence of the novices. This is roasted and eaten with roasted bananas, burning whatever may have remained in the fire before leaving. Whatever was talked about in the sacred grove remains a secret between the participants alone, and is never discussed. This serves to instil into the initiates a sense of veneration for their ancestors, and is an important ingredient in their religious formation. It also serves to make them feel that they have reached a new stage when they can be entrusted with the clan secrets and responsibilities, and indeed allowed to tread on sacred territory.

Back in the homestead where the initiate will be circumcised, the novice's father will have fixed *lukangu* (ritual pole) consisting of a forked branch of a *lusoola* tree (*markhamia platy calyx*), in the middle of his own courtyard. This is planted in the courtyard only when a man becomes an elder upon the circumcision of his son. If the novice is his first son to be initiated, then the father by performing this ceremony formally becomes an elder. A son is considered a manifestation of fecundity, and for the son to reach initiation a man will now have come of age and reached the stage of elderhood. The status of an elder does not simply depend upon age but the achievements therein. A man who does not bear children is said "to have wasted the yeast" he was smeared with, as it will not have borne any fruit.[150]

Lukangu is regarded as the sacred pole where the living dead and other supernaturals congregate, and is the place where all public sacrifices in the homestead are offered. It is the external counterpart to *intzeko* (central upright pole of the house), believed to be the congregating spot for *basambwa* (ancestral spirits).

Lukangu (ritual pole) is where the father or ritual elder sacrifices *iyemulukangu,* a bull slaughtered in thanksgiving to the ancestors. The blood is left to flow and sink into the ground at the bottom of the *lukangu* as appeasement to them. The entrails of the sacrificial animal are divined for tokens. The father cuts out the heart and lungs of the sacrificed animal and hangs them on the *lukangu.* Then he takes *buse* (chyme) and smears it on the forehead, chest and feet of the initiate amid invocation of the ancestral spirits. He also smears him with yeast. This is an auspicious sacrifice coming as it does on the morning that the initiate is to be circumcised. The day is loaded with expectation, excitement and trepidation. With all these informing the mood, amidst the rite of smearing, the father or ritual elder proceeds to pray over the initiate. The prayer states the origin and significance of *imbalu.* Then he enumerates the norms of manhood, admonishing the initiate to internalise, uphold, defend and always propagate them. The following is a sample of the bidding prayer during this rite:

Imbalu iyebakhale,	*Imbalu* belongs to the ancestors
Iyebakuka	It belongs to the grandfathers
Imbalu iya Nabarwa	*Imbalu* belongs to Nabarwa
Basambwa bakhurangilile	May the ancestors lead you
Bakhuambekho	May they touch and enable you
Beme ibweni, beme inyuma	May they stand in front and behind
Bakhue tsikhabi	May they give you blessings

---

[150]Ludwig Wamono, interviewed by author on 4th October 1999 at Bukhisa village.

Witse *imbalu* iyefwe ing'ene	Endure *imbalu* the way we all do
Wele akhue lisaye	May God bless you with children
Akhue sikuka	May he bless you with sons
Ukobola isi inyanga yama	May you endure like the sun
Ulame, ulame, ulame	May you live long
Ubone bisoni ni biimiila[151]	To see your children's children's children

After that the maternal aunt whose bride wealth his father used to pay for the boy's mother shaves the initiate's head. By this action the community will be telling him in no uncertain terms that he is no longer what he has been hitherto, as he is ushered further and deeper into the sacred rites that constitute passage into adulthood.

4.5.4.4. Ibukhootza, *Visit to Maternal Clan*

The initiate then visits the maternal clan to formally request for permission to be circumcised and to receive the blessings of the maternal ancestors. It is mandatory for the mother's brother, the one who used the bride wealth of the boy's mother, to give a cow to at least the first son of his sister. After all he will only be returning some profit from the cows his mother brought home as bride wealth. The cow is slaughtered and a knowledgeable maternal elder divines its intestines for omens. Yeast is smeared on the novice and beer blown upon him while invoking the blessings of the maternal ancestors upon him, closely following the pattern of exhortations given by the yeast-man. Chyme is smeared upon the limbs of the initiate by the maternal uncle amidst admonition and exhortation, as he addresses the novice by the maternal names given him.[152] The following is a sample of such exhortation by the maternal uncle:

---

[151] Fab Ronald Walukhaso and Praxeda Namonywe interviewed by author on 28th August 1998 in Musiru village.

[152] In Masaba culture, the child is given names of maternal ancestors by the paternal grandfather, though the child is officially known by the paternal names. The maternal relatives will always call the child by their own names, just as the mother does time and again. This goes to show the importance, which is accorded to the

Iwe naoyu, iwe naoyu	You are my grandfather *(mentions names)*
Khotsa, basambwa bebukhotsa	Nephew, may your maternal ancestors
Bakhuambekho Bakhurangilile	Precede, guide and protect you
Ifwe banawoyu sikhuli bari taa	We your maternal relatives are not cowards
Sikhurya *imbalu* taa	We do not fear *imbalu*
Nawe ulinde *imbalu* nga naffe	You should emulate us
Khwalinda lukosi	We are peaceful and honourable
Khwaakosa babewana beffwe	We honour our nephews
Ifwe nga bakhotsa bowo	We as your maternal kin
Khukhulombela tsikhabi	Invoke peace and blessings upon you
Ulame wikele baale	May you live a blessed long life
Urubure babandu ukhutyukhe	May you sire many sons and name us
Ulama ulama ulama[153]	May you live long

Prayers are said for the boy to prove himself a man, bring fame and respect upon both clans and for him to be productive so that both clans would thrive. A feast is served and eaten before the initiate is formally sent back to be circumcised. Giving him two short twigs known as **tsisoso**, which are symbolic of the maternal ancestral blessings does this. **Luliki** (underside of a cow) is cut and hung on the boy's shoulder for all and sundry to see how well the maternal uncles have given honour to their sister's son. A maternal clan, which does not show honour to their maternal nephew, is looked down upon as being poor and close-fisted, and this brings ridicule to the boy's mother. Members of the maternal clan escort the initiate's party, with the elderly falling back while the young and strong carry on all the way to

---

maternal clan in the life of a person, and to underscore the multiplicity of belonging in the life of an individual.

[153] Lawrence Wabuti interviewed by author on 22nd August 1998 in Mbale town.

witness on behalf of the maternal clan and to bring back news about the circumcision ritual.

4.5.4.5. *Mwitosi,* Sacred Swamp

From the maternal clan the candidate is led to the common playground for the final time to meet his fellow initiates. All the candidates from the neighbourhood meet upon the playground to dance together while they wait for their fellows who have visited their maternal clans to arrive. It is a performance that is reminiscent of the *isonja* dance, a final show of resolve to tell one another that they were serious about going through with it, and that they indeed are still in the race for manhood. It also certainly provides mutual encouragement to the novices before the final leg of no return. Those who arrive earlier continue dancing until the others arrive, and when all are gathered, they part and proceed to their different common sacred swamps for the very last smearing rite, this time of mud.

Meanwhile the sacred swamp will have been consecrated and dedicated with sacrifices, incantations and invocations by the ritual elders charged with its custody. The mud will have been trampled upon until it froths and bubbles from within. It is said that *kimisambwa kyembalu* (the ancestral spirits of *imbalu)* make the mud well up only during this season, to signify their pleasure and preparedness to bless them.

Before jumping into the mud, the candidate is divested of most of his paraphernalia except the bare minimum. Those who come carrying *tzindiki* (the undersides) of the cows slaughtered for them at the maternal clans', are also divested of them by the same maternal aunt who shaved the boys earlier in the day.

Individually, and strictly according to family seniority, the novices jump into the air twice, and on the third jump land in the mud. Every candidate is blessed by beer being blown over him before being smeared singly, and according to laid down protocol. The elders charged with smearing the novices with mud dutifully go about their job amid the usual string of admonition to the candidate to prove himself a man, knowing that the whole world will be watching. The tone of the admonition will have shifted from the one of the earlier two days. This time the advice is more in keeping with the realisation that the hour of truth has finally arrived, and the boy needs to be encouraged to stand the ordeal with bravery and single-hearted resolve. The pervasive message will now be how much "hotter than fire", and how long like "dawn till sunset" the ordeal lasts. It is as though everybody now accepts that he is serious and that they need to assure him that he is right in his resolve, and that they are right behind him all the way. The emphasis now is placed upon bravery, single-mindedness, and internal resolve, as the difference between *businde* (boyhood) and *busani* (manhood) is touted with the latter being proffered as the only adult thing to do.

The elder begins by calling the novice by name so that the novice knows that the exhortation is meant for him personally. Things will have now come down to the individual level and no longer to groups or pairs. It is now the individual novice for himself alone, just as it is him to face the knife alone. Things depend upon his own determination and decision, as nobody else can help him: not his father, not his friends, nobody but him.

The elder formally recognises the ancestors in the novice by referring to him as father, and then as grandfather. The following is a sample of what the *umulongi* (ritual elder charged with smearing the candidates with the sacred-clay) says:

Iwe nawoyu, iwe nawoyu	You are so and so *(mentions names)*
Iwe papaa! iwe kukaa	You are my grandfather, my father
Iffwe Banamboko	We are Banamboko
Iffwe lumwani	We endure for ever
Litosi lyesi ikhuaka lino lye bakkuka	I smear you with sacred ancestral mud
Bakuka bakhuambekho	May the ancestors touch you
Bakhue tzikhabi	May they shower you with blessings
Wime *imbalu* iyebakhale ing'ene	Be brave like they were
Nikhwama ano khuri	When we leave this sacred-swamp
Ulikhutsya *imbalu*	You are going for *imbalu*
Nikhawama mwitosi muno khuri	As we leave this mud
Uli khutsya khulwanyi	You are going to be circumcised

Ne *imbalu* pilo pilo pilo	But *imbalu* is very painful.
Nesibakhala imumilo taa	But they do not cut the throat
Newe sili unyoile khukhwingila taa	Nor are you going to be the first
Bakuka bowo bosi bengila *imbalu*	All your ancestors were circumcised
Naffwe fwessi khwaingila *imbalu*	We too are all circumcised
Imbalu iyebakhale, iya Nabarwa	*Imbalu* belongs to Nabarwa
Witze *imbalu* iyeffwe ing'ene [154]	Be brave like your ancestors were

Then each novice thanks the elders in song before climbing out to be dressed for the last time and led away to the courtyard to be circumcised. A very solemn and rather eerie song called *sisioywa* is then intoned, ushering in a completely new mood. The mood is no longer of happy excitement but rather that cold calculating determination and expectation. From this point on there is no looking back as the clan will have invested too much time and effort, and the novice will have been given ample time to reconsider his decision. A nucleus party leads the initiate to the homestead using a path that they beat on the spur of the moment, avoiding usual paths for fear of witchcraft against the initiate.

This is a sample of the *sisioywa,* the solemn chant sung while leading the candidate to the courtyard.

Wangwe wamusiru wekhale, ooh ooh	The wild leopard is waiting, ooh ooh
Wekhale, ooh, wekhale ooh ooh ooh	Waiting, ooh, waiting ooh ooh ooh
Wangwe wamusiru khalingo, ooh ooh	The wild leopard is at home, ooh ooh

---

[154] Augustine Wandende, interviewed by author on 26th November 1998 at Nakaloke village.

Khalingo, ooh khalingo ooh ooh ooh	Is at home, ooh, at home, ooh ooh ooh
Wangwe wamakana wekhale, ooh ooh	The fierce leopard is waiting, ooh ooh
Wekhale, ooh, wekhale ooh ooh ooh	Waiting, ooh, is waiting ooh ooh ooh
Wangwe wamakana khalingo, ooh ooh	The fierce leopard is at home, ooh ooh
Khalingo, ooh khalingo. ooh ooh ooh	At home, ooh, at home, ooh ooh ooh
Isolo isasake iyo yarura, ooh ooh	The spotted animal emerges ooh ooh
Yarura ooh yarura ooh ooh ooh[155]	Emerges ooh emerges ooh ooh ooh

The emotive content behind this figurative language derives precisely from the fact that a leopard is an animal the Bamasaba hold in great fear as a dangerous animal of prey. This symbolism is discussed in detail elsewhere in this work.

4.5.4.6. Khukhwingila, *Circumcision Rite*

From the sacred swamp, the candidate is led directly to the circumcision spot in a circuitous way that finally makes the party emerge from the east. The party approaches the homestead from the higher ground, and never from the lower one. Normally houses stand facing the valley and never facing the hillside. Like many other communities, for the Bamasaba the east signifies new life, new beginnings, birth and immortality. The sun may appear to have gone down but it surely rises promptly in the east the following morning. The Bamasaba will look and spit towards the sunrise in the east before setting off on a journey in the early morning.

The party picks *tsimbobwe* (thick ends of banana fruits), which they throw into the crowd waiting at home, to make way for the novice and his party. It is also a way of scaring away people suspected to harbour evil intentions

---

[155] Ibid.

as such people would attract a full barrage of these missiles without the possibility of pin-pointing anybody in particular. People may take cover from these missiles but the parent and elders stand firm.

At the circumcision spot, which is at the bottom of the *lukangu* (ritual pole), are placed *ityanyi* herbs, in the middle of which is an egg. The herbs are believed to be potent medicine for enhancing bravery in the novice and drive away any evil spirits that may have been sent his way by the enemies of the family or clan.

Uwesanda (the ritual gourd-bearer) meets the procession as it approaches the precincts of the homestead and escorts them back to the homestead while blowing the ritual beer, which he carries in the gourd, upon all and sundry. By this time it will be only a small group of chosen elders and strong young men known for their bravery during their own circumcision. The rest of the people will be expectantly waiting at home, with the elders jostling for strategic positions in front of the spot, and elbowing away anybody suspected to be evil-minded. Members of the *bakulo* (joking enemies) will be pushing and insulting all and sundry to gain a foothold in front of the novice hoping to get an excuse to prove that this is a clan of cowards.

Circumcision is the moment of truth so it is highly charged with excitement and expectation. The fickle-hearted who fear to see blood normally watch from a safe distance away from the scene of the action. All along the crowd is gathered, the novice leaps into the air thrice landing upon the egg and breaking it. He plants his legs apart, places a club across his shoulders, with his eyes firmly fixed ahead and unflinching. The elders tell him to correct either the angle of the neck or the stare of his eyes, and tell him to relax the lower muscles of his tummy. Even the slightest quiver of the eyelids would be interpreted as fear, and would brand a youth as a coward. This would be shameful to the novice himself and by extension to the clan as they would be branded cowards. Every man wants to be regarded as a "total man" and nobody wants to live under such a cloud of shame, continually taunted by *bakulo* (joking partners) and never given respect by peers. Manliness is measured in terms of how one stands the ordeal, so *imbalu* is the defining factor of bravery. The escorts tell him what to do as they gradually and surely bring him to the spot where he will stand. The novice is given time to regain his breath after the marathon from the sacred swamp to the courtyard, before the circumciser and his assistant emerge and approach him.[156]

On touching his penis the elders shout in unison, *"wakhusaba wakhusaba wakhusaba"* (he is begging you), or *"wakhwimakho wakhwimakho wakhwimakho"* (he is upon you). The assistant pushes the foreskin back and puts dust to remove any dirt collected under the foreskin and to increase the gripping power. Using his sharp thumb-nail he measures the estimated extent of the cut then he releases for the elders to say whether they agree with the size or not. The elders watching intently either approve or suggest an alternative extent as preferences differ from parent to parent.

Then the circumciser cuts off the foreskin as the crowd roar *"wakhurema litayi, wakhurema litayi, wakhurema litayi"* (he has cut the foreskin) or *"wakhwoneka wakhwoneka wakhwoneka"* (he has deflowered you). He steps on it to foil any attempt by evil-minded people stealing it to bewitch the novice. After this the novice dances again briefly and throws a cock he has been holding upon the house before he stands again for the dreaded and infamous inner incision.

The elders shout in unison, *"mulekhele mulekhele mulekhele"* (leave it to him), as the circumciser goes in to make the dreaded *kumurundura* (inner incision). This necessitates using the thin pointed edge of the knife to make the incision, and is undeniably the most painful part of the whole operation. The novice is repeatedly cautioned to guard against it, as it is at this juncture that most novices show fear or lose control altogether, howl in pain or kick out.

When the surgeon is making this incision the elders put up an endless din of *"sililililili sililililili sililililili"* to imitate the noise made by the knife as it grates through tough fresh hide. If the surgeon is an expert, the operation takes about a minute or so, and he blows his whistle to signal the successful end of the operation.

The novice is then made to sit down on a banana stem and is given *kamayeku* (a sweet brew of fermented millet meal and yeast) to sip. After all the vigorous walking, running, singing and dancing, not to mention the tension and the ordeal, a novice would be exhausted and some refreshment

---

[156] In some cases the party stops a short distance away to give the novice time to catch his breath, or to wait for the circumciser in case he will not have arrived.

will be highly timely at this juncture. This drink, sweet yet half intoxicating is relaxing to the nerves and is also known to be highly nutritious. Relatives and friends come forward, some with gifts to congratulate the newly circumcised upon his bravery and his successful accomplishment of manhood. When he is relaxed, he is led away to the hut where he is to remain in seclusion for a time while he heals. Then the congregation find themselves places in their respective groups to drink beer, which the novice's parents will have brewed for this singularly important occasion in their lives and that of the clan in general.

There is, however, no whistle if the novice shows cowardice by either crying out or sitting down during the operation. In the event of such an occurrence, the relatives walk away to escape the curse such an unfortunate state of affairs is believed to bring upon the clan. They leave the novice at the mercy of *bakulo* (joking enemies) and other strangers who seize him, gag him or stuff his mouth with dust or mud, and have him forcibly circumcised. The *bakulo* then gleefully and certainly maliciously loot the homesteads of whatever they can lay their hands on. The novice and indeed the whole clan can never live down such shame, as the *bakulo* will make their lives miserable at every turn with insults. In such a case, a black goat must be slaughtered that same evening as a purification sacrifice to avert the curse occasioned by such an occurrence.

4.5.4.7. Intzeko, *Central Pillar of the House*

To show the central importance given to circumcision, *imbalu* by the *Bamasaba*, the mother of the novice, provided she is alive, is required to attend her son's initiation, and to perform certain rites which go with it. Even when she is separated from the boy's father and is married elsewhere, she has to temporarily leave her husband and attend her son's circumcision. On the night preceding the operation day she is required to have ritual sexual union (actual or symbolic) with the man with whom she bore that son. It is a re-enactment of the sexual act, which led to the birth of the boy. At circumcision the following day, the boy will be born anew, this time as a social child. But society cannot give birth to him until the parents have symbolically done so through this ritual union. At the time when the son is undergoing circumcision, she sits at the base of the *intzeko* (central pillar of the house), with her legs outstretched like a woman in labour. She must mimic the posture assumed at childbirth.

She holds to it without moving or talking as it is believed that if she does she precipitates her son's own movement during circumcision. At the sound of the whistle, she and other women spring up and rush out of the house carrying **kimikango** (mingling sticks) and singing in jubilation. They rejoice, make ululation, sing and dance in celebration as they run round the homestead beating eaves of houses and granaries, in mock pursuit of the proverbial leopard which threatens their baby and has eaten off part of his penis.

4.5.5. *Phase Five:* Mwikombe, *Convalescence Period*

This phase comes after the physical operation and lasts all the way to the hatching ceremony. The Bamasaba say that, *imbalu ing'ene ili mwikombe* (the real *imbalu* ordeal is in the convalescence hut). While the physical cut lasts a minute or so, the convalescence period lasts months of sleepless nights. The difference being that the former is a public performance, which is intensely under public scrutiny while the latter is within the privacy of the *likombe* (convalescence hut). The former attracts many social taboos while the latter does not, though it has its own norms. For instance, during the ritual of circumcision, even the slightest betrayal of pain meets with public disapproval and ridicule, but crying and groaning under pain during convalescence would be commonplace. For instance an erection during sleep may result in the wound opening up and bleeding, with the attendant excruciating pain. Problems which were not evident at circumcision come out during this time. For instance novices bleed profusely if major veins were severed during the operation and had not been tied properly by the surgeon. It is also widely believed that some medicine men have the ability to make a novice bleed as punishment for insolence to adults. Indeed, it is not unknown for a novice to die from excessive bleeding.

In the past, treatment of the wound consisted of *khukhupa inguu* (applying *inguu*), a certain herb, which was dried, crushed and applied upon the wound. But this was feared for its extreme burning sensation and the consequent excruciating pain upon a raw wound. It was believed that in picking the leaves, the attendant had to wait when there was no wind or breeze to ruffle the leaves. He would then pick the leaves without shaking the bush, otherwise the leaves would assume an unbearably burning sensation. Many feared to apply it, with the inevitable consequence of the wound festering! If the wound did not heal properly it left shameful ugly leopard-like spots upon the scar. This was regarded as a shameful thing indeed.

An elder leads the novice to the *likombe* (convalescence hut). The hut is blessed by spewing beer upon it amid invocation and supplication to the ancestors to bless it and see the convalescent quickly through confinement. The newly initiated is made to walk round before entering it.[157] He remains in seclusion for three days before being allowed to wash off the yeast and other dirt accrued during the three days of intensive dancing and visiting relatives. On the third day there is a ceremony called *sisyalukho* when relatives and friends come carrying gifts of food, chicken, eggs and the like, to see and congratulate him.

The surgeon also comes back to purify him of his ritual impurity following his shedding of blood. In case he has sired a child before the purification, a fee of a goat was imposed upon him and paid by the father before the purification ritual took place. On this particular day the *umufulu* (newly initiated) was shown all the minor paths leading out of the homestead, symbolising that he could now use short cuts out of and into the compound. Uncircumcised boys were not allowed to use short cuts out of and into the compound, but had to come and go only through the main entrance.

4.5.5.1. Khuusaabisa, *Purification Ritual*

The novice is considered to be ritually unclean after his exposure to the rituals and to the supernatural forces involved, so he must not touch food with his hands until he is ritually cleansed. This rite of purification by the circumciser is known by the term *khusaabisa* (washing or purifying). It used to take place on the third day known as *sisyalukho*. But because of the increased number of initiates involved, it may take place any evening between the day of circumcision and the third one. This purification ceremony consists of certain elaborate acts. It begins with the surgeon pouring beer upon the hands of the *umufulu* (newly circumcised) and

---

[157] Gabriel Wekesa Lumbasi, interviewed by author on 22nd August 1999 in Nakuru town.

asking him to wash his hands with it. The surgeon then strongly enjoins it upon the **umufulu** not to forget his (the surgeon's) name since it is him who has brought him from childhood to manhood. It is him who has made him a man, and given him status and identity as a Mumasaba man. Then he goes on to admonish the novice in an elaborate way.

The following is a sample of the admonition and ethical imperatives by the circumciser during the purification ceremony:

Syalelo ise Wepukhulu wa Musilo	Today I Wepukhulu son of Musilo
Uwesikuka sye bakimbafula	Of the clan of rain-makers
Nnakhusaalile iwe	Have begotten you
Mwambu wa Namuleme	Mwambu son of Namuleme
Uwesikuka sye Banamboko	Of the clan of Banamboko
Nakhurusile mubusinde	I have removed you from childhood
Nakhukwarisile ingubo ye busaani	Clothed you in the robe of manhood
Isese kukao	I am your grandfather
Ukhebilila lisina lyese ta	Never forget my name
Ise ukhuele busani ni lisina bari nawoyu	I have given you a definite name
Bunywanywa nitsyebubwana ururekho	Shun insolence and childish behaviour
Wibirise ng'omusani ni lukoosi	As a man, behave honourably
Uwe babandu lukoosi	Honour people
Nabo kane bakhuwe lukoosi and	They too will honour you and
Busaani lukoosi isi babandu boosi[158]	Manhood is honour and peace to all

---

[158] Wakhasa Walwanda, interviewed by author on 26th September 1998 at Bumukoya village.

He warns him against insolence towards young and old, and against whatever is incompatible with the adult status. He then hands him the surgeon's knife, the very one having been used for circumcising him. While holding it the circumciser solemnly tells him:

Kumubono kuno nikwo kukukhuele busani	This knife has brought you manhood
Nasiryo wibirise busyele ng'omusani	You should conduct yourself as a man
Ukhaakha kumubono kwose imbilu ta	Do not smear my knife with soot
Ukharera khuswala khumubono kwose ta	Do not bring shame upon my knife
Kumubono kuno kwakheba baakali	This knife has circumcised many
Kwarerera baakali busani ni lukoosi	It has brought manhood to many
Iwe wekelile umusaani	You have now joined the rank of men
Uwe basaani basyo lukoosi	Honour your fellow men
Nabo bakhwisemo lukoosi[159]	And they will reciprocate with honour

He then hands him a spear and shield, telling him,

Lifumo lisi ukhuambisa lino	This spear that I hand to you
Nilyo lisi basani belindila busolo	This is what men use in protection
Nilyo lisi basani bahimila tsisanyi mwiswa	It is what men use for hunting animals
Sikhuambisile lifumo lino	I have not given you this spear
Ndi utsye ulumbe babandu taa	So that you may attack other people

---

[159] Ibid.

Sikhuambisile lifumo lino	I have not given you this spear
Ndi utsye wirire babandu taa	So that you may kill people with it
Umusani ulinda lukosi ni babandu	As a man you keep peace with people
Nabo baakhuwa lukosi	So that they too may respect you
Busani lukosi	Manhood is peace and harmony
Ingabo yino niyo isi basani betsetela	This shield is for defense
Umusani nga busolo bwolile witseta[160]	A man defends himself

He then hands him a machete, telling him,

Kwarang'a kusikhuambisa kuno	This machete which I hand to you
Nikwo kusi basani barambila kimilimo	This is what men use for working
Kusi basani basawulila kimikunda	What they use for slashing the bush
Na bakhasi babwe balima	So that their wives can dig
Kusi basani baremera kimirongoro kyentsu	It is what men use for cutting poles
Sikhuambisile kwarang'a kuno	I have not handed you this machete
Ndi uremere babandu ta	To cut other people with
Busani kimilimo[161]	Manhood is about work

---

[160] Lawrence Tsemale and Augustine Wandende, interviewed by author on 26th September 1999 at Bunamboko village.
[161] Ibid.

He then hands him an axe and tells him:

Isoka isikhuambisa yino	This axe which I hand you
Yini niyo isi basani baremera bisala	This is what men use for felling trees
Isi baasakila tsikhu	It is what men use for cutting wood
Nabakhasi baatekhela bilyo balya[162]	For their wives to cook for them food

He then hands him a hoe, telling him:

Yino imbako	This is a hoe
Imbako isikhuambisa yino	This hoe which I hand to you
Niyo isi basani barambira kimilimo	It is what men use for working
Isi basani balimila kimikunda	It is what men us to dig their gardens
Urambe kimilimo, ubaye, ukoye	Grow crops to feed relatives
Ukoye kamalwa balebe banywe	Brew beer for people to drink
Bulebe inda, bulebe indekhelo	Kinship is about eating
Umusani kimilimo	Manhood is work
Ulime, ulye ni balebe.[163]	Dig, plant and feed the relatives

Then he hands him a bamboo stick containing a drinking straw, telling him:

Luno lusekhe	This is a drinking straw
Lusekhe lusi ikhuambisa luno	This straw which I hand to you

---

[162] Ibid.
[163] Ibid.

Nilwo lusi basani banywela kamalwa	This is what men use for drinking beer
Nawe ukoye babandu banywe	Brew for relatives to drink
Ngonywa kamalwa ulinda lukosi	When drinking beer keep the peace
Ulekhe khulomana nibasyo mumalwata	When drinking avoid quarrels
Kamalwa busale ni lukoosi	Drinking is about friendship
Kamalwa sikali busolo ta[164]	Drinking is not about fighting

Beer is an important and indispensable forum for socialising and for relaxing. It is where men meet other men to exchange news and views on a variety of issues.

He then hands him fire saying:

Kuno kumulilo	This is fire
Kumulilo kusikhuwa kuno	This fire which I hand to you
Unyole akhaba kulosi kukwafwa imoni	Find even an old woman with a squint
Kukhutekhele bilyo	To cook food for you
Kukhusalile babandu	To produce children for you
Utyukhe baakuka	For you to name the ancestors
Sikhuele kumulilo kuno	I have not given you fire
Ndi wosyele tsintsu tsyabene ta	To burn people's houses
Busani lukosi[165]	Manhood is about peace.

---

[164] Lawrence Tsemale, interviewed by author on 4th November 1999 at Bunamboko village, and Leo Wawomola interviewed on 6th November at Butiru village had similar ideas on the text of this *khukambila* (exhortation).

[165] Ludwig Wamono, interviewed by author on 6th November 1999 at Bukhisa village.

As the exhortation demonstrates, the emphasis is placed on marriage and not on love or beauty. What is important is that she cooks and bears children. This is a way of cautioning the newly circumcised against procrastinating with the excuse that he is still looking for a beautiful bride to marry.

Victor Turner has aptly pointed out that the period of convalescence is a transformative one through which the initiate transits from childhood to manhood.[166] It is pervaded with strict prescriptions and prohibitions. For instance *umufulu* (a convalescing initiate) does not eat food anywhere else but in his *likombe* (convalescence hut), or in that of a fellow *umufulu*. He must not sleep or seek shelter from rain anywhere else except in his *likombe* or that of a fellow *umufulu*. If he sleeps or sheltering elsewhere except his own *likombe,* he must pay a fine of a chick or egg to his *umutiliini* (personal attendant) before being let into his *likombe*.[167]

4.5.6. *Phase Six:* Khukhwiyalula, *Hatching Ceremony*

When most of the newly circumcised have healed, the ceremony of *lusantza* (burning of dry leaves) is performed. This feast is known as *lusanza* in reference to the *kamasanza* (dry banana leaves), on which the *bafulu* sleep during convalescence. The ceremony is also known as *khukwiyalula*, literally meaning "the hatching rite". It is as if the newly circumcised are "hatched" into men. This is the ceremony where the newly circumcised are welcomed back and incorporated into society as full members after several weeks of living in seclusion.

On the night preceding this day, the dry banana leaves or mats are collected and burned in a huge bonfire. All night the *bafulu* keep vigil around the fire, eating roasted chicken and plantains, as they sing songs of *imbalu* and generally make merry for the last time as carefree youth.

Great caution is taken to make sure that the ashes from this bonfire do not fall in the hands of evil-minded people. So the ashes, bones and other remnants of the fire and feast are carefully and painstakingly collected and hidden. The area is dug up to make it difficult if not impossible for

---

[166] Victor Turner, *The Ritual Process: Structure and Anti-Structure.* New York: Aldine Publishing Company, 1979, p. 95.

[167] Steven Namonyo, interviewed by author on 21st August 1998 in Bugema village.

anybody to know the exact spot where the fire in which the mats were burnt actually was. At dawn, the newly initiated go to wash in the river where the water runs briskly. A pond or stream where water is either stagnant or slow cannot do. Running water signifies passage and hence purification. They come back singing, *"Imbalu ye Bamasaba khwaakitabusa, likobi lye Bamasaba khwalitabusa"* (we have accomplished the tradition of the Bamasaba, we have paid the cultural debt). They also come back, calling each the name of his circumciser, saying he had "eaten off" part of their penises.[168]

Beer will have been prepared for this last feast of welcoming and receiving the newly initiated into society. During the drinking and festivity of this day, the hitherto *bafulu* are formally received into the community of men by formally being dressed in *isumbati* (the robe of manhood).[169]

4.5.7. Phase Seven: Ineemba, *Convocation/Commissioning Dance*

This special dance which takes place at the end of the circumcision year is the official and symbolic closing of the season. Each and every newly initiated individual is supposed to attend this dance at least once. If one cannot attend in person a proxy is paid to attend on one's behalf. The symbolic significance of this dance is also discussed in detail below.

Ineemba is the final rite in the circumcision calendar, and takes place in the dry months of December or January after circumcision. This dance comprises drums of unusual sizes, the longest being about six feet long, accompanied by several smaller ones. It brings together all the newly hatched members of society from a radius of several miles, with every newly circumcised being required to attend the dance at least once; otherwise he is seen as not having been officially commissioned by the ritual.

This dance, which formally marks the end of the circumcision season and the convocation of all the newly initiated, is staged in most major centres so that all the *batembete* (newly circumcised), literally meaning the delicate ones, can attend. It is obligatory for them to attend and participate in the

---

[168]Lawrence Tsemale, interviewed on 4th November 1999 at Bunamboko village.

[169] Augustine Wandende, interviewed by author on 26th November 1998 at Nakaloke village.

ineemba dance for all the three days when it lasts in any particular centre. If one is unable to attend on any of the three days, one is required to pay a proxy to attend on one's behalf. One can also attend *ineemba* in another centre other than one's own.

It is held during the dry first months of the new year when there is less work and when people have time for leisure. It brings together the *batembete* from a large radius. It is more than leisure as it is an ideal opportunity to meet relatives from different ridges over a wide radius, and it also affords all and sundry the opportunity to meet prospective marriage partners. The *batembete* are normally rich from all the gifts bestowed upon them and are in position to entertain one another, not to mention the local beauties that grace it.

This is a very majestic dance where the *batembete* dance waving long sticks in the air. Round their necks they wear long garlands of *libombwe*, a fast thriving creeper, and they compete to see who has the biggest and longest of the garlands. The size of the garland indicates the amount of love bestowed upon one by one's relatives and friends. Being post harvest time, different types of local brew and dishes are normally plentiful and available for everybody to quench their thirst and replenish their energy after the long journeys and the dancing. At the end of each song, they all give a long drawn-out shout while pointing their sticks to the northeast. That is the direction whence the ancestors and *Nabarwa,* the woman through whom *imbalu* was introduced among the Bamasaba, came.[170]

4.5.7.1. Bubakooki, *Institution of Age-Sets*

Babakoki are people circumcised during the same year. It has nothing to do with biological age, but everything to do with social age. This is simply because for one reason or another, some people get initiated late, say in their twenties, while others do so in their late teens. This is because some novices begin the process but never complete it. These are known as *bakonela* (those who have "slept over"). In the past some of these people would do it for many years until it became necessary for the clan to simply seize and have them circumcised by force. The alternative was not to let them go through the process: as soon as such a candidate known for having

---

[170] Leo Wawomola, interviewed by author on 6th November 1999 at Butiru village.

reneged on his declaration of intent before indicated willingness again, the circumciser was summoned and he was promptly circumcised before he would change his mind yet again.

This institution is very important and members of age-sets know one another over a myriad of villages, either because they danced *isonja* together, or met somewhere during the time of dancing and visiting relatives. But they certainly met during *ineemba* where the newly initiated meet to congratulate one another upon their achievement of manhood. The *babakoki* address one another by the endearing appellation of *bakoki* (buddy or comrade). Society has safeguarded this relationship by instituting obligations, rights and duties upon the members of such groups. These include among others:

a. No member is allowed to marry a daughter of his *bakoki* as she is regarded as a daughter to him.

b. Whenever any member of the age group has a son initiated, the *babakoki* should be given *lubaka* (something given in recognition of their being members of the same age group).

c. Whenever a member's daughter gets married and the father collects bride wealth, he has to brew beer and invite the *babakoki* to drink and make merry.

As was the case with other African communities, daughters are not highly regarded among the Bamasaba. A man who has only daughters is not highly regarded in society and is seen by some as having no child. It is believed that daughters are meant to get married and go away to enrich other clans with children and labour. They are therefore referred to as "*mulyango kwangelekha*", literally meaning "the house across the ridge". Sons are needed to defend the family and clan against internal and external aggression by protecting the clan's interests, and especially by bringing forth children to name and so immortalise the ancestors. Women do not own land, for they cannot defend it, so a daughter does not inherit her father's land. If he has no son among the daughters, such land reverts into the possession of his brothers.

So sons are needed to inherit the land and other possessions of the father, and most importantly to perpetuate the father's lineage by naming him after death. A man without a son cannot officiate at any of the rites of *imbalu*, for he is considered as having 'no voice with which to speak among men'!

In a nutshell, a man's personal immortality is assured only through a son, and people will go to great lengths to beget a son.

    d. It is prohibited for an uncircumcised person to claim *lubaka*, or for anybody to claim *lubaka* from a person of a different age set, as this would be tantamount to obtaining it by false pretence.

    e. *Babakoki* are not allowed to fight, or to shed each other's blood.

    f. While playfully wrestling, they are not supposed to lock legs, or carry each other on their backs. [171]

4.5.7.2. Kamengilo, *Imbalu Topical Names*

The history of *imbalu* is invariably the history of the Masaba nation. Every circumcision year bears a topical name arising from an important and noteworthy event that took place during that year or there about. These topical names are also the age-set names by which all those initiated in a given year are known. They have been handed down through an oral tradition enshrined in legends, stories, invocations, prayers, myths, and riddles. These circumcision age-set names were, therefore, the calendar by which every other events in the corporate sphere of the Masaba nation are fixed: dates when children were born, when people died, and so on. Before literacy culture set in, novices were required to know a string of these names by rote. It was their point of reference for placing people and helped to regulate social relationships. Anybody circumcised before one was one's senior and expected to be treated as such. Contravention of this protocol had severe sanctions as it was construed as insolence, a serious social aberration.

From childhood, people were trained to remember events with precision and competed to see who had the most agile memory. In time the historians of the community were identified and given due respect for their talent. These became points of reference whenever information about certain events was needed or disputed. These experts had many points of reference to cross-check the dates of events, but *kamengilo* were the most secure as there would be people who remembered them. Realising that many of the old people who bore invaluable information were passing away, members

---

[171] L. W. Wawomola and L. Wamono, interviewed by author on 6th November 1999, at Butiru village.

of Masaba Historical Association started to trace and record the history of *imbalu*.[172]

The description of *imbalu* would, therefore, not be complete without including these topical names, as they are the calendar of the corporate history of the Masaba community. They are listed hereunder, and where possible the major event after which each was given is explained alongside.

Year	*Name of Age-set and Meaning*

1801   **Bawila**
There came a group of strangers that may have come from the North, possibly of the Teso or Karamojong extract.

1803   **Bamiila**
There was another group of strangers whose origin was not known, and who were named *bamiila*.

1805   **Banapera**
There came another group of strangers that were referred to as Banapera. These are believed to have been perhaps Itesots or Karamojong.

1807   **Bapokoto**
It was the first time the initiates wore *tsipokoto* (wooden arm bands) when dancing, hence the name.

1809   **Banalume**
It is said that during this season, the weather was overcast most of the time, and there was a lot of dew throughout the day. The word *lume* in Lumasaba means dew.
Another explanation is that many people fell sick and those who had some herbal knowledge asked for *syelume*, something given to a herbalist for braving *lume* (dew) to look for herbs.

1811   **Bamarango**
During this circumcision season many initiates showed fear and the surgeons smeared *kamarango* (thighs) of the initiates with blood in contempt.

---

[172] Leo Wawomola, interviewed by author on 6th November 1999 in Butiru village.

1813	**Bamalyabi**
	There came another group of unknown people who were referred to as *Bamalyabi*, hence the name of the circumcision season.
1815	**Banamang'ulye**
	Kamang'ulye are a shrub with soft leaves mostly used in toilets. During this circumcision season these shrubs were plentiful, hence the name.
1817	**Bamakanda**
	There was another group of unknown people who were referred to as *Bamakanda*, hence the name.
1819	**Bamumulya**
	There was yet a group of people named as such, who came into the district.
1821	**Bamalaala/Baneusi**
	Bamalala refers to the fact that the newly circumcised, for the first time, used *kamalaala* (banana fibres) for their beddings.
	Baneusi comes from the fact that many initiates showed fear and shouted (*khukhwiusa*) during the operation.
1823	**Bakosoa/Bamakumba**
	There came foreign people whom the Bamasaba called *Bakosoa*.
	They were called *Bamakumba* because there were many bones (*kamakumba*) as a result of many deaths of people and animals. In those days the practice was to throw corpses away, to be eaten by vultures and hyenas, so bones abounded.
1825	**Barome/Banerome**
	It is said that at this time the deaths of people and animals continued. *Barome* refers to the fact that people mourned their dead who had been thrown in the *mwirome* (bush).
	Banekokhe refers to the fact that the animals, which died of the epidemic, were burnt, so there were heaps of ash (*likokhe*) everywhere.

1827	**Bamakala/Banang'oma**
	There came another group of foreign people who introduced beans, which are known locally as **kamamakala**.
	The name **Banang'oma** refers to the fact that at this time there was an invasion, and so people used to beat drums to mobilise for war.
1829	**Batongolo**
	During this circumcision season, the newly initiated used **tongolo** (leaves of sweet potatoes) as relish, hence the name.
1831	**Balisa I**
	There came another group of people who were known as **Balisa**. This clan of people is said to still exist in Kimilili in neighbouring Kenya.
1833	**Bamakombe/Bawuma**
	It is said at this time there were many comets seen in the sky. As these comets had tails of fire, the people thought these were spirits flying about.
	There was also a lot of mist making people fear that their death (**kamakombe**) had come. Because of this type of fear, while dancing the initiates did not sing but simply hummed (**khuwuma**), hence the appellation.
1835	**Bakhalangaki/Balokha**
	During this season there was famine leading many initiates from the drier lower parts of the district not to be circumcised. Those from the wet higher regions (**angaki**), however did. Normally the higher regions being closer to the forest enjoy more rainfall, so the famine was not that severe. The name indicates that there was a division between the upper (**angaki**) and lower.
	It was also called **Balokha** because there came a group of people who would shout when speaking (**khulokha**), and had very uncouth behaviour.
1836	**Basawa**
	Because of the famine in the previous year having forced initiates from the drier lower regions to postpone their initiation, there was **imbalu** the following year. The name

derives from the fact that initiates started using *zikasawa* while dancing.

1837   *Bakolongolo/Namanda*

The word **khukolongokha** means "all without exception". In this season there was more food and all the initiates who had postponed their initiation because of famine got initiated.

There was also migration of people towards the plains as the people who had inhabited these plains had perished from famine, and others had also migrated in search of food.

The other name of *Namanda* derives from the fact that the livestock epidemic continued to decimate herds. These were burned, so there was heaps of charcoal (**kamanda**) all over the place.

1839   *Bakikwameti/Bananzukhi*

There was a group of foreign people who were referred to as **Bakikwameti**, probably of the Masaai extract from Kenya.

Bananzukhi is derived from the fact that there were swarms of bees (**inzukhi**) and a lot of honey during this season.

1841   *Barome II/Baneyombo*

There was a lot of wailing (**liyombo**) because of the many deaths at the time.

1843   *Basoi/Banetuwa*

There was yet another group of foreign people called **Basoi**. There were also lots of bushes of the cactus type (**kamatuwa**) in the district at this time of circumcision.

1845   *Bawututu*

There were many owls (**wututu**) in the district at the time. The presence of these birds in abundance was significant because they were associated with death, and their feathers believed to be poisonous.

1847   *Bananyeli I*

It is believed that at this time women started to wear bangles (**binyele**) on their arms.

1849   *Barenyere*
There was a group of foreign people who were referred to as
such.

1851   *Basama*
It derived from the word *khusama* (to bark). At this time
there were many wild animals, which barked like dogs.
Many of them died, and people who ate the meat of these
animals also fell sick, barked and later died. These animals
may have suffered from rabies.

1853   *Bananzaru*
This derived from a group of people who arrived in the
district, believed to have been of the Nilotic extract.

1855   *Banangosya*
There were an exceptionally high number of vultures
(*tsingosya*), which used to feed on corpses.

1857   *Banakhoba*
During this particular season many initiates exhibited fear
and were circumcised by force while bound with *tsikhoba*
(cords).

1859   *Banasike*
At this time there were lots of locusts (*tsisike*), which
destroyed many crops, hence the name.

1861   *Nabusima*
There was serious famine, with the main type of food being
millet meal known locally as *busima.*

1863   *Barokhi/Balisa*
A new group of people arrived in the district. They were
referred to as *Alok*, and may have been of the Luo extract.

1865   *Bamatanda/Balokha*
Kamatanda were young locusts. There were many locusts,
which ate up crops, hence the name. *Balokha* are a group of
foreigners who returned to the district. These people are said
to have shouted (*khulookha*) when talking.

1867   *Bawalumbe/Ndalila*

There were many deaths caused by smallpox and dysentery. *Ndalila* refers to the famine, which prevailed at the time, as people were too sick to work in their gardens.

1869   *Basalekwa*

It derived from the name of a group of people whom the Bamasaba called *Basalekwa*, who came into the district at this time.

1871   *Bananyeli II*

There was a group of people who resembled those who had come in 1847.

1873   *Bazengweli*

A tall and naked people, probably the Pokot (Suk) of present-day Kenya, invaded the district.

1875   *Bakhalundu*

During this season many people died of pestilence (*tsinundu*), hence the appelation.

1877   *Bakulebu/Banamekhala*

Bakulebu because at this time there was a war between the Bamasaba and the Teso of Tororo, known by the Bamasaba as *Bakulebu*.

Banamekhala refers to the fact that during this season many initiates feared circumcision and were circumcised while seated (*mekhala*).

1879   *Babanyange*

There were droves of swallows known in Lumasaba as *tsinyange*. These normally migrate at particular seasons of the year. During this season there were many birds, which the Bamasaba call *tsinyange*. These are white birds, which like grazing among cattle and near wetlands, and are associated with prosperity among the herds.

1881   *Bamaina*

The word *Maina* means the deity of animal husbandry. This deity has his shrine on the dung-heap behind the house where animals are kept. During this season there was relative calm and prosperity in herds in the district as the enemies of the Bamasaba had been repulsed.

There was peace as the kingdom of Mumia wa Siundu in present day Kenya had been well established then, putting an end to insecurity. The Bamasaba then thought that *Wele Maina* had come among them, bringing peace and prosperity.

1883   ***Bamiinyi/Banafula***
It is said that there were many birds known as *tsimiinyi* in the district.

Banafula refers to *ifula* (rain) because there was a lot of rain during this season. Normally this season experiences the dry spell where harvests are carried out so this was unexpected and exceptional, hence the topical name.

1885   ***Bakhaele/Basiindi***
Bakhaele refers to the disease (*khaele*) that decimated people and herds. It has its origin in the word *khuela* meaning to be decimated.

1887   ***Bazuma/Bachuma***
At this time many people went to present day Kenya to look for paid employment. This type of economic migration was known as *khuchuma*, hence the name.

1889   ***Bamatsukhu/Bamutuli/Bakhalikhi***
Bamatsukhu refers to the fact that there was a disease that affected the lungs (*kamatsukhu*) of cows.

Bamutuli refers to a disease that decimated chicken. And *Bakhalikhi* refers to the fact that many initiates who feared applying a painful herb known as *inguu* on the wounds because of its severe burning sensation had their male organs rot.

1891   ***Basawa II***
There was a repetition of the name that had been applied to the season of 1836.

1893	***Bamalyongobi/Nabyuma***
	Cattle died from a disease known as ***Malyongobi***. Because of the carcasses of dead cows, there were many green flies known locally as ***nabyuma***.
1895	***Bamase***
	The word ***emase*** derived from the Teso language meaning locusts. During this season locusts destroyed crops.
1897	***Bamarofu/Misiko***
	During this season there was a bumper harvest of bananas, so there were ripe bananas (***kamarofu***) in plenty.
	Misiko is a corruption of the Swahili word ***mizigo*** meaning luggage or loads. This was because during this season there were caravans of people carrying loads or luggage for Europeans.
1899	***Nabusima/Nalufumbi***
	During this season there was famine again with the main food being millet meal (***busima***). As it was dry there was dust (***lufumbi***) all over the place, hence ***Nalufumbi***.
1901	***Namilundu***
	This is the time when Semei Kakungulu, a Muganda chief sent by the King of Buganda, arrived in the district with guns (***kimilundu***). This was in accordance with the 1900 Agreement where the King of Buganda was mandated to rule the country on behalf of the British Crown. Among his responsibilities was that of "pacifying" the hinterland of the country for the British colonialists.
1903	***Matongo/Silikhale***
	During this season the initiates wore beads known in Lumasaba as ***matongo***. Asians sold these beads. ***Silikhale*** refers to the time when formal government started, and was corrupted from the Swahili word ***serikali*** meaning government.
1905	***Bisutse/Namapati***
	There were many wild animals of the fox family called ***bisutse*** in Lumasaba. These animals were a threat to both

humans and domestic animals. People were mobilised to hunt and kill them hence the topical name *bisutse*.

Namapati refers to the first houses made of *kamapati* (corrugated iron sheets), which were built in the district.

1907   *Nabitiri/Manyonge*

Bitiiri are iron wrist rings, which became fashionable at this time.

The word *manyonge* derived from another type of iron wrist rings worn by women at the time.

1909   *Namisinga/Biketi*

People learnt how to use *kimisinga* (beehives) for honey.

The name *Biketi* derived from the word ticket. This was precisely because people were required to pay poll tax and were issued with tickets.

1911   *Nalubya*

During this circumcision season the telephone line was constructed from Jinja to Mbale. The word *lubya* is Lumasaba for wire.

1913   *Khawoya*

During this season many fowls died from a disease known as *khawoya*, hence the name.

1915   *Nalusafu*

During the year, Ugandans were forced to work without pay on government projects. This took place once a week. The name *lusafu* was derived from the free community work.

1917   *Nabitete/Nabikaandi*

Bitete means grasshoppers. During this year grasshoppers ate up crops and other leaves.

1919   There was hardly any circumcision due to severe famine that had started the previous year. This famine was known as *intzala yamutuka*. This was a corruption of the word "motor car" which was pronounced as *mutuka*. It was the first time a motorcar was seen in the district.

1920   *Nandeke*
            It was the first time that people of the area around Mount
            Elgon saw an aeroplane. In Lumasaba *indeke* literally
            means a bird.

1922   *Namikhinga*
            The word **kimikhinga** means tails. There was a plague
            epidemic spread by rats. The government required people to
            catch and kill rats. The tails of these rats were taken to the
            district headquarters as proof that each one had killed so
            many rats. Rat tails became a way of poll tax, hence the
            topical name.

1924   *Namirumba/Naluwalo*
            This was the time when people were organised to work in
            luwalo (turns), to plant *mvule* trees along the roadways.
            Mvule trees are known as **kimirumba** in Lumasaba.

1926   *Nefumi/Walumbe*
            During this season there was a lot of **lifumi** (mist) with the
            sun hardly appearing throughout the day. People were afraid
            that *walumbe* (death) had come. Others say that there was
            an eclipse.

1928   *Nabiliba/Murutu*
            This is the time the railway line passed through the district
            towards Soroti. The word **Biliba** was a corruption of
            sleepers, the metal bars used for building the railway.
            Murutu refers to the dynamite used for blasting through
            rocks in order to build the railway line.

1930   *Nafesa/Nakhweru*
            The name *Nafesa* is a corruption of the Swahili word *fedha*
            meaning gold. It was in reference to when Europeans started
            prospecting for gold (*fedha*) in the district. The name
            nakhweru derives from the type of locusts known locally as
            nakhweru, which invaded crops in the district at the time.

1932   *Nabwonya*
            People mobilised to kill **bubwonya** (swarms of young
            locusts), which were destroying crops.

| 1934 | **Nabisakati** |
| | This was the time that people started bulding *bisakati* (sheds) in which the initiates would be circumcised, to reduce exposure and especially shield them from the eyes of women. It had hitherto been done in the open. |

1934 **Nabisakati**

This was the time that people started bulding *bisakati* (sheds) in which the initiates would be circumcised, to reduce exposure and especially shield them from the eyes of women. It had hitherto been done in the open.

1936 **Nabirala/Nangiti**

Following successive seasons of famine, the chiefs mobilised people to build *birala* (granaries) in their homesteads and at the administration centres. These acted as food reserves in which they stored millet to be used in case of famine.

Nangiti referred to the event when *ingiti*, or *ikhiti* (wild hippopotamus), killed Chief Isaya.

1938 **Namisanga/Nalubawo**

This was the time women started wearing **kimisanga** (ivory bangles) on their wrists.

Nalubawo referred to the fist time when those who feared being circumcised at home went to the hospital to be circumcised. *Lubawo* means wooden plank and referred to the wooden table on which the circumcision was done in the hospitals.

1940 **Busoolo/Keya I**

This was the time when strong young men were conscripted into the King's African Rifles (K.A.R.) to fight in the Second World War. This abbreviation was corrupted to **Keya**.

1942 **Busoolo/Keya II/Naluwenda**

Busoolo means war. The Second World War was still in progress, and people were forced to sell their cows to feed the soldiers.

Naluwenda referred to the demarcation of the government level of the forest on Mount Elgon beyond which people were not allowed to farm or occupy. This was done in order to preserve the forest from destruction by invaders as the pressure for land intensified.

1944	**_Nabikapu/Mutanganyi_**
	There was famine again and people walked around with fibre bags (**_bikapu_**) for carrying maize flour. This maize flour was yellow which made people believe it had been mixed with other things. **_Mutanganyi_** was a corruption of the Swahili word **_kuchanganya,_** which means to mix.
1946	**_Ly'embwa_**
	At this time the government Department of Veterinary Services mobilised the killing of stray dogs, and the injection of domestic ones as a measure against rabies
1948	**_Musambwa/Naikote_**
	This was the time when **_Dini ya Msambwa_** (Religion of the Ancestors) founded by Elijah Masinde from neighbouring Kenya started in the district. He and his followers climbed the Bukusu hill and sacrificed a white sheep to the ancestors. This is the hill from where the forefathers of the Babukusu tribe of Bungoma district in Kenya migrated.
	It was also called **_Naikote_** because it was the first time that **_naikote_** (bore holes) were sunk in the district.
1950	**_Masanyalase_**
	This word **_amasanyalaze_** is a Luganda word for electricity. This was the time the electricity line reached Mbale, the capital of Masabaland.
1952	**_Kolasi/Mowlem_**
	This is the first time a tarmac road (**_kolasi_**) crossed through the district. It is the time when the **_Mowlem_** Construction Company built the tarmac road from Tororo through Bugisu to Soroti, hence the name.
1954	**_Kwini/Lukholeele/Yunioni_**
	This refers to the occasion when Queen Elizabeth II visited the country to inaugurate the Owen Falls Power Station in Jinja. **_Lukholeele_** refers to the fact that for the first time **_basinde_** (initiates) gathered to dance at the District Headquarters in Mbale.
	Yunioni refers to Bugisu Co-operative Union's coming into existence to buy coffee and cotton from the farmers.

1956   *Koheni/Bamutesa/Banambozo*
This refers to the fact that the Governor of Uganda, Sir Andrew Cohen, visited Mbale to witness the circumcision ceremonies. He was the first governor to do so, and this age-set was named in his honour.
Bamutesa because Sir Edward Mutesa, king of Buganda, visited the district.
Banambozo refers to the nickname given to La Fontaine, a European anthropologist who did her research in the district.

1958   *Nalukhobo/Nabunyala*
This is the time when the District Council (*Lukhobo*) was given more authority, and when indigenous District Commissioners were appointed to replace Europeans.
Nabunyala referred to the authority (*bunyala*) given to the blacks through their District Council to manage their own affairs.

1960   *Legco/Nakhungu*
This was the time when the first district representative was elected to sit in the Legislative Consultative Assembly (Legco), hence the name.
Nakhungu referred to the *tsikhungu* (locusts), which destroyed crops in the district during this year.

1962   *Banauhuru/Banachachacha*
Uhuru is a Swahili word meaning independence. This is the time when Uganda attained its independence from Britain.
Banachachacha because of mini skirts called *chachacha*, which were in fashion.

1964   *Umuinga*
This was the time the first *Umuinga* (paramount chief) went round the district blessing the initiates at the County Headquarters before they brewed beer for circumcision.

1966   *Muwambe*
It derived from *khuwamba* (to seize). During this year many people, some of whom old men who had defaulted, were seized by force and circumcised. Ad hoc militant groups even stopped vehicles to check if the travellers were

circumcised, and if any were found to be uncircumcised were forcibly circumcised on the spot.

1968   *Banang'oma/Bamwaga*
This was the time the initiates went around escorted by *tsing'oma* (drumming bands). *Bamwaga* refers to the undulating type of dance popular during *imbalu* at that time.

1970   *Banakhururwe/Banamwesi/Banakilo*
Nakhururwe referred to the heavy rains and the resultant *tsikhururwe* (landslides) in the district where many people were swept away.
Banamwesi referred to the time when man landed on the moon (*kumwesi*).
Banakilo derived from the metric system, which was introduced at this time, as a conversion from the old British system of measurement.

1972   *Nabahindi/Nabufu*
This referred to the exodus of *bahindi* (Indians) when dictator Idi Amin Dada, the then President of Uganda, chased them away, confiscated their properties and distributed them to his friends and soldiers.
Banabufu refers to the famine, which ravaged the country at this time. People subsisted mostly on maize, cassava, or millet flour flour, known as *bufu* in Lumasaba.

1974   *Bananyilili*
This referred to the long lines people used to form in front of shops to buy essential commodities, at petrol stations for fuel, and bus stations for transport as all these things were in severe shortage under Idi Amin's rule.

1976   *Bahudula/Baweyodela/Banamagendo*
Hudula means to snatch in Lumasaba, and refers to the snatching (2-7-1976) by Israeli commandos of the passengers of an Israeli plane hijacked to Entebbe by Palestinians.
Baweyodela refers to the fact that due to the biting scarcity of commodities, people used to walk long distances into

Kenya to acquire essential commodities. *Kukhiyodela* means to fend for oneself in Lumasaba.

Bamagendo stems from the word *magendo,* which was coined to refer to the illegal trade carried out by petty traders who would criss-cross the Kenya-Uganda borders on foot carrying commodities.

1978   *Nabusoolo/Sabasaba/Nabidomolo/Basimama*

Nabusoolo refers to *busoolo* (war) between Amin's forces and Tanzanian forces, where shells referred to as *sabasaba* were employed. Nabidomolo refers to the introduction of plastic jerrycans known locally as *bidomolo* to replace tins. *Basimama* stems from an outbreak of scabies at that time. People suffering from it would stop to scratch before proceeding. The word *simama* in Swahili means to stop.

1980   *Banabisasi/Nabikona*

Bananas were so expensive that people could not afford to buy whole bunches but instead bought clusters known locally as *bisasi*.

Banabikona derives from the banana leaves from which people used to drink locally distilled gin, as glasses had become too expensive.

1982   *Bamakang'a/ Ndiikyo/Namwilulo*[173]

Bamakang'a derives from a popular song at that time referring to the unusual practice of young men preferring *makang'a* (older women) to girls. It was because the older women were economically able to take care of them while girls were an economic burden on the young men.

Ndiikyo is Lumasaba for "that is how it is", and was another popular song referring to the practice of young men preferring "sugar mummies" to girls.

Banamwilulo stems from the uncharacteristically long time it took the circumcision season to end as it dragged on into the new year.

---

[173] Lawrence Tsemale, interviewed on 11th September 1999 and on 4th November 1999 by this author in Bukhaweka village.

1984	**Bamutoto**
	Since 1954 the Farewell Blessings of the initiates were given at the District Headquarters in Mbale. But since 1984 the ceremony was switched to Bumutoto believed to be the birthplace of **imbalu**.
1986	**Bamuseveni**
	This was the time the National Resistance Army of Yoweri Kaguta Museveni captured power in Uganda.
1988	**Balakwena**
	Alice Lakwena, a spirit medium from Acholi district, led an army to overthrow the government of Museveni. She marched on Kampala via Mbale but was defeated in Iganga, hence the topical name.
1990	**Bamusisi**
	This comes from the Luganda word **musisi** meaning earthquake. There was an earthquake, which shook especially the Western part of the country leading to loss of life and property.
1992	**Banapotolo**
	There were many "patrol" groups rounding up poll-tax defaulters in the district. **Potolo** is a corruption of the word "patrol".
1994	**Banamilengo**
	Because foodstuffs were too expensive, many food items were measured in small quantities or heaps known in Luganda as **omulengo**, hence the derivation.
1996	**Banamagambila**
	This was the time the Constituent Assembly was elected to draft a new constitution in Uganda. **Kamagambila** is Lumasaba for laws.[174]

---

[174] The author is indebted to Mr. Augustine M. Wandende and the Bugisu District Cultural Office for permission to peruse the records on the circumcision topical names.

4.6. CONCLUSION

Following the Gennepian scheme, this fuller description demarcates the three phases of separation, transition and incorporation: Phases one to three mark the separation, four and five the transition, while six and seven mark the incorporation. This detailed description of *imbalu* has set the ground for an interpretation of the ritual. Having seen what the Bamasaba do, we may now move on to examine what *imbalu* means to them, and what the different actions symbolise. Then we can interpret the actions and rites not as disparate entities, but appreciate their deeper and fuller meaning and significance for the community that practises them.

CHAPTER FIVE: MASABA *IMBALU* – AN INTERPRETATION

5.1. INTRODUCTION

> Initiation rituals and secret signs most often refer to the traditions of origin of the society, its history and early heroes ... Neither the organisations nor their rituals can be understood except in the light of these traditions, mythical though they are. Each society's history, as perpetuated inside it, serves to justify a claim to power through ancient knowledge.[175]

This chapter discusses the significance, symbolism and interpretation behind *imbalu* in order to get to the central cultural values, which are being dramatised. It surveys the ritual of *imbalu* from its preparation stage up to the commissioning dance, so as to bring out the under-girding cultural and religious significance. The over-riding socio-religious and socio-cultural values that it holds for the community who practise it are brought out and recognised for what they are. This ritual must be seen to possess a central value for it to be accorded such importance in the collective life of the community, since

> Rituals reveal values at their deepest level ... men express in ritual what moves them most, and since the form of expression is conventionalised and obligatory, it is the values of the group that are revealed.[176]

The themes of identity, social control, power and culture, which form the basis of, and indeed pervade the rituals, will be surveyed and brought to the fore. These are informed by the religious beliefs and worldview of the Bamasaba, for as Okot p'Bitek observes,

> The religion of a people is perhaps the most important aspect of their culture. What they believe governs their lives. It provides their 'worldview' – the general direction along which they live their lives,

---

[175] J. S. La Fontaine, *Initiation*. Manchester: Manchester University Press, 1986, p. 41.

[176] Monica Wilson, "Nyakyusa Ritual and Symbolism", in *American Anthropologist*, vol. 56, no. 2 (1954), p. 241.

and relate to each other and the universe ... The knowledge of the religions of our people is the key to the knowledge of our cultures.[177]

Actions and gestures will be examined with a view to bringing out their deeper and symbolic meaning, delineating the socio-religious nature of *imbalu* from its economic, psychological, educational and other functions. The chapter, therefore, answers the central question, namely:

What significance does *imbalu* hold for the Bamasaba as a community?

An answer will be attempted with broad concepts of culture, identity, followed by an explication of how these concepts find expression in the pattern of symbolism that pervades *imbalu*. It will then link the concept of male power and authority with the role of women in this ritual where only males are initiated into adulthood.

Where no informant is cited for an interpretation, it should be taken that the particular interpretation concerned is by the author in his capacity as an informed insider himself having undergone the rituals.

5.2. *IMBALU* AS CULTURE SIGNIFIER

Imbalu is a core cultural signifier and embodiment of the worldview of the Bamasaba. It is argued that the ritual stages signify the affirmation of the people's culture which is sacralised to lend weight to the cultural norms by giving them divine origin and sanction. The novice is enculturated into the Bamasaba world with its patriarchal gender ethics, its emphasis on fecundity and biological reproduction of future bearers of the culture and its moral ethic on which the survival of the community rests.

As mentioned in an earlier chapter, Arnold van Gennep defines rites of passage as rites which accompany every change of place, state, social positions and age, and divides them into:

1. separation or pre-liminal phase
2. transition or liminal phase, and
3. incorporation or post-liminal phase.[178]

---

[177] Okot p'Bitek, *Africa's Cultural Revolution*. Nairobi: Macmillan Publishers, 1973, p. 86.

[178] Arnold van Gennep, *The Rites of Passage*. Chicago: Chicago University Press, 1960, p. 2.

Masaba *imbalu* falls within this scheme, with regard to these three phases, and will be analysed accordingly.

5.2.1. Separation, Transition and Incorporation

The rites of separation begin when the **umusinde** (novice) is separated from his earlier group at his candidacy when he gets the clan's permission for initiation. From this stage forward as he acquires **bitzentze** (thigh bells) and other paraphernalia in preparation for **isonja** (group dance), he is regarded as a candidate. The shaving of hair on the morning of circumcision is the ultimate ritual separation from childhood and marks the irreversible transition to adulthood.

There is a correlation between ritual and ecology. The geographical location of Masabaland, coupled with the factor of its dense population,[179] directly influences the type of separation which takes place. As Victor Turner, while comparing **imbalu** with Mukanda rites among the Ndembu of Zambia observes,

> ... demographic factors affect both the siting and the symbolism of the circumcision rites, for the Ndembu seclude their novices in lodges far from the inhabited territory, and make an important ritual distinction between the domestic and wild domains, while the Gisu, with hardly any bush to speak of, seclude their novices within the lineage dwelling-areas and do not make a symbolic distinction between bush and residential area.[180]

The phase of transition forms the intermediate period which Victor Turner refers to as "between and betwixt". In **imbalu** this transition is best marked by the actual physical operation of **khukhwingila imbalu** (circumcision).

The **umufulu** (newly circumcised) is neither **umusinde** (boy) nor **umusani** (man). He is neither what he was before, nor what he intends to become, so he is indeed in an indeterminate position. This is what in van Gennep's typology would fall between the two borders, in a 'no man's' land. He wears a skirt like a lady but would not be classified among them. He is ritually unclean and may not live with people nor eat with them. He has to observe

---

179 H. B. Kabera, *The Population of Uganda by Districts*. Kampala: Department of Geography, Makerere University Press, 1983.

180 Victor Turner, "Symbolization and Patterning in the Circumcision Rites of two Bantu-speaking Societies", in Mary Douglas (ed.), *Man in Africa*. London: Tavistock Publications, 1969, pp. 230-231.

both sexual and dietary prohibition during this indeterminate period of convalescence, in transition towards adult life. The hut where he stays is referred to as *likombe* (the place of the dead), for the novice is ritually dead.

The phase of incorporation in *imbalu* would be identified as *khukhwiyalula*, the "hatching" period. It is when the initiate is formally received back into society, this time as an adult. The boy who was separated from society several months earlier is no more, and in his place there now emerges a man. He is now referred to, not under the father's name as the son of so and so, but by his own name, for he is a fully-fledged man in his own right. He has a new name, new dress, new abode, new social status, and indeed new person-hood.

He may not sleep in *likombe* (convalescence hut) ever again, nor is he allowed to sleep in his parents' house ever after, since he is no longer under the parents' jurisdiction. With regard to the economic and political implication of manhood, it is clear that the rites,

> symbolise the removal of the boy from jural identification with his father to a position of his own in the community. After circumcision he takes his place as an equal among men, eligible for all the privileges associated with adulthood ... more importantly, he must now set up his own household.[181]

There is a new status as he is now an adult man in his own right. He should now not shake hands with elderly women as they now take on a new perspective: they are now seen as his prospective mothers-in-law. Gender roles now strictly apply to him, and he must not touch a cooking pot. If hungry and there is no woman to cook for him, he may only eat plantains roasted over a fire.

All these restrictions are geared towards forcing him to get married as soon as possible. Since he must not sleep in his parents' house, he is not considered as one of the children in the home strictly speaking, for he is now an independent man, on the same footing with his father. If his father slaughters a goat or cow he must give him a share of meat like he does with all his other neighbours and relatives.

---

[181] Suzette Heald, "Witches and Thieves: Deviant Motivations in Gisu Society", in *Man*, ns 21, no. 1 (1986), p. 70.

Therefore, he is not expected to eat in his parents' house anymore. Of course if he is around when the food is served he is welcome like any other guest would be. But his parents would not entertain him coming to knock at their door to ask for food. The parents begin eating supper early before he comes back from his walks so that he may not find food. If he dares to knock at the door the mother will tell him they have eaten everything, even when there is food. She will throw in the advice that he should find his own wife to open for him when he comes home at night. The father on his part will growl to him about the bad manners of knocking at other men's doors at night.

A wife is referred to by the official title of **umubwani** (one who kindles the fire), and the kitchen is her uncontested territory, where men are strictly excluded. A Mumasaba man does not interfere with his wife's business in the kitchen, as it is tantamount to chasing her out of it, a shameful thing when the complaint is brought to the elders' attention. Roles are spelt out very clearly.

5.2.2. Imbalu *as Link to Ancestral Land*

Imbalu is intimately tied in with Masaba worldview, a holistic vision of the universe where beliefs, values and practices are all interwoven together to give meaning to life. Life itself is viewed as a journey towards collective immortality with the ancestors. It is these ancestors who are posited as the authors of **imbalu** and other customs, a heritage bequeathed to their offspring to safely guide them into collective immortality. These prescriptions and proscriptions are contained in the cultural code of conduct, whose express intention is to safeguard life, promote it and order community. For instance, it is believed that whoever dies without offspring or without having been circumcised will not be accepted in the world of the ancestors, as he will have betrayed their cause by not fostering clan continuity.[182] Therefore **imbalu** as a cultural ritual is aimed at instilling these ancestral norms and worldview into successive generations. **Imbalu**, land and the obligation to be fecund are three central pillars that go in constituting the worldview of the Bamasaba.

---

[182] L. W. Wawomola and L. Wamono, interviewed by author on 6th November 1999 in Butiru village.

Culture is an integrated whole comprising elements seen as central to the identity of a particular community. The central ones are the building blocks of the culture, while the less important ones are the sand and cement that hold this edifice together. In combination they go into lending a particular culture its physiognomy. Historical and geographical factors of a community determine to a very large extent the composition of elements which give a particular culture this physiognomy. The history of the Bamasaba is a history of continually trying to push further the boundaries of their inhabited world beyond the narrow confines of the ranges and ridges of Mount Elgon, while keeping what they had from outsiders. Their *Itesot* neighbours to the west and the *Jopadhola* to the south were traditionally pastoralist communities. These needed ever more land, especially the lush plains towards *Kachumbala* to the west and *Bukedi* to the south, for grazing their herds. The topical names of *imbalu,* which are an embodiment of Masaba history, are replete with references to wars with these communities, as they tried to push the Bamasaba further up into the ridges. As their numbers grew, so did the need for more land increase. Evidence from the topical names of the age-sets shows recurrent incursions by strangers, followed by equally recurrent defeats at the hands of the Bamasaba warriors. Being a sedentary population where agriculture is the mainstay of productivity, the homesteads, which are normally found within the farms, become the location of shrines, which they have to safeguard.

The survival of the community depended upon the availability of land, indeed on the ability of its younger generation to win more of this scarce resource. Land became a major issue, its acquisition and protection for the sustenance of the community a matter of grave importance. *Imbalu* then bred acquirers and protectors of the land. *Imbalu* then was used as the measure of a boy's maturity, and marked the time for handing to him the worldview, norms and value ethic of the community as handed down from the ancestors through successive generations. The instructions and ordeals are all geared towards making him a convinced and toughened man, ready to take up his responsibility towards the community. Among these was that of protecting the community and its interests by taking on any adversary, and their neighbours fear the Bamasaba. Having faced the knife without flinching, the neighbours discovered that a knife or spear did not scare them but instead spurred them on to prove their manliness.

130

Cultural practices normally crystallise into customs. These customs get sacralised over time so as to lend divine credibility and sanction to them, and to give them the power of obligation. *Imbalu* is a Masaba custom, which has been sacralised and given ancestral sanction and power to make it binding upon all Bamasaba males. The covenant entered into by the initiate is continually celebrated and renewed every two years to rejuvenate it and give it currency especially in the face of changing times. The belief that they are *basaani* (men) while their neighbours are but *basinde* (boys)[183] is always a rallying factor, which gives them the impetus to fight to the bitter end. This is dramatised by the apparent ease with which they stand the ordeals and justified by the ferocity with which they fought their neighbours. Masaba *imbalu* is a communal ritual aimed at instructing and preparing young men for the important duty of taking charge of the community's affairs. It is, therefore, a cultural ritual where the community brings the initiate before itself, puts him through initiatory instructions and ordeals, with the purpose of conferring upon him a new status as an adult. Society is the matrix, which gives birth to this individual, humanises and helps him to grow to maturity within it and according to its norms and values. The initiate is expected to internalise and subscribe to its worldview, uphold its norms and values, defend them, and indeed to propagate the community in all dimensions.

Societies attach a lot of significance to ritual because of its expressive value, believing that it will bring out the desired state of affairs. In ritual, something is being said and done; something of importance is being symbolically asserted. The same honesty that marks the ritual approach allows people to be themselves in the presence of one another, acting out with their bodies what they think with their brains.[184]

The liminal phase has been especially identified as being important in shaping identity, as well as building group solidarity and cohesion. Victor Turner in particular shows how social bonds, what he terms *communitas,* are engendered out of the spontaneous sense of unity and solidarity, especially during the transition phase, arguing, "Among themselves,

---

183 J. B. Purvis, *Through Uganda to Mount Elgon*. London: T. Fisher Unwin, 1909, p. 271.

184 Roger Grainger, *The Language of the Rite*. London: Longman and Todd, 1974, p. xi.

neophytes tend to develop an intense comradeship and egalitarianism. Secular distinctions of rank and status disappear or are homogenised".[185] They feel they belong together, and as an age-set they feel more than capable of taking up the responsibilities that society has entrusted to them. The age-set system makes this easier as they are encouraged by one another, finding strength, confidence and encouragement in numbers.

Ritual is important too, because of its extra degree of intensity, normally brought about by the fact that its behaviour pattern is a contact between the secular and the sacred. It is, therefore, able to affect the bodily posture, the gait, indeed the whole disposition of the general demeanour of the participants.[186] Believing that this is an ancestral requirement with whom they now identify gives them the confidence required to transcend the experiential as they have faith in the supernatural.

5.2.3. Sexuality, Fecundity and Community

Imbalu is closely associated with sexuality and procreation, since marriage and sex are a *conditio sine qua non* for the continuity of the community and the immortality of the ancestors. Sex and fecundity are fundamental elements in the origin of the life of the community and of its sustenance. La Fontaine seems to capture the theme correctly when she says that in creating new life, sexual intercourse mobilises mystical powers. The dramatisation of sexual acts or their performance in ritual contexts is to be understood as a means by which the ritual action is infused with potency and generative force. Yeast and chyme are understood from this perspective as generative elements. Therefore, sexual symbolism is not to be understood so much as referring to human sexuality, but rather as the ritual attempt to harness supernatural powers to effect the desired end.[187]

The physical cutting is done on the sexual organ, which is perhaps the most painful spot on the body because it is associated with fertility. Initiation is about the mysteries of life and death, and the sexual organ is the gateway to

---

[185] Victor W. Turner, *The Ritual Process: Structure and Anti-Structure*. New York: Aldine Publishing Press, 1979, p. 95.

[186] Margaret Mead, "Ritual and Social Crisis", in J. D. Shaughnessy (ed.), *The Roots of Ritual*. Grand Rapids: W. B. Ferdmans Publications, 1973, p. 87.

[187] J. S. La Fontaine, *Initiation*. Manchester: Manchester University Press, 1986, p. 116.

life. The physical cutting on the sexual organ is thus understood as commissioning it to carry out its purpose in the scheme of things by fostering more life. Laurenti Magesa puts this point very well when he notes that,

> It is not surprising that one of the areas emphasised in instruction is sexuality. Instruction in this area is exhaustive as the transmission of life and the preservation of the life force depends on sexuality.[188]

Therefore, *imbalu* is aimed at bringing about responsible husbands and fathers whose sexuality and sexual activity will ensure the continued flow of the ancestral stream of life. Fecundity as symbolised by the potency contained in yeast is a key theme in the instructions, and runs through the fabric of the various actions and rites. Marriage and procreation are especially explicit in the exhortations of the ritual elders, the maternal uncles, and the surgeon during the day of purification.

The community will have invested their hope and future in the young persons, as the future wellbeing of the community depends upon them. The future of the older generation in terms of personal and collective immortality also depends on their fecundity, to constitute what has been referred to as the community of the living dead. Among the Bamasaba when a male child is born they say *wakobosile sianga* (he has returned the skull). Traditionally dead bodies were thrown away to be eaten by vultures and hyenas, after which the skull was later collected and hung between forked branches of a tree near the homestead. The birth of a male child was referred to as bringing back the skull of the dead elder as the boy would be named after him. When a boy child is born the father is jokingly told that he is now free to die if he wants, as he will have accomplished his obligation to society by leaving behind the medium through which he himself will be propagated, and the clan will continue to thrive.

This point explains why marriage in Masaba culture is consummated by the birth of a child, a male child to be precise. A marriage which is not blessed with a child is not consummated, and the man can, if he wants, ask for his dowry back to pay for another wife. In any case if he still wants the wife, he can keep her but marry another with whom he can beget children. It is

---

[188] Laurenti Magesa, *African Religion: The Moral Traditions of Abundant Life*. New York: Orbis Books, 1997, p. 98.

not very far from the biblical story where Abraham's wife Sarah gave him her maid for him to get children with. The memory of the dead can only be kept alive through procreation and successive naming, and this explains the religious and central importance of sexuality and fecundity in *imbalu*. To the Bamasaba, marriage and sex are not ends in themselves, rather they are seen as means towards procreation. To them, marriage without the intention of procreation would be quite incomprehensible. *Imbalu* is a means through which the traditions and values of the community are passed down to the novices for onward transmission to subsequent generations.

Marriage has a multiplier effect upon kinship in more ways than the biological. In the understanding of the Bamasaba, marriage is not a personal affair, but is rather a communal affair as it is the coincidence of several clans who become related through the two young people. A wife belongs to a man, but she is also the responsibility of the entire clan. A man would not be permitted by the clan to mistreat his wife while they keep quiet. If for instance he beats her to death, the matter would not end with the individual in question being charged with murder in a court of law. In the case of such an unfortunate occurrence, the clan of the woman would seek revenge upon the clan of the man. Houses would be torched, animals killed or looted, while crops would be destroyed. The police would have a hard time controlling the emotions generated by such a death. As the saying goes, *"niwira uwomumya usikhawo uwowo"* (if you kill a stranger's person you pay with your own)! In a nutshell, there is no existence without belonging to a community, and the actions of one member have direct bearing upon the community in general, and other individuals in particular.

5.2.4. Community, Ancestors and Legitimating Myths

Myths are central in rituals because they embody claims to its divine origin and sanction. Indeed, ritual is commonly validated by its supposed antiquity, when people see it as being part of their history, even if they may not quite understand why they must do certain things in that particular way. Monica Wilson has amply asserted this point when she says,

> The force of ritual comes partly from its antiquity, real or supposed, and the problem facing all who celebrate rituals in a fast changing

society is how to combine relevance to changing circumstances with the sanctity of tradition.[189]

The novice is told through didactic songs and proverbs that *imbalu* is the legacy of the ancestors with whom he wants to identify. Their legendary heroic deeds are recounted through such songs as well as in myths.[190] Myths about the origin of the Bamasaba in general and of *imbalu* in particular bring to the present something from the past, and convey a message to the performing community concerning the importance of this ritual. By making recourse to the ancestors, they situate *imbalu* within the history of the community, playing the central role of explaining its importance to the community. Myths are an essential element in the ritual because they bridge the historical gap and link the initiate to the ancestors, thereby binding the two together. Victor Turner puts it well when he says,

> Myth treats of origins but derives from transitions ... Myths relate how one state of affairs became another, how an unpeopled world became populated; how chaos became cosmos; how immortals became mortal; how the seasons came to replace climate without seasons ... and so on. Myths are liminal phenomena: frequently told at a time or in a site that is betwixt and between.[191]

In the concrete case of *imbalu*, the myths of origin explain it as a sacred custom; a cultural heritage bequeathed to the community by the ancestors, and one which every Masaba man must perform freely and proudly.[192] Internalisation of the cultural requirement is important, and personal subscription to the norm is crucial in the efficacy of the ritual. One does not only go through it as a requirement, but has to subscribe to it as a cultural value if one is to identify with it. The responsibility of defending and propagating the values of society are incumbent upon every member. That is why,

> The strength to endure the ordeal with courage must come from himself; if his heart is not in it, then no one can help him. The boys' songs as they dance in the months before the rituals express glory in

---

189 Monica Wilson, "The Wedding Cakes: A Study of Ritual Change", in J. S. La Fontaine (ed.), *The Interpretation of Ritual*. London: Tavistock, 1972, p. 188.

190 See 4.5.4. above for an example.

191 Victor Turner, "Myth and Symbol", in D. Sills (ed.), *The International Encyclopedia of the Social Sciences*. New York: Macmillan Publishers, 1968-1979, p. 576.

192 See for instance 1.2.3 above.

the independence of their choice and their own determination to 'face death'.[193]

The life experiences of the ancestors are brought forward to guide the present, as the initiate is eager to identify with them and to accept this cultural requirement as his own. The ancestors are invoked to be present and to participate in the rituals they have enjoined upon their successive offspring. Ancestral origin and authority give the rituals credibility and sanction. This point is driven home when the songs urge all and sundry to *syheta umwana afane babawe* (circumcise the son to resemble the father).

Imbalu could be perceived as a form of animation of relationships. On the vertical axis, the initiate builds a relationship with his ancestors who are an extension of his kinsfolk, and with the Supreme Being. At the horizontal level he has to take an active and personal role in the exercise of developing relationships with his kinsfolk. The novice who has hitherto been a non-person claims his father's relatives as his own. The new member is recognised by society, and is helped to foster relations with members of the paternal as well as the maternal clans. Where he was earlier seen as a child he now assumes a new identity as a man. A special close relationship is cultivated with his age-set mates with whom he must live in solidarity and mutual dependence. Magesa captures this point when he says,

> ... initiation also underlines the realization that within the social organization an individual is required to show special loyalty to certain personal or group-relations as a way of strengthening the whole society ... The most significant group relation, established by the very fact of initiation, is the institution of age-sets ...The socio-religious importance of age-sets is that they are used to manage social complications that could be detrimental to the force of life, thus, they promote the overall life of society.[194]

Imbalu is a period of good will, when relationships are made and/or strengthened. The rounds made by the novice to visit the different relations far and wide is testimony of this animating exercise. A visit to a relative is perhaps the most expressive sign of friendship. The Bamasaba say that, *"Bikele bibisaula intzila itzya w'omulebe"* (it is feet which clear the path

---

[193] Suzette Heald, "Witches and Thieves: Deviant Motivations in Gisu Society", in *Man*, ns 21 no. 1 (1986), pp. 69-70.

[194] Magesa, *African Religion*, pp. 104-105.

to a relative's home). It is understood as bringing *basambwa* (ancestors). Since *basambwa* are credited with the origin of the clan and with the authorship of the customs by which the members live in harmony among themselves, a visit by a relative is associated with blessings. The novice brings not only himself and *basambwa*, but also the party of participants, who are a microcosm of the entire clan. In a sense, the entire community: living, departed and yet-to-be-born is congregated in the home of the relative.

Movement from the novice's home to those of various relations and back marks the connection of these points by the factor of relatedness. The food that is cooked and eaten together is actually a communion meal, since there is the strong belief that the departed are themselves palpably present. Communion is a celebration of life and relationship that gives birth to more and better life. At the heart of these visits and communing is the over-ridding factor of identity with them. By claiming them as one's very own blood, he identifies with them in their joys and sadness.

Initiation does not only leave an indelible mark on the body of the initiate, but leaves an indelible mark on the body politic of the community too. With the initiation of novices the entire community is re-invigorated, imbued with new life through the strengthened ties among kinsmen, age-set mates and friends. As war unites a divided nation to face a common enemy, *imbalu* rallies people, making them forget their domestic differences. Lots of grudges and other problems between individuals and families dissolve during these festivities, as *imbalu* over-shadows all other considerations. Lots of new relationships are engendered between families arising from the gifts extended to, and brought home by the initiates. The far distant relatives who are visited are brought nearer into the web of relationships, as relatedness is brought to the fore while space is relegated to the abstract.

The children of these families come to know one another, many for the first time but certainly not for the last, thereby inaugurating what would for many of them be life-long relationships. Friends and neighbours of these relatives come to welcome the initiates and other relatives. These are sucked into the relationship web creating friendships beyond consanguinity. It is not only the worldview of the community and its customs that are passed on, but the network of relationships are themselves handed down to successive new generations.

Without such a strategy these links would wither and die as children grow up not knowing their distant relatives. At the vertical level, through invocation, libation and sacrifice, relationship with the ancestors and Deity is also renewed and strengthened. This covenant of identity and mutual relatedness is renewed and invigorated at every successive initiation ceremony.

Among the newly initiated themselves, the institution of **bubakoki** (age-sets) establishes bonds of comradeship far and wide. Though different in physical age, the knife brings all who were initiated during the same season social equality not possible even among blood brothers. The reasons for the disparity between the physical ages of the age-set buddies are diverse. Some novices get initiated in their teens while others do so in their twenties, either because the latter procrastinated for long, or because they started but never completed the process. These are known as **bakonela** (those who have "slept over"). In the past some of these would do it for several consecutive seasons until it became necessary to forcefully circumcise them. It became a norm that as soon as such a cowardly novice declared his intention again, sometimes after intense teasing leading to resignation, he is circumcised immediately before he changes his mind yet again.

Compliance with the cultural requirement of initiation is taken so seriously that defaulting cannot be condoned. In 1966 an incident occurred which illustrates the seriousness with which **imbalu** is regarded in the community. There was a nation-wide crackdown where defaulters were rounded up and forcefully circumcised. Among them was an old circumciser who had conned his way by pretending he had been circumcised in the hospital. Fearing that he might die before being initiated, the wife informed his relatives that he was still **umusinde** (uncircumcised) after all! They seized and checked him to ascertain the wife's claim. And behold, he was indeed still uncircumcised! He was subsequently made to dance, and was marched to a playground where he was circumcised.

Because of many cases of forced circumcisions the year was given the topical name **Muambe** (seize him). Since then there is less patience for those who, after collecting gifts from relatives, renege on their resolve. People have neither time nor material to waste on such people and the indignity of being seized drives many to resignedly yield.

5.3. *IMBALU* AS AGENT OF IDENTITY

The notions of culture, identity, and power are so intertwined as to become virtually inseparable. One informs the other and one cannot be unravelled without necessarily affecting the others adversely. Identity is a spiral which begins with the immediate family, spreads outwards to the kins group, the village, the clan, the joking relations and the age-set group. The rounds that the novice makes in tracing members of his kin's group is to touch the lymph nodes of community, identity and power. He claims as his own the relations who have hitherto been of his father's, as he himself was but a non-person, simply an appendage of his! Now that he wants to become an autonomous human entity, he alerts them by going to them and taking *kumukheti* (stick of *imbalu*) to them.

It is like taking stock of his relatives, since it is the father who sends him to all these relatives to visit them with the explicit purpose of informing and asking for their blessings. But this has the implicit purpose of soliciting for support in his intended project of becoming an autonomous member of the community. With their support, material and moral he can proceed to face the knife knowing they are solidly behind him. This affords him material, social and psychological security. He now identifies with them, and this has the effect of bolstering his power too.

The age-set mates are a big addition upon the people he now identifies with, and opens the circle of relationships ever wider as he is unable to know them all. It is a special social group, which transcends the parochial confines of family, village and clan to embrace others far and wide, giving him the conviction that relatedness is an open circle. Society has multiple roles in the whole exercise, as it is the sponsor of the novices, the one who tests them, and the one who confers the status upon them. At the same time it is society which is the matrix within which the same novices will incubate, so to say, before being hatched.

Imbalu creates worthy adults who will take their duties as Masaba men seriously, and in accordance with the dictates of the community. Having instructed him in the ways of the community, society requires that he should internalise their cultural beliefs, values and worldview, and indeed subscribe to them. He is expected to foster, live by, protect and propagate them to subsequent generations. The myriad *babakoki* (age-mates) around him ensure that he does not bring their group into disrepute, and the *umukhebi* (circumciser) that he does not bring shame upon his *kumubono* (knife). His maturity is, therefore, not an event but a process, nor is it a one-man affair but a communal one as society has a stake in it. Freedom then does not mean licence to do as he pleases, but to do what the community expects of him. The good is what engenders the community and safeguards its interests. Conversely, the bad is what endangers the community and undermines its interests.

Isonja is a public gathering of all those who intend to acquire identity as full members in the community. These identify with one another as comrades at arms in their search for manhood, which comradeship will endure throughout their lives. Not only do they identify with the community of Bamasaba, but they also identify with one another as *babakoki* (members of a particular age-set).

Isonja is responsible for inaugurating and building identity among the novices themselves, as well as making them integral members of the wider community.

Identity then has more than just one dimension. At the personal level the novice identifies with the family as a focal unit whose interests constantly overlap.

The new member is identified by society as a new and integral member of the community. The new status changes his earlier relationships in a radical way, as he has to forge new relationships. His relationship towards his father now changes as the father now regards him as a fellow man, and no longer as a child. The clan now treat him as one of their own, a clansman. He is now allocated ancestral land from the share that his father himself acquired from the boy's grandfather. This land is not a question of the father's charity but a right grounded in customary law. It is therefore an obligation and duty for the father to pass on to his sons what he himself received from the ancestors. Receiving a share of the ancestral land is in itself a mark of identity with them and their heroic feats. Besides *imbalu*, land is perhaps the second most important item in the life of the Bamasaba.

5.3.1. Manliness as Identity

Imbalu is presented as that which separates men from boys, the brave from cowards. The initiate is made to feel that *imbalu* is an attainment, a goal to be coveted and achieved as a symbol of maturity and communal identity. This is reinforced by the fact that the uninitiated hold no esteem in the society of the Bamasaba, for they are regarded as children, grown up children if they are physically mature. This creates a longing for identity and esteem, which society alone confers upon those who successfully undergo the ordeals inherent in *imbalu*. There is a sense of solidarity and communion between the initiate and the corporate community, engendering communal spirit and corporate identity.

> Rituals articulate and reiterate a system of meaning, and prevent it being lost from sight. They act out and sacralise sameness. They restore, reinforce, or redirect identity. They maximise order by strengthening the place of the individual in the group, or society, and vice versa by strengthening the bonds of a society vis-à-vis the individual. They unify, integrate, and sacralise.[195]

The novice aspires to the acquisition of what is touted as a higher status where he identifies with men instead of boys. The individual is absorbed in the common cultural fabric where the community assimilates him when he assimilates its values, beliefs and worldview. By linking the past with the present, the community fills the emotional void of rational existence by surrounding stressful situations with emotional support from peers and ancestors.

Imbalu is likened to death and is often referred to as "fire" and "death". The novice is told over and over again that the operation is not only "fire" and "death" but that it lasts from sunrise to sunset. This "timelessness" of the ordeal coupled with the fact that the ancestors and elders underwent it, help to put the challenge of manhood in context, as *imbalu* is regarded as the hallmark of full manhood and of Masaba identity. Only those who have brought themselves to reconcile with this requirement by building up unshakeable resolve dare come forward. The community throws down the gauntlet and only those who are brave, the dare-devils, pick and throw it back at community. In doing this they will be justifying their challenge by pointing out that all his forefathers did it, and therefore he too will do it.

An initiated man is required to exhibit certain sentiments seen as manly, and curb others considered unmanly by the community. A challenge to a man's manhood is undeniably the most brazen of all challenges and is a

---

[195] Hans J. Mol, *Identity and the Sacred*. New York: The Free Press, 1977, p. 233.

declaration of war. Circumcising communities tend to place an inordinately high premium upon manhood and manliness. Such a challenge tends to evoke very strong emotions in a person to whom manhood has been preached as a value above others. Such a person can go to great lengths to prove his manliness. Even the question of death seems to acquire a new meaning as it is presented as a component part of the challenge. It is seen as being quite normal as one dies to join his ancestors in personal and collective immortality. This viewpoint is shared by John Beattie, who considers the expression and reinforcement of certain sentiments and values necessary for the smooth running of the performing society as a major function of ritual. This is achieved especially through indoctrination.[196] Evoking the community's memory as a way of reminding the members of their deepest identity is one of the basic functions of myth. It achieves this by recourse to their collective evolutionary history, thereby forging and integrating the corporate identity of the community.[197]

5.3.2. Music, Dance and Identity in Imbalu

The Bamasaba refer to their circumcision ritual as *khukhina imbalu* (dancing). Like a symphony with different movements, varied rhythm and tempo, it is imbued with music from beginning to end. The music and dance enable the *imbalu* initiates to go through the ceremony with ecstatic enthusiasm without stopping to ponder the extreme pain at the end of the line. By always looking to the higher ideals such as pride of family and community, identity with adults, independence from the father, and the general idea of belonging to something larger than self, the initiates are numbed to the ordeal.

This symphony opens with *isonja,* an inaugural public and collective affair where the novices are introduced to and tutored in the art of composition, dance and drama. They are also introduced to teamwork and communality since *isonja* is a communal affair.

Whereas *isonja* takes place in the evenings, the *imbalu* symphony picks momentum during the second phase when the novices accompanied only

---

[196] John Beattie, *Other Cultures*. London: Routledge and Kegan Paul, 1977, p. 206.
[197] Dan Sperber, *Rethinking Symbolism*. Transl. A. L. Morton, Cambridge: Cambridge University Press, 1975, p. 145.

by their near of kin without *namyenya* (song leader cum composer) visit far away relatives. By visiting these far away relatives, the novices are tracing kinship in time and space. Space, in terms of distance between kin and kith, and time in terms of how long it takes them to go and come back, are eliminated in favour of kinship. As the saying goes, *Aali umulebe mbawo lukongo taa,* (where there is a relative there is no mountain).[198] Kinship is about identity, and it brings the power of belonging to a group where one feels affirmed and secure. The teaching during *imbalu* lays stress upon the communitarian dimension of life as opposed to the individualistic tendency. This comes out clearly especially during the exhortation of the circumciser during the rite of *khusaabisa* (purification). The stress is that people live as families and clans, not as discrete individuals. Laurenti Magesa captures this spirit when he says,

> Learning the values of co-operation and sharing and the central importance of belonging to a family, a clan, and a community as an integral and responsible member constitutes this initial phase of the initiation process. Just as one is nothing without belonging to a community, the community disintegrates somewhat without the membership and contribution of everyone.[199]

The tempo increases markedly with the phase of thrashing millet for beer as seriousness and anticipation set in. Only those who are serious reach this far, many having quietly fallen by the wayside. This momentum heightens with the brewing of beer, and reaches a climax with the actual circumcision rite itself on the third day.

5.3.3. Sacralising Identity by Covenanting

In *imbalu* the supernaturals are invoked to witness and safeguard the vows against contravention, visiting havoc upon those who break them. In it, as in other elements of a religious nature, the supernaturals play the important role of sanctioning the vows by lending credibility and authority to them. The physical marking of circumcision is the community's way of putting a seal upon those who have formally and ceremonially danced their way into the inner recesses of the community. It is an indelible mark of identity with

---

[198] A common Masaba proverb meaning that however steep a mountain is, it cannot bar one from visiting a relative.

[199] Laurenti Magesa, *African Religion*, p. 96.

the community and with the ancestors upon whose command the ritual is held. Blood represents life, which is itself a religious element, as without life there would be no celebration at all. Shedding of blood by the novice signifies the sealing of a covenant bond with the living community and the ancestors. Mutilation signifies separation from the earlier position,

> which automatically incorporates him into a defined group; since the operation leaves ineradicable traces, the incorporation is permanent ... it is clearly a 'sign of union' with a particular deity and a mark of membership in a single community of the faithful.[200]

The mingling of his blood with dust is an inseparable covenant band with the ancestors who have become *liloba* (soil). It is a giving of some individual's life to reinforce the community's life as union with the supernatural. The ritual is, therefore, a medium where the human and the divine are interfaced in the same entity.

The physical cut is, therefore, a mark of membership among the community of men, and a sign of union with the ancestors. In a certain sense, as David Chidester says, "The physical body becomes a social symbol of personal transformation and group solidarity."[201] For ritual death is valuated not only as an initiatory ordeal necessary for a new birth, but also as a privileged situation for the novices as it allows them to be identified with their ancestors.[202]

The conviction that the new status is superior to the earlier one makes it possible for him to understand the ordeals of initiation as the pangs of a new birth. Physical, social, and psychological maturity are seen as personal achievements since the strength to endure the ordeal with courage must come from the novice himself.

In the case of *imbalu*, the ancestors and *Wele* (Supreme God) are the supernatural by whom the vows are contracted in the presence of the elders who are the living representatives of the ancestors. The surgeon is an important personage as he is the efficient cause by which the child is made to become a man. He is a ritual priest with the cumulative authority of the

---

[200] Van Gennep, *The Rites of Passage*, p. 72.

[201] David Chidester, *Patterns of Action: Religion and Ethics in a Comparative Perspective*. Belmont, California: Wadsworth Publishing Company, 1987, p. 132.

[202] Mircea Eliade, *Rites and Symbols of Initiation: The Mysteries of Death and Rebirth*. New York: Harper and Row, 1958, p. 37.

elders and ancestors behind him. His profession is regarded as a calling by *kumusambwa kwembalu* (the spirit of *imbalu*) associated with the ancestors. The act of circumcision is the centre of the rituals and their justification. The rite of *khusaabisa* (purification) where the novice is made to hold the surgeon's knife while the latter instructs him in the meaning, value and virtues of manhood is a formal way of covenanting.[203] It is reconciliation with it, and seeing it not only as an instrument of pain but as that of transformation.

Whenever an initiated man does something childish, people will remind him of this rite and its covenant. This speaks volumes, for it is an indictment of the person's unbecoming behaviour as the person in question is seen as having contravened the vows by which he was bound by the surgeon while he held the knife. Words have power and words spoken in a ritual setting are binding and efficacious. For instance a parent must not grumble about a child as it is understood as a curse. In contradistinction, a positive word from the mouth of somebody older and related by blood is understood as blessing. Therefore, all the words spoken by the elders at the different forums during the festivities constitute blessings, and are binding upon the novice, for they are spoken in the presence of the supernaturals and the living representatives of the community.

Holding the circumciser's knife while being told the prescriptions and proscriptions of adult life is an effective way of vowing to uphold them. Its nearest equivalent is perhaps holding the Bible or Koran when being sworn into office. Such a one is bound to uphold the tenets of office as enshrined in the vows by protecting them with all one's strength and ability.

5.3.4. Significance of Sacrifice in Imbalu

There is an essential similarity between ritual and sacrament, for in both it is an outward sign pointing to an inner reality. It retains the idea of

---

[203] Ogbu U. Kalu, *The Embattled Gods: Christianization of Igboland 1841-1991.* Lagos: Minaj Publishers, 1986, pp. 307-309. The author is well aware of the argument by scientists such as Van Baaren (*Religion and Reason,* pp. 35-46) against the importation of terms such as covenant from religion into the science of religion. This term is used here as a descriptive category in reference to the relationship, implicit and explicit, which exists between an individual and his community on the one hand, and between the community and their divinities on the other.

mystery, for it cannot be fully understood.[204] As it has been observed, a ritual, an object, a person or place, in as far as it symbolises something else that is sacred or mysterious, can be considered sacramental.[205] This is because it manages to bring the human and the superhuman together in some human-divine interaction. It is, therefore, at once a definite focus of interest, a means of communion and communication, and a common ground for understanding. At the personal level, sacrifice makes an individual's life and world meaningful, for it opens new avenues beyond the empirical, giving meaning and purpose to his existence.

Sacrifice plays an important role in *imbalu*, because it is a means of expressing the concept of communality. This is at the two levels of humans among themselves, and also of humans and supernaturals. This is precisely because identity operates at horizontal and vertical lines. The horizontal dimension joins the individual socially to his community and his age-mates. He is also vertically bonded to the ancestors and to God. This relationship is then sealed with blood and therefore with sacrifice. Sacrifice becomes a ratification of identity so that it is now rooted in a religious ritual, as the social event is sacralised. It should be noted that what happens in sacrifice is largely informed by the people's religious beliefs and worldview. Sacrifice may be for any number of reasons, but suffice for us to examine propitiation, purification, communion, and thanksgiving sacrifices in *imbalu*.

The Bamasaba view sacrifice, especially one where blood is shed, as being a very efficacious mode of religious expression and interaction with the supernatural. Blood signifies life and when the life of a sacrificial animal or bird is shed, it is believed to augment that of the persons involved as sacrifice is self-giving. This belief in the efficacy of blood is even evident in interpersonal relationships. A person will consider himself having been an honoured guest if, and only if some animal or bird is slaughtered for him. In that respect, a small chicken slaughtered for him is worth much more than a chunk of meat bought from a butchery. The hen will be referred to as *bukeni* (banquet), something specially prepared for the guest; and the meat from the butchery as *tzinyenyi* (relish or sauce). In the

---

[204] Mircea Eliade, *The Sacred and the Profane: The Nature of Religion*. New York: Harcourt, Brace and World Inc., 1959, p. 4.

[205] Joseph Martos, *Doors to the Sacred*. New York: Doubleday, 1981, p. 12.

absence of a hen, an egg is boiled in the meat and is served first by the host to the guest. This symbolises a hen, though still in potency. Then the meat is served after the egg. The presence of the egg in the meat alters the nature of the whole dish from an ordinary meal to a formal one.

Sacrifice normally begins by some sort of consecration. One way is by laying on of hands, and the other by holding the neck of the sacrificial object during slaughter. This action of freely giving the sacrifice changes the object from what it ordinarily is to a symbol that it is meant to be. A casual observer may see an animal being slaughtered, but he needs 'inner eyes' to actually behold what is taking place. In the eyes of the believing community, there is no longer an animal but rather a sacred sacrificial victim. The result is consecrated meat, which only those who are ritually permitted and are ritually clean can partake of. This is also done in a prescribed manner, for they are sharing in a meal with the superhuman. The elements necessary for sacrifice, namely the sacrificial victim, a ritual leader, faith of the sacrificing subjects, intention for the sacrifice, and indeed the recipient/s of the sacrifice are all in place.

There is a prescribed way of handling it, within a given frame of space and time, by people who are ritually permitted to do so. All the others are tabooed from even coming near, let alone touching or eating it, lest they incur ritual guilt and bring ritual impurity upon the entire sacred sacrifice. It is this idea of self-giving that makes it mandatory for the sacrificial victim to have stayed at least a night in the homestead of the person sacrificing it. It is the same reason behind the stipulation that the one sacrificing has to observe ritual purity immediately before and during the time of sacrifice. One aspect of such purity is abstinence from sexual relations on the eve of the sacrifice.

Propitiation sacrifice includes the animal slaughtered by the father of the novice, at the foot of the *lukangu* (ritual pole) on the day of circumcision. It is meant to make the ancestors look well upon the novice, the family and the clan, and not visit harm on them. The father acknowledges the ancestors as being part and parcel of the community, and as playing a central role in the lives of their offspring. For as Placide Tempels observes: "The dead constitute the invisible part of the family, clan or tribe, and the invisible part is the most important".[206] The one sacrificing must be in a state of ritual purity, hence the invocations, libations, smearings, and prayers. This is a normal requirement whenever humans come into contact with the superhuman, meant to ward off the negative effects this may bring upon the community. The guilt of one member is not an individual but a communal affair with consequences for the entire community. Each person's actions influence the general welfare of the community and the necessary conditions of life: rain, harvests, farm produce and peace.[207] It is as if the blood of the animal is given to appease the supernaturals so that the life of the humans may be upheld. Hanging the heart and lungs of the sacrificial animal on the *lukangu* (ritual pole) in the compound signifies the giving of the entire animal to the supernaturals. The heart is the pump that keeps life flowing through the organism, and the lungs represent the breath of life, so they signify life.

The heart is also understood as the repose of a person's most secret intentions and emotions. It is where love, hatred, jealousy, evil, piety and other equally secret intentions and emotions, both positive and negative, reside. It is the seat of both good and bad intentions. As Jean Comaroff says of the Tswana, the heart is the physical and experiential centre of being, it registers impressions that impinge on the person from outside and radiates influence beyond the self.[208]

The lungs, on the other hand, signify breath, the vital force without which a living creature ceases to be alive. The Bamasaba see these two organs as the centre of life in a living creature, human and beast. They constitute the animal itself so to say. Hanging these two on the *lukangu* signify telling the supernaturals that this animal in its entirety is but a symbol of the giver's wholehearted self-giving, indeed indebtedness to them for his vital force. In his mind would be the three most important elements: long and healthy life, wealth and finally immortality. Health is infinitely more than merely being healthy in body, for it entails a healthy mind and

---

[206] Placide Tempels, *Bantu Philosophy*. Paris: E.T., 1959, p. 69.

[207] Aylward Shorter, *Songs and Symbols of Initiation: A Study from Africa in the Social Control of Perception*. Monograph 1. Nairobi: CHIEA Press, 1987, p. 6.

[208] Jean Comaroff, *Body of Power, Spirit of Resistance*. Chicago: University of Chicago Press, 1985, p. 128.

environment, including the health of his wives, children, animals and gardens.

The Bamasaba believe that the ancestors possess power to bless and protect the living, or to visit harm upon them, depending on whether they are remembered and honoured, or denigrated and neglected. Belief that as spirits the ancestors are better placed to intercede with *Wele* (Supreme God) on behalf of their living offspring, makes it expedient for them to be venerated. Belief in *Wele* (Supreme God) is routed through the ancestors owing to the practical approach where communication is easier between equals. Contact between the humans and the supernaturals ought to be channelled through an intermediary. Belief in a transcendental Creator God, is not at all contradicted or diminished by the invocation of *basambwa* (ancestral spirits) for practical everyday living. These are the logical points of reference because firstly, they are relatives, and secondly, they were themselves humans only recently, so they understand human problems well.

Communion between the human and the ancestors is further demonstrated by the sacrifice of a fowl slaughtered in the ancestral burial grove, on the day of circumcision. The ancestors are acknowledged when they are individually called by name, and invoked amid libation. The fowl and the bananas are roasted and eaten only by the elders and the novice/s, in the company of the ancestors. It is evidently a communion meal between the elders, the novice/s and the ancestors to whom they have been introduced.

All the members share the cow the father slaughters for the *babakoki* (age-set mates) as a thanksgiving to *Wele* (Supreme God) for blessing this particular member with life and children. Reaching elderhood through the initiation of a son is considered a blessing.

Purification sacrifice is offered for instance when a novice has defiled during the operation. A black goat is sacrificed to cleanse the *lulwanyi* (courtyard). Likewise, a novice who sires a child before being circumcised is also regarded as having incurred ritual guilt. A goat is given to the circumciser who will slaughter it and smear some chyme on the novice, throwing the rest of the chyme on the house to ward off ritual guilt.

Thanksgiving sacrifice is typified by the goat or cow *iyelusantza* slaughtered on the day of incorporation. Certainly on this day there is joy and thanksgiving for the successful initiation of the novices who will be incorporated into the community of *basani* (men) on this day.

5.3.5. Traditional Religious Beliefs

As this is a religious cosmology, and religion is about things which matter most to people, the people's aspirations are verbalised, expressed and re-enacted in religious idiom. So while *imbalu* is a social event, it is above all a religious ritual interlaid with sacred elements including *inter alia* vows, shedding of blood, symbolic activities, sacrifice, invocation, prayers, smearings, blessings, purification, contact with the supernatural, shaving, circumcision, taboos, and ancestor veneration. All these find their basis and springboard in the religious beliefs of the Bamasaba, their values and indeed in their worldview since, as Beattie argues,

> Rituals almost always embody beliefs, and these beliefs may provide acceptable explanations for events which would otherwise be inexplicable ... they provide an antidote to ignorance and doubt. For most people, in all times and cultures it is important to know, even know wrongly, rather than not to know at all.[209]

Rituals are, therefore, used to communicate something of a religious value to other members of the community, through word, symbol, or action. The people involved in *imbalu* are saying something and doing something they value and believe, something they desire and hope to achieve, both here and in the world to come.

Religious behaviour has to do with reciprocity between the human and that which he considers to be the recipient of his prayers and worship. This interaction takes the form of prayer, invocation, sacrifice, praise and so on. After all what is ritual but that which humans do in their interaction with that which they regard as the superhuman.[210] For the form of interaction, what is regarded as sacred space and time, and the recipient of their overtures are determined by what their culture stipulates them to be.

Likewise, the ordeals of *imbalu* are themselves expressed in religious terms since they are couched in symbolic form. The presence and decisive role of the ancestors in this whole enterprise pervades this ritual with

---

[209] Beattie, *Other Cultures*, p. 206.

[210] Evan M. Zuesse, "Ritual", in Mircea Eliade (ed.), *The Encyclopedia of Religion*. Vol. 12. New York: Macmillan, 1987, p. 405.

religious undertones. This is where the words of Victor Turner ring with marked insistence when he says,

> in ritual context, almost every article used, every gesture employed, every song or prayer, every unit of space and time, by convention stands for something other than itself. It is more than it seems, and often a good deal more.[211]

The conviction that *imbalu* brings about a new status which is superior to the earlier one makes it possible for the novice to understand, and to gallantly endure the ordeals of initiation regarded as but the pangs of social birth.

Above all, religion is concerned with a beyond, with man's relation towards that beyond, and with what these particular people consider to be the practical implications of that beyond for their life. *Imbalu* is not understood only as a means of becoming a man, but above that as linking the individual to his ancestors among whom he expects to share a collective immortality.[212]

5.4. SYMBOLIC ACTIONS IN *IMBALU*

The compound concepts of culture, identity and power are vividly brought out in the pattern of symbolism. A symbol is a language for ultimate reality, for it reaches out for that which is not immediately known. It pushes forward the frontier of knowledge and grasps the reality of things as it attempts to get to the real nature of life and the meaning of existence itself. Symbolism is the language of religion because it alone goes beyond the frontiers of empirical objectivity and seeks the appropriation of the transcendent. Symbols tend to bring the external world of religion into our physical world, so they are a medium between the two worlds.

It is the concern of religion to get beyond the appearance to the ultimate reality, as man makes an audacious bid to bind himself to creation and the Creator. In religion man is trying to enlarge and to complete his own

---

211 Victor W. Turner, *The Forest of Symbols: Aspects of Ndembu Ritual*. London: Cornell University Press, 1973, p. 15.
212 Thomas F. O'Dea and Janet O'Dea Aviad, *The Sociology of Religion*. Englewood-Cliffs, New Jersey: Prentice-Hall, 1983, pp. 1-2.

personality by finding the supreme context in which he rightly belongs.[213] As it has been observed,

> Much ritual symbolism draws on the simplest and most intense sensory experiences, such as eating, sexuality, and pain. Such experiences have been repeated so often or so intimately by the body that they have become primary forms of bodily awareness. In ritual, they are transformed into symbolic experiences of the divine, and even into the form of the cosmic drama itself. We may therefore speak of a "prestige of the body" in ritual. In the bodily gesture, the chant, dance, and stride of participants, primordial presences are made actual again, time is renewed, and the universe is regenerated.[214]

All the actions that take place during the *imbalu* period are geared towards effecting the desired change and transformation, and they are performed in such a way as to leave a permanent imprint on both the body and psyche of the initiate. There are numerous instances where symbolism is employed to dramatise death and burial on the one hand, rebirth and resurrection on the other. For instance entry into *mwitosi* (the sacred mud), entering *likombe* (convalescence hut) backwards to symbolise re-entry into the womb, *khukhwiyalula* meaning hatching himself, among other symbols of separation and transition, make him to understand that this passage is an irreversible growth. He will have crossed an unbridgeable gulf separating his earlier condition from the new one.

The symbolic meaning of the old items is quite elaborate. Old items contain ancestral power handed down the line through successive generations. By using these old items the candidate shares in this ancestral power and identifies with it. He acknowledges the sacred custom enshrined in the rite of *imbalu*, while he himself now becomes a medium for propagating it to successive generations. This he does by being faithful to the traditions of the community, their cultural values and virtues, as well as their worldview. By using these items he also shares in the cumulative historical characteristics, virtues, valour, prosperity, fecundity, and life of the ancestors in particular, and the community in general. He becomes an incarnation of the ancestors after whom he is named, as they act as models

---

[213] G.W. Allport, *The Individual and His Religion*. New York: Macmillan, 1973, p.142.

[214] Evan M. Zuesse, "Ritual", in *The Encyclopedia of Religion*. New York, 1987, p. 406.

for inspiring him. The past is, therefore, brought to bear upon the present as the candidate claims the traditions of his people. These items, then, act as a bridge between the past and the present, between the ancestors and the candidate. The candidate himself, on the other hand, bridges the past and the future. He himself becomes a medium of propagating this same power to the younger generations by being faithful to the traditions of the Bamasaba, their cultural values and virtues, as well as their worldview.

By using the old vessels the elders are saying symbolically that the ritual is not created by them, but rather that they are only deputising for the ancestors whose legacy the ritual is. They are but stewards mandated to perform this sacred ritual, and to hold it in trust for subsequent generations. The initiate receives the instructions, values and power, which he makes his own, and then transmits them to subsequent generations. This power and life must continue to flow as they mean the continuance of the community. Whoever receives them yet becomes a dead end by not bringing forth life is considered a traitor to the community, and such a person was never given a normal funeral.

The symbolic meaning behind running to and from the stream is that the candidate is eager and cannot wait to become a man. Scooping water with his bare hands symbolises the need for patience even when in a hurry, but also signifies the ability to be innovative and self-reliant in times of need. Not looking behind means that this candidate has resolved to become a man and sees nothing positive in the life he is leaving behind, nor will he be distracted by anything. A Masaba man is expected to be decisive and set upon what he intends to do without undue distraction by other things.

Carrying the pot on his bare head symbolises readiness to do hard and uncomfortable work and to bear hardship manly. It has the further meaning of being serious and forthright in matters of importance. Life will have taken on a new dimension to which the initiate had better acquaint himself early enough. Gone will be the days of comfort, complacence and undue consideration for his personal welfare. Instead, life will have become downright serious and often rough. Not looking back has the added symbolic meaning of never backsliding into actions, which are childish, as he will have emancipated irreversibly.

Brewing of beer symbolises growth and maturation. Roasted dough, which is insipid on the first day, is by the fermentation power of yeast, transformed into potent and intoxicating beer on the third day. This process is irreversible so the candidate's maturation too is irreversible.

Placing the pot beneath the *lukangu* (ritual pole) in the middle of the courtyard symbolises exposure to the whole public and to the community of the invoked supernaturals who are believed to abide there.

Initiation is a public ceremony in which the whole community has a stake, and it is they who ceremonially remove the candidate from the inferior stage of childhood and install him into the coveted one of adults. Society is the matrix within which he will be helped to realise the maturity he is called to, to experience and understand his own identity as a full member of the community with all the rights and duties this places upon him. His identity is founded upon, and is subordinate to that of the community into which he is assimilated. He assimilates the community's experiences and values transmitted from earlier generations, while the community in turn assimilates him as he lives by its values and aspirations.

By his initiation the community is re-initiated, renewed and newly imbued with life and hope. By witnessing the initiation of young members the older folk relive their own initiation and realise the passage of time as they will now have become a generation of elders with new and specified roles in the community. Successive initiation ceremonies avail the older men the opportunity of ongoing formation. As they now mete out instructions and exhortations, they are challenged to re-examine their own lives to see as to whether they have lived these values. That is why the community will only allow people who have internalised the values they preached. The candidate only has to look at the personal life of the preaching elder to understand what was being said by the admonishing elder. It is not a matter of 'do as I say but not as I do', but as Aylward Shorter has said, experiential teaching.[215]

5.4.1. Kumwiikhoyo, *Suspension of the Moral Code*

Mircea Eliade explains initiation ritual in terms of death and rebirth, and says that,

> Every ritual repetition of the cosmogony is preceded by a symbolic retrogression to Chaos. In order to be created anew, the old world

---

[215] Shorter, *Symbols*, p. 5.

must be annihilated ... Initiatory death provides the clean slate on which will be written the successive revelations whose end is the formation of a new man.[216]

The return to chaos includes, among other things, reversal of habitual behaviour. Suspension or relaxing of social decorum, for instance avoidance of fathers and mothers-in-law, verbal permissiveness, respect of personal property, and concern for personal sensibilities are certainly a reversal of habitual social behaviour and constitute a sort of social chaos, as boundaries of interaction are temporarily removed. This also includes suspension of gender and age differentiation as men adorn women's clothes and women men's. The fact that ancestors and even God himself are believed to be present at these rituals is a reversal of the rules of interaction between the human and the superhuman.

Evans-Pritchard has documented expressions of obscenity in several communities and observes that "these prescribed acts and songs of obscenity are made to emphasise the suspension of the ordinary laws in the 'marginal periods' in passage rites."[217] He posits an explanation for this state of affairs, which I find quite plausible and interesting:

> We have noticed that that collective obscenities generally occur as part of large ceremonial undertakings, such as those associated with death, the birth of twins, drought and initiation into manhood. Now these are all occasions of emotional stress fraught with grave danger both to the individual who experiences them and to the society. The pent-up emotion of anger, fear, sorrow, grief reaches a point where some activity is essential; yet, unless this activity is guided into harmless channels it may prove to be fatal to the individual and disruptive to society. On such occasions society condones, or even prescribes, actions which it ordinarily prohibits and penalises.[218]

Suspension of the code of conduct serves certain purposes too, among them freedom to instruct the novices without undue regard to social encumbrances in speech and expression. Concern with socially permissible language can be an impediment in instruction precisely because there are strict proscriptions in reference to words deemed as sexually explicit hence

---

[216] Eliade, *Rites and Symbols of Initiation*, p. xiii.

[217] E. E. Evans-Pritchard, *The Position of Women in Primitive Societies and Other Essays in Social Anthropology*. London: Faber and Faber Ltd., 1965, p. 92.

[218] Ibid., p. 95.

socially offensive. Lifting or relaxing these requirements helps to create a relaxed atmosphere, which enhances the festive mood of the ritual.

5.4.2. Khuuakha, *Smearing with Yeast*

The traditional items worn by the novice symbolise continuity with and fidelity to the ancestral tradition. The thigh-bells make a jingling musical rhythm to the accompaniment of song and drumming, thereby providing music to which the participants dance. The animal skins and other paraphernalia have the overall effect of making the candidate look spectacular and "less-than-human".[219] They make the candidate feel that he is no longer, or rather not yet, a human being. It leaves a lingering sense of repugnance whenever he remembers how he looked and how he was treated, and ascribes this to the condition of ***businde*** (boyhood).

This makes the acquisition of manhood something of a hard-won achievement to be proudly treasured, while ***businde*** and all that is associated with it are made to look undesirable for a grown-up. This coupled with the insults and social prohibitions that go with the state of childhood go a long way in socially coercing him to take the plunge.

The smearing with yeast has differing explanations from my informants. While Wawomola[220] felt it signifies blessing, Tsemale described it as symbolising fecundity, pointing out that even a girl is smeared with yeast before she is escorted to her husband's for marriage. Since marriage is seen in terms of procreation, a girl is smeared before marriage to express the wish that she may be fertile and give birth to many children.[221] I think both explanations have a point. Yeast as a strong catalyst possesses power of transformation, so it symbolises power of maturity and transformation. The boy is expected to mature like the beer that he has brewed, and like it to be transformed on the third day. Yeast transforms beer from some tasteless and insipid mixture on the day it is brewed into a powerful and intoxicating brew on the third. Likewise, the boy is expected to be transformed on the third day from a weak, fearful, childish youngster on the first day into a

---

[219] L. Wawomola and L. Wamono, interviewed by author on 6th November 1999 at Butiru village.

[220] Ibid.

[221] Lawrence Tsemale, interviewed by author on 11th September 1999 at Bunamboko village.

strong, fierce and mature man on the third. Just like beer undergoes a physical change, which is irreversible, so the boy should also undergo a change by growth from a child into an adult, a change which is irreversible. Above all, as beer is potent brew so the novice should be potent and fecund. This rite also gives the elders the opportunity to invoke the ancestors to publicly point out and condemn the weaknesses of the novice. It is an opportunity for officially setting off the intense rituals, which mark the countdown to the day of circumcision for all and sundry to witness.

Mircea Eliade points out that the white paint (yeast) is meant to make them resemble ghosts.[222] From this day the novice is considered formally a non-person and is associated with the dead. This is in congruence with the Masaba idea of being confined to the *likombe* (symbolically place of the dead) during the convalescence period.

5.4.3. Khuukambila, *Invocation and Exhortation*

The word *khuukambila* has the denotation of admonition or exhortation. But it is linked to the word *likambila,* which means law. The admonition, therefore, has to do with the laws of the community with regard to accepted adult conduct, and manly conduct in particular. The public condemnation of faults is given in the spirit of correction, and aimed at encouraging the individual to reform, indeed conform. Faults committed before *imbalu* are regarded as childhood acts for which he is exonerated but not without some retribution. For instance an elder who has been keeping a grudge with the initiate may give him a serious slap to remind him of the particular misdemeanour. A slap has a double effect at this time. The elder finds a legitimate way of venting his anger upon the initiate, thereby defusing a grudge that might lead to a conflict or a curse in future. Such a misdemeanour is condemned in the strongest terms because it is a serious flaw in conduct. These and any others faults are condemned as he is told in no uncertain terms that such conduct would not be tolerated. And he cannot have the excuse of saying he was not aware of them as nobody ever brought them to his notice.

Uncircumcised boys are normally very careful as elders may even provoke them to see what type of youth they are. All these failings are paraded

---

[222] Eliade, *Rites and Symbols*, p. 37.

before the community during the smearing sessions to get all round condemnation. As the officiating elders go about doing their job, everybody will be keenly watching the countenance of the initiate for any signs of defiance, arrogance, hatred or anger.

Anthony Matanda explained yeast in connection with discomfort. He was of the opinion that the feel of dry yeast upon the skin is very uncomfortable and helps as a psychological reminder to the novice that he is no longer his old self. Other discomforts include lack of, or little sleep, thereby keeping the novice on his toes as people keep on reciting the litany of the ordeal so that his whole being, physical and mental, are saturated with this one message of *imbalu* as an ordeal.[223] This repetition time and again by different people in different ways is a method of intense instruction if not outright indoctrination.

5.4.4. Litosi, *Sacred Mud as Link with Ancestral Land*

The ancestral swamp, which is the last stop before the ordeal, is fraught with symbolism. The sacred swamp marks a link between the living, the ancestors and land. The fact that it froths after the ritual elders have tromped upon it and blessed it with beer while invoking the ancestral spirits betokens its potency. This indicates the presence of *basambwa* (ancestral spirits) and their blessings of the rituals.[224] The ancestral spirits of *imbalu* are believed to have prepared the mud as it is said to froth from within. Though the elders trample the mud till it froths, yet this does not diminish their belief in the myth that it is the ancestors who make it froth. This is the function of aetiological myths in such a ritual whose aim is the sacralisation of society's customs to give them divine origin and sanction. That is why Hans Mol says that,

> Irrespective of whether a particular myth is primarily a narrative, an iterative tale, or a speculation about existence, it is always an implicit or explicit statement about man's place in his environment. And this universal function of making statements about man's place is the common character of myths.[225]

---

[223] Anthony Matanda, interviewed by author on 20th August 1999 in Buketera village.

[224] Fab Ronald Walukhaso, interviewed by author on 8th November 1998 in Musiru village.

[225] Mol, *Identity and the Sacred*, p. 246.

Descending into the sacred swamp by the initiate for another round of invocations, prayers and exhortations culminating in being smeared with mud, signifies death and burial of childhood. This is close to what Eliade describes when he says that,

> The central moment of every initiation is represented by the ceremony symbolising the death of the novice and his return to the fellowship of the living. But he returns to life a new man, assuming another mode of being. Initiatory death signifies the end of at once childhood, of ignorance, and of the profane condition.[226]

His emerging from the mud symbolises leaving childhood behind and being reborn as an adult. Just like he will not go into the sacred mud again, so should he no longer stoop to childish behaviour and thoughts.

The continued invocation that started at the first smearing as the elders invite the ancestors to be present and bless the rites shows how humans exhibit their need for supernatural succour to augment their efforts. This is a time of tension and expectations, the time for divine intervention. It is the demarcation of where human ability ends and where divine intervention clearly takes over. It is quite significant that the rituals are intensified from the day of brewing, reaching its apex on the day of circumcision as the tension reaches fever heat. This is precisely because rituals arise and function in situations of emotional stress, and are needed to open up avenues for escape by shifting the situation from the empirical to the supra empirical. These rites fill the emotional voids of instrumental rational existence, and direct through surrounding these stressful situations with emotional support.[227]

The act of putting mud on the novice makes him look even spookier. This coupled with the eerie *sisioywa* (poignant song) send chills down the spines of even circumcised men, and many are known to hide when they hear it. The symbolism and emotive significance of this chant lie in the imagery employed. It invokes the name of the fiercest and deadliest animal of prey known to the Bamasaba. The leopard is a taboo animal whose mere mention evokes fear! It is forbidden to talk about it especially at night for fear that it might appear. It is because leopards are among the most feared animals of prey that decimated herds and killed people over the years. It is

---

[226] Eliade, *Rites and Symbols of Initiation*, p. xii.
[227] Ibid., pp. 244-245.

accurate and sure when it pounces, and goes straight for the jugular vein, quickly subduing its prey! It is also very orderly and leaves little blood in the wake of its hunt.

The song depicts the fatal leopard as lurking in the dark patiently stalking the initiate, and waiting to pounce and devour him. This is meant to test his courage in the face of danger. The circumciser wears a leopard skin, and his actions are likened to that of the leopard, as he too is quick and sure! Helmut Straube sees the wearing of animal skins in initiation ceremonies as bringing home the numinous dimension of the rituals.[228]

The imagery of the leopard, therefore, has several unmistakable messages for the novice. All of them spell trouble for him, so his courage and bravery are here called upon. The actions of the circumciser are compared to those of the leopard, indirectly warning the novice that there is no way he can escape paying the "cultural debt". But at the same time telling him that just like the leopard kills its prey quickly, the circumcision operation lasts but a short while.

Approaching the home from the east after the swamp has the significance of new life, new beginning, birth and immortality. Leading the initiate by a different route also means that there is no looking back anymore.[229]

5.4.5. Khukhwingila, *Day of Circumcision*

Pointing out the skulls or graves of the ancestors helps to instil into the novices the sense of belonging, identity, and reverence. Libation, invocation and indeed the sacrifice make the novices feel grown up enough to share in the secrets of the community. Clan secrets are imparted to them here under vow never to divulge them to women or the uncircumcised. Normally rituals make what is dramatised look real, so introducing them to the ancestors makes them feel like they know them personally. The meal of roasted meat and plantains eaten here is a communion meal with the ancestors, binding them to secrecy.

---

[228] Helmut Straube, *Die Tierverkleidungen der Afrikanischen Naturvölker*. Wiesbaden: Franz Steiner Verlag, 1955, p. 194. The wearing of animal skins fits into the idea of sacredness being ascribed to an object by the people. In the case of the initiate wearing animal skins, it seems to make him look "less-than-human". But the same skins being worn by the circumciser have a different symbolic interpretation.

[229] Lawrence Tsemale and Damascus Wandende, interviewed by author on 29th July 1999 at Bunamboko village.

Shaving of the novice's hair by his paternal aunt, the one whose bride wealth constituted the dowry that the father paid for the boy's mother, has a powerful significance. This aunt is like a "female father" to the boy so to say, and is not permitted to shave her nephew's hair. Her shaving of his hair, the first and only time she may do so, underlines the ritual import of the act, symbolises the ritual severance of ties with his earlier status. It marks the transition from childhood to adulthood, a discontinuity between two states of being. Shaving is a dominant symbol of severance of relations. For instance after the death of a person, after the mourning period there is a ceremony where all the immediate family have their hair shaved to show discontinuity with the departed member. Only after this ceremony can the members of the immediate family disperse to their different places of abode.

The requirement that the father and mother of the novice should perform ritual sexual union on the eve of the son's initiation goes to show how important sex and sexuality are emphasised in *imbalu*. It signifies their begetting him again as an adult this time, marking the passage of time and change of status. Just as birth follows sexual union, so rebirth must follow ritual sexual re-union between the parents. After his initiation, even in the event that the father and mother may have separated, the boy will have the authority as an adult to build a hut for the mother in his own homestead.

5.4.6. Khuusaabisa, *Rite of Purification*

This is when the *umufulu* (newly initiated) is ritually cleansed, to ever after remain clean. It is, above all, the day he formally ratifies a covenant with the community. This may not be a formal verbal formula, but it is binding in as far as the initiate assents to the words uttered by the circumciser, by holding the knife that was used to cut him. It has been argued that "the essence of an oath is that it commits the individual, binding him or her to other members, and its breaking usually involves powerful sanctions..."[230] Besides the novice himself, the most important person on this is the circumciser, the person who administers the oath to the new member.

---

[230] La Fontaine, *Initiation*, p. 16.

The novice is taken out of the *likombe* (convalescence hut) and made to walk round it. This signifies defeating of all enemies surrounding the homestead, since a homestead is a man's territorial kingdom. The convalescence hut symbolises the mother's womb, so entering it signifies a return into the womb. But it also signifies the tomb where the newly initiated has been relegated after his ritual death, hence the prohibition of touching food with his hands till after purification. He will sojourn and remain in *likombe* (convalescence hut) until the time of being hatched and incorporated into society. He is in a transitional situation, between van Gennep's social and religious "no man's land"[231], and Victor Turner's "between and betwixt"[232], as he has neither status nor gender. He looks like a male but wears skirts from his sisters; he is neither what he was before nor what he is to become, neither a boy nor a man!

Likombe literally means where the dead reside.[233] Since the symbolism of death to childhood and rebirth to adulthood are at the core of initiatory ordeals and instructions, his emerging from it later clearly signifies resurrection from the dead and birth (rebirth) into society as an adult. This is the goal and purpose of all the rites of initiation.

The pouring of beer upon the hands of the newly initiated signifies ritually washing his hands of any earlier guilt and impurity incurred during childhood. In case the novice has fathered a child before circumcision, he is considered to be under ritual guilt. A fine of a goat is imposed upon the father before special purification rites are performed for the boy. In the event that he already has a wife, illegitimate pre-initiation sexual intercourse has brought them ritual impurity, so the wife too is cleansed together with him. This purification rite cleanses them of all such guilt and allows them to begin as new people. If he has no wife, then a sister stands in for a wife, and is cleansed together with him. She is regarded as his wife since she has the responsibility of bringing home the bride wealth with which he will pay dowry for his own wife. The sister has a special place in

---

[231] Van Gennep, *The Rites of Passage*, pp. 1 and 21.

[232] Victor Turner, *The Ritual Process: Structure and Anti-Structure*. New York: Aldine Publishing Company, 1979, p. 95.

[233] While the word *likombe* remains in current usage for the convalescence hut, this literal meaning behind *likombe* seems to have been lost. Lawrence Tsemale, interviewed on 11th September 1999, agreed that the literal meaning is convincing though people do not give too much thought to it.

her brother's household and addresses the wife as "my wife" for the aforesaid reason.

The circumciser both purifies and covenants the newly initiated by making him hold the circumcision knife while he enjoins upon him the cultural beliefs and norms of the community. This is like a formal swearing ceremony, as the one administering the oath and the one making it are formally mentioned by their names, clans, totems or special clan identity marks. The circumciser symbolically gives birth to the *umufulu* on behalf of society, for he is the efficient cause of his new adult status. The admonitions have both domestic and social dimensions, as both can bring shame and ridicule upon the circumcision age group in general, and upon his knife in particular.

His social father formally hands the traditional weapons and other tools of a man's daily life in the community to him. They are mentioned by their names and their uses and misuses clarified. These tools and weapons cease to be secular implements and instead assume a socio-religious dimension. The possibilities of using or misusing them are present, but he is strongly enjoined to use them for the correct purposes, while their misuse is strictly prohibited. Working, drinking of beer, eating food, hunting, marriage and the begetting of children now become duties and social obligations. Work becomes an extension of a person's self, the means by which he furthers himself and establishes power in society. It is a means of production for him to feed his family, pour libation and offer sacrifices to the ancestors, feed his kinsmen and friends to strengthen kinship and friendship. As the saying goes, *"bulebe inda"* (kinship is the stomach). This plays on the double meaning of the word stomach, which also refers to the womb. It means that kinship is not a matter of being of one stomach (womb) but by filling stomachs together.

Drinking beer stops being just a pastime and acquires the social dimension. That is why only initiated men are allowed to carry *litaya* (bamboo stick with a drinking tube inside). It becomes an important forum for meeting other men to exchange news and views, indeed to forge lasting friendships and alliances with, especially members of one's own age-set. It also becomes a means of promoting kinship and friendship by brewing beer to which one invites them in one's home as honoured guests.

It might be argued that the things the novice is told are things he already knows through socialisation. Be that as it may, the difference lies in that this time he is formally told these things in a ritual context. Taking an illustration from another context, a couple must have loved one another before coming to the altar to make their vows. They are, however, still asked the seemingly superfluous question as to whether they love each other and whether they want to marry. Their assent in this ritual context amounts to a vow. This is what makes the difference between what we know informally and that which we formally assent to ritually. The novice certainly knows and has used the implements, which he is handed during the purification rite. But they are now handed to him in a ritual setting, their names, uses and misuses spelt out to him.

With regard to the drinking straw handed to him, it should be noted that uninitiated boys are not allowed to drink beer with men but can only do so in calabashes, as no circumcised man can suffer a *musinde* touching his tube. It is these insults and taunts which drive many to pay the cultural debt to escape incessant humiliation. Timothy Wangusa makes it clear in his novel how a novice who was asked to lay down the dancing regalia and enter his mother's house reacted by thinking,

> Into my mother's house! No! Never! Never! Never! To return to the insults?...*Ndi musinde wowo?* Am I your uncircumcised boy? Do not touch my millet-brew tube! Do not touch my gourd, my plate! I cannot share the same woman with you! Do not touch me with the filth from under your foreskin![234]

The advice by the surgeon to the newly initiated to get "*akhaba kuloosi kukwafwa imoni*" (even a one-eyed old woman) is to caution him against delaying to marry and have children on the pretext of looking for a beautiful one. This underscores the importance attached to marriage and procreation for which *imbalu* is understood to be a prelude. Procreation is a communal obligation aimed at keeping the stream of life flowing. The common good therefore precludes personal sentiments as beauty coincides with functionality. The qualities of a wife almost invariably boil down to the basics of whether she is hard working and fecund, and the rest is superfluous.

---

[234] Timothy Wangusa, *Upon This Mountain*. London: Heinemann, 1989, p. 62.

5.4.7. Khukhwiyalula, *The Hatching Ceremony*

This is a very important ceremony for the simple reason that it is the time when the newly initiated are "hatched" into society. The burning of the bedding of dry banana fibre signifies yet another threshold between the transition and the incorporation phases. It is another symbolic obliteration of the novice's past so as to allow him to begin a new life. The term "hatching" used to refer to this ceremony is itself a graphic witness to what it is understood to denote. Hatching creates the concept of emerging like a chick does out of an egg, which the mother hen has incubated in seclusion over a time. Symbolism borrows its figurative language from nature, and the word graphically drives the point home as the novices is almost literally "hatched" by society after a time of "incubation". The time of convalescence "incubates" them through pain and suffering to grow up and to be finally hatched into the community as adults. The ordeal of the physical cut is but the first step upon this journey that culminates in the "hatching" process.

The input of the elders, the experiences of the novice himself during the intensified pace of the rites leading to circumcision are but the raw material. These are mulled over, meditated upon in sacred time and space during convalescence. As Timothy Wangusa exclaims,

> ***Imbalu*** is agony! You have it on the courtyard, then you have it in the house. It's weeks of pain! Applying ***inguwu*** to the wound, that powder of the bitterest herb in the world! You put it on the wound and it smarts as if this world was buckling and cracking up. And you willingly make sure it smarts! For manhood is pain! Wilful pain![235]

Ritual death occasioned by these ordeals of initiation as described above,

> produces a decisive alteration in the religious and social status of the ... initiated ... The novice emerges from his ordeal endowed with a different being from that which he possessed before his initiation; he has become another.[236]

One characteristic of symbols is that they are not created but are born out of life and are built into people's experience. This makes them universal and versatile. For instance the idea of washing in swiftly running water

---

[235] Wangusa, *Upon this Mountain*, p. 61.
[236] Eliade, *Rites and Symbols of Initiation*, p. x.

denotes the washing and whisking away of the impurity occasioned by the shedding of blood and sojourn in the world of the dead. Running water, its passage, and washing represent ritual purification.

5.4.8. Ineemba, *Convocation and Commissioning Dance*

Since rituals are said to be analogous to culturally produced texts, which may be read to endow meaning upon a people's experience[237] as the final rite in the circumcision calendar, *ineemba* has a lot of symbolic significance. It lasts three days, just like the beer that takes three days to mature. The symbolism of the figure three is explained as representing the tripartite dimensions of the community.[238]

Just like university departments examine and promote students, the hatching ceremonies are performed in individual or collective homes. So like a graduation, *ineemba* is a convocation of all the newly "hatched" members of the community. This is the ceremony when they are, if we may borrow the phrase, to be formally and publicly given power to be men and to do all that appertains to this social status. It is certainly an important forum for them to meet their *babakoki* (age-set mates) from the different ridges of their locality. Friendships are formed or enhanced here, some of which endure throughout life. It enhances a sense of identity, the spirit of solidarity and comradeship among the different members of the age-set, which ties will be cemented through further and future meetings here and there. This sense of solidarity is important as these young people begin to build their networks of relationships, social, economic and political. *Bakoki* is always a brother and is the person to go to, whenever one finds oneself in need.

Ineemba, therefore, is multi-functional. It is a very solemn and majestic dance to which they gently sway to the gentle rhythm, proudly donning long garlands of *libombwe* betokening their expected fertility in the near future. This dance is also aimed at providing the newly circumcised with the opportunity of meeting prospective wives. Indeed, girls look forward to this dance to clinch marriage proposals. At the end of each dancing session, they all give a long drawn-out shout while pointing their sticks to the north

---

[237] Bell, *Ritual Theory*, p. 15.
[238] Lawrence Tsemale, interviewed by author on 29th July 1999 in Bunamboko village.

-east, paying homage to the ancestors by pointing in the direction from whence *imbalu* came.

5.5. *IMBALU*, MALE POWER AND AUTHORITY

It might be argued that at the centre of *imbalu* is the linking of the young male person to the patriarchal power structure of Masaba community. Since it stands at the sacred gates of the Masaba community, going through *imbalu* bestows cultural identity upon the individual, and with it *bunyali* (power) in various forms.

The word *bunyali* carries the concept of ability to do and to hold. It can be summarised as power, that which legitimately enables one to do and to hold. Firstly it gives the individual social status and assigns him power to be an adult. Now that he has been allowed into the interior of the community, he is recognised as an autonomous person, and his status entitles him to act responsibly on his own without dependence upon his parents or tutors.[239]

> Through the instrumental value of transition rituals social status is defined and power assigned ... power should be viewed as one's own capacity to perform social acts, a capacity regulated and constrained by the limits established by membership in the age class system ... The potential capacity to perform social acts provides an individual with the fundamental right to act socially.[240]

This power is the capacity to perform social acts within the confines of the regulations and norms of the community with regard to his social status as a newly initiated member. Though an adult and full member there are still other things he may not as yet do. For instance he now has the power to drink beer with other men.

Before initiation a *musinde* (uncircumcised youth) can only drink beer in a calabash, charity of the men perhaps after performing menial jobs like boiling water for them. He is allowed to drink from a man's drinking straw, as a *musinde* is not allowed to carry one. And if he did the men would not

---

[239] Bernardo Bernardi,"Initiation Rites and Post-Pubertal Transition", in Ugo Bianci (ed.), *Transition Rites: Cosmic, Social and Individual Order*. Rome: L'erma di Bretschneider, 1986, p. 85.

[240] Ibid., p. 85.

allow him to put it in the pot of beer, with the justification that since a *musinde* pollutes, his *lusekhe* would contaminate their beer. Beer itself is associated with the concept of power.

The fermentation process, which brings about the alcoholic content in beer, is an aspect of power, the power of intoxication, and may only be partaken of by those who have power too. It has the effect of subduing all and sundry, as even the physically strong get inebriated to the point where they start singing circumcision songs once again like *basinde*, in itself a social aberration. That explains why brewing of beer is such an important symbol of the maturation process of the novice. If the beer failed to mature it would be taken as particularly bad omen for the novice in question.

That explains why brewing has many prescriptions and proscriptions, just like sacrifice does. For instance the person who brews beer must refrain from sexual relations till the beer is mature. Sex is believed to take away the fermentation power thereby rendering beer powerless and incapable of intoxicating.

The Lumasaba word used to refer to beer that has failed to mature is *khutooya,* the same word used in connection with a person who is physically or mentally impaired, for instance an arm or leg, which lacks the power of free movement. An initiated man who does not exercise these powers is referred to as one who is so impaired, one who only wasted yeast as the symbolism was not actualised in real life.

Imbalu also confers upon the newly initiated the power to marry and raise a family. The power to become a parent also opens up avenues of holding positions of power in the community. Upon the circumcision of his son, the father will attain the power of elderhood. After that he may sit in council as an elder and make decisions which have implication for other members of the community. Elderhood opens for him the possibility of holding political office as a lineage head or even as *umukasa* (chief). Therefore it confers upon an individual both actual power to do and hold, but also potential power, which will be actualised in time and space as he is gradually, advances into ever-higher positions of power and responsibility in the community.

Imbalu and attachment to land are two of the major elements that distinguish the Bamasaba, and are closely related. As Timothy Wangusa attests,

Ask a Mumasaba where he came from and he points to the mountain. Ask him to name the most precious thing on earth and he names the earth itself. Ask him to swear and he is sure to swear by his circumcision.[241]

Imbalu bestows upon a young person power to share in the inheritance of the forefathers by inheriting a part of the ancestral land given to his father.

Many wars have been waged against their neighbours in defence of the borders, and indeed in pursuance of ever extending the border marks. *Imbalu* was an instrument in producing tough, fearless and admittedly ferocious warriors who would fight to protect the land they possessed, and beyond that who would ever extend the borders with the neighbours. Victor Turner observes that the Bamasaba,

> are penetrating other districts in considerable numbers – with an average density of at least 250 per square mile of cultivable land, rising in parts of the Manafwa valley to more than 700 per square mile.[242]

There is severe land shortage, and the fertility of the land makes it even more sought after, rendering it one of the most sensitive issues among the Bamasaba. Many homicides in the district have their cause, directly or otherwise, over land. Even women who normally do not own land fight over it with their co-wives as they want ever more land for their sons.

La Fontaine observes that the fathers' reluctance to sub-divide the land to his son creates bad blood between them, leading to the many cases of parricide and inter-generational conflicts between them. She avers that,

> As far as father and son are concerned, the crucial factor is that initiation gives a young man the right to claim his patrimony. In handing over a portion of his land and stock to his son, ... diminishes the capital with which he may acquire power in his village. ... One means of resisting the onset of this decline is to delay the initiation of sons....[243]

Land is wealth and it is power, especially as most of the land in the district is volcanic soil good for the growing of food and cash crops, especially coffee which is a source of economic wealth. Land boundary disputes

---

241 Timothy Wangusa, in the foreword to the Masaba Historical Research Association Newsletter (unpublished).

242 Turner, in *Man in Africa*, p. 230.

243 J.S. La Fontaine, "Parricide in Bugisu", in *Man*, vol. 2, no. 1, (1967), pp. 254-255.

normally run along predictable grooves of manhood and manliness. If they cannot agree they should call in another kinsman to arbitrate, otherwise the argument degenerates into an exchange of challenges at each other by reference to their manhood thus, *"Ngewe umusaani tuuma lulwakha khubone"* (if you are a man cross the boundary), or *"Iwe umusaani nase umusaani"* (You are a man and I am too). This is usually a declaration of war, as no man would want to be seen to be less than a "total man"! At this juncture a homicide would be only waiting to happen.

Ownership of land and hence its defence are prerogatives of men. Though women are usually the ones who alter boundaries when digging, land disputes normally exclude them. The party who feels his neighbour's wife while digging has encroached upon his land will not assault her. Instead he will ask her to stop digging, and to go call her husband to sort out the matter.

5.6. THE ROLE OF WOMEN IN *IMBALU*

In a community where power and authority are invested in the male, it could be argued that *imbalu* is a ritual which marks the division of the sexes and justifies male domination. But it should be borne in mind that,

> Initiation rites establish a distinction between childhood and adult status which is a matter not of physiological development but of social definition. This distinction and the related one of gender, the social roles designated by the terms 'man' and 'woman' which is also constructed by initiation, are fundamental to the organisation of society. They are thus of significance to all who participate, not merely to those being initiated.[244]

Though men are initiated to mark a stage of maturity while women do not have such a public ritual, it is still widely agreed that they also have rituals which mark their maturity. For instance, both menstruation and childbirth are perceived as a form of initiation. Girls are expected to start observing avoidance of their fathers from their first menstruation because menstruation blood is ritually polluting. Special care is exercised with menstruation blood just as it is done with that of male initiation, since both are ritually powerful and ritually polluting. It should be protected, lest it

---

[244] La Fontaine, *Initiation*, p. 116.

falls into the hands of evil-minded persons, who can use it for destroying the generative force inherent in it. In the case of childbirth, the pain is compared with that inflicted by circumcision, but the argument is that the former is not voluntarily undertaken, thereby reducing its significance as an initiatory ordeal.

Women are intimately linked to *imbalu* since the myths and traditions of origin trace it to a marriage between a Masaba and *Nabarwa*, a woman of Elgonyi Maasai ancestry, and the exhortations during *khuuakha* (smearing rites) stress the fact that *imbalu* came to Masaba through a woman. During *ineemba* (final communal dance) every dance ends with the newly initiated pointing their sticks to the north-east where *Nabarwa*, the lady credited with bringing *imbalu* to the Bamasaba, came from.

Kinship and community are central concepts in *imbalu*. While children are seen to belong to men in this male dominated society, it is also widely admitted that women are the generators of kinship. It is they who engender relationships, thereby contributing in a large measure to social organisation. La Fontaine notes that, "the affinal ties created by a marriage produce links between distinct and often antagonistic groups and as such are part of the social organisation."[245] Women are, therefore, credited with the multiplier effect of relationships through marriage. When Bamasaba meet, they first exchange greetings, and then identify themselves. Self-introduction makes clear how they are related to one another, by blood or marriage. This determines how they should treat one another.

Women are peacemakers and community builders. In the instance of *bukulo* (joking relationships), inter-marriage marks the improvement and indeed normalisation of relationships between feuding clans. Members of these clans become in-laws.

By wearing women's beads from around their loins and kerchiefs from their heads, an initiate identifies with his female kin. As La Fontaine notes,

> The observer can see in the beads, which are associated with an intimate part of a woman's body ... an identification of the initiand with the women of his group ... The dress of an initiand therefore carries a whole range of meanings which identifies him with women in general and with female kin in particular ... He seems an

---

[245] Jean La Fontaine, "Gisu Marriage and Affinal Relations", in Meyer Fortes (ed.), *Marriage in Tribal Societies*. Cambridge: Cambridge University Press, 1972, p. 88.

individual with both male and female attributes, a brother/sister composite which represents both male and female aspects of his lineage.[246]

The point of comparison between male and female may lie more in the aspect of **bunyali** (ability or power). In terms of resolve and courage, this is measured, demonstrated and confirmed by how one handles the ordeals of circumcision. Since women do not undergo circumcision, they are seen as having less courage.

Another aspect of power is in the socio-economic arena, where every man strives to cut a niche for himself in society. As Victor Turner observes, "Gisu society is 'achievement-oriented' for males who have undergone circumcision".[247] A man is respected because of what he owns in terms of land, wives, sons and herds. These were traditionally the benchmarks of manhood and success. Even today, Masaba men "are widely known for their competitiveness and their assertive natures, their society rewards individual achievement.[248]

Seen from this angle, not only do some men have more power than women, but they also have more power than other men. In a socio-economic structure where land is the traditional benchmark of wealth, women are disadvantaged by not owning land. Based on the argument that they do not own land because they cannot defend it, this denied them socio-economic power.

Suzette Heald observes that in some communities circumcision is equated with virility and warriorhood. The male organ is metaphorically compared to a sharpened spear to be used against other men and indeed women.[249] But in the case of **imbalu**, she notes that,

> One of the more unusual features of **imbalu** is the way in which it valorises male gender and masculine heroism but in such a way as to draw the sexes together rather than radically opposing them. The image of complementarity is sustained. If women are weaker than men it is because they do not face the knife but this does not detract from their identification with the ritual ... The complementarity of

---

246 La Fontaine, *Initiation*, p. 120.
247 Turner, in *Man in Africa*, p. 233.
248 La Fontaine, *Initiation*, p. 144.
249 Heald, *Manhood and Morality*, pp. 64-65.

the sexes and the necessity for their co-operation remains the keynote.[250]

Where manliness tends to advocate the suppression or repression of such emotions as love, sympathy and the like which are associated with femininity, complementarity is indeed imperative in the family. Fathers provide the physical power of discipline where mothers usually tend to balance that with tenderness and love. A woman also tempers the man's tendency for confrontation with her more conciliatory approach to issues. That is why it is the practice to have an unruly boy circumcised and married early as a means of taming him.

In a way, *imbalu* is a dramatic reinforcement of gender distinctions, as perceived by the initiating community. A close look at the different phases of *imbalu* reveals that women are actively involved and represented in the rituals, as mothers, sisters, wives or wives-to-be, etc. Right from the stage of *isonja* (initial communal dance), it is the female folk who share with the initiate beads from around their waists, which they string for him to wear across the chest. Women wear beads around their waists, as their smooth and slippery feel is believed to increase erotic arousal. Since *imbalu* is understood as a gateway to fecund sexual life, sharing these beads with women symbolises fecundity of the initiate.

During the second phase of *khuwentza* (searching for) *imbalu*, the female kin provide a larger portion of followers who sing the choruses, and dance to the songs. They provide the necessary labour for cooking and serving at initiation parties. There is a clear-cut division of labour: the men slaughter, skinning and cut the animals, while women do the cooking. As the physically better endowed, men carry meat from the relatives, or pull the animals given as gifts. In effect, they do the heavy jobs, which need more strength. In a family it is the men who do the slashing of forests for the women to dig. The men also do the weeding, the harvesting, and the building of granaries necessary for storing grain.

During the third stage of *khukhupaka*, the initiate and his colleagues thrash the millet for beer, while the job of grinding falls upon the women.

During the phase of *khukoya* (brewing) while the initiate fetches water, which he mixes with the dough, the women grind the sprouted millet,

---

[250] Ibid., pp. 64-65.

which the mother applies to the beer to start the fermentation process. Some of the yeast is used for smearing the initiate and his near of kin. Noteworthy is the fact that during this important smearing rite, the boy's sister stands beside him and is smeared together with him. This is a powerful symbolism underscoring the indispensability of the womenfolk in the ritual. The sister is cast in the role of a wife. It is with the cows she brings home as bride wealth that her brother will acquire a wife for himself. For this reason, she is justified in calling her brother's wife her wife.

The special role of women is also recognised when the boy's paternal aunt performs the ritual of shaving him, to sever his childhood and usher him into adulthood. The women cut off the hair of childhood long before the men cut off the skin of childhood. Though the boy may be close to the mother, he is socially even closer to the paternal aunt. While he practises social avoidance with the mother, and may not discuss intimate sexual matters with her, he freely does so with the aunt as there is no social avoidance with her.

The mother's ritual importance is recognised through the special role of adding yeast to the beer, to mark the countdown to the boy's initiation. Her indispensable role in his initiation is evidenced in the symbolic act of conceiving him the night before circumcision. She symbolically gives birth to him socially on his circumcision day by holding onto the central pillar of the house. She goes through the pangs of childbirth, symbolically but also literally. She is consumed by anxiety, worrying whether his initiation will be successful or not.

In the rite of *khusaabisa* (purification), the role of women in the overall purpose of initiation is clearly spelt out. For the Bamasaba, initiation is seen as the affirmation by society that an individual has reached a stage where he not only may but also must marry. Marriage is central to the society, to the point of being the culmination of the purification cum covenanting rite. The newly initiated is told by the circumciser to immediately find a woman to bear children to further the clan. The exhortation by the latter that *akhaba kukwafa imoni* (though she be one eyed) lays emphasis not on beauty and other personal attributes, but on the functional aspect of gender. A woman is cast in the all-important role of homemaker, one who kindles the fire to warm up the home. For that reason a wife is referred to as *umwene ango* (owner of the home). Her special role of kindling and cooking is connected with the kitchen, which is respected by Bamasaba men as the preserve of women. A man does not make a habit of going to the kitchen, and even during a quarrel a man must not follow her when she flees to her kitchen. The appellation of *umubwani* (the one who kindles the fire) carries with it the concept of one who warms the house, literally and metaphorically. Fire has the symbolic concepts of warmth in this mountainous location, which is cold much of the time.

But fire has the added symbolism of food and nourishment, hence a family spirit. Marriage is understood in terms of raising a family. A home with a woman but minus children is not warm. It is quiet and devoid of the warmth brought about by children. That is why on marriage a young couple are normally given some child to temporarily make the place warm, while the couple expect their own children. Marriage is consummated after the birth of a child, especially a male child. Without an issue, a marriage is not consummated, and the man can return the wife to her parents and ask for his bride wealth back to pay for another wife. If the woman is good and the husband or the clan like her, she may be retained but the man must marry another wife to beget children.

Women have a very central and indispensable role in *imbalu*. Women give birth to physical children, while men bring forth social ones. While a child is conceived and brought into physical existence by the women, men bring him into social existence. In this scheme, the mother's brother plays the role of a "male-mother", while the paternal aunt plays that of a "female-father".

While in Masaba culture children belong to the father, the mother's role is not under-looked. For instance while the child is given ancestral names of the father's clan, it is also given names of the mother's clan. The maternal uncles have a big say over their sister's children. For instance, it is virtually inconceivable that a boy would be initiated without first receiving the blessings of the maternal uncles.

During the stage of convalescence, the men will concentrate on taking care of the wound, which they themselves inflicted, while the women take care of the wounded. The men nurse the manhood while the women nurse the man. There is a whole world of difference in perspective here. It is like women go to the core of life, and are interested in the whole, while men are engrossed in external parts of it. It will be incumbent upon the womenfolk to make sure that the newly initiated is fed well to enable him recover from his ordeal, while the men rejoice in their art and continue to perfect it.

It would not be easy to decide as to whether it is men who produce for women, or the women for men. During the festivities of *imbalu*, women good-naturedly tell men that *khwabasilila mwikhoyelekho* (we gave birth for men to rejoice in). Men, however, counteract by claiming that *khubakhebela mwikhoyelekho* (we circumcise for women to rejoice in). I quite agree with Jean La Fontaine when she argues that,

> The link between initiation and the allocation of roles is not a simple matter. The rites form part of a complex cosmological and social order ... The separation between men and women in ritual sustains a social division of labour which makes the sexes socially indispensable to one another. Men may define themselves in opposition to women by virtue of the secret knowledge which they alone possess, but they are intimately associated with women in joint domestic enterprises.[251]

But perhaps women produce physical children for the men to make social men for the women. Whatever the case may be, there is no denying the fact that the two genders complement one the other. There would be neither physical nor social children without each playing their respective roles to the full.

5.7. CONCLUSION

Imbalu is about transition from childhood to adulthood. But it is also about transformation from a child to an adult as the novice is expected to go beyond mere transition to complete and irreversible transformation.[252] The notion of *busani* (manhood) entails more than physical maturity. Adulthood is not measured in terms of years but in terms of whether one has internalised the tenets of culture crystallised into customs which are sacralised to give them divine authority and sanction. It entails the acquisition of a cultural grammar used as a point of reference for subsequent experiences. The maturation process consists of successive social graduations where society acknowledges achievements by publicly

---

[251] La Fontaine, *Initiation*, p. 118.
[252] Eliade, *Rites and Symbols of Initiation*, p. 37.

conferring new statuses upon individuals by socially ordained representatives, in culturally stipulated ceremonies. These milestones towards elderhood and ancestor-hood are guided by custom.

Imbalu is, therefore, a way of cultural identity, power dissemination and governance, social stratification, and social control. The biological mother gives birth to a biological child, and society gives birth to a social child whom it brings up into a social adulthood. Emile Durkheim asserts that man is a man only because he is civilised, and

> a treasury of knowledge is transmitted to each generation that it did not gather itself ... it is to society that we owe these varied benefits of civilisation ...[253]

Therefore, adulthood is not an event but a process, which begins in society's womb, progresses through society's lap, to and through the tomb where the same society reverently places the individual to join the collective immortality of the ancestors. The individual will have moved full circle from the living to the departed, only to return in the yet-to-be-born members of the same community.

Though only males are initiated, *imbalu* is a cultural festival for the entire Masaba community, males and female alike. In it all have complementary roles to play, and all contribute to the overall success of the ritual.

[253] Emile Durkheim, *The Elementary Forms of the Religious Life*. London: George Allen and Unwin, 1976, p. 212.

CHAPTER SIX: THE QUESTION OF CHANGE

6.1. INTRODUCTION

> Sixty years of incorporation into the wider society of Uganda, first under colonial rule and then in an independent state, have altered, but not diminished, the significance of initiation for the Gisu ... it focuses on the ordeal of submitting to circumcision, without flinching and in full public view.[254]

Culture is crafted in a people's attempt to come to terms with their environment. It is the sum total of their achievements, material and mental, under-girded by a system of values they consider important, indeed indispensable. In discussing culture, Bruce Lincoln identifies ethics and aesthetics as being core elements, since these are the "two areas in which groups articulate their characteristic and defining preferences or what some are inclined to call 'values'."[255]

The first argument here is that values underpin a moral universe, and that the guardians of the community device strategies of maintaining their universe. The second concern relates to the impact of change upon those strategies of universe maintenance.

Every society has its way of making sure that its norms and values are observed and not flouted, precisely because an individual is less than society. It does this through several means of social control, namely, socialisation, restrictions, punishment, and rewards.

a. *Socialisation* is where the salient values of the community are inculcated into the people.

b. *Restrictions* are used to restrain people from flouting society's salient values.

c. *Punishment* are meted out to those who flout these norms and values, and

d. *Rewards* are accorded to those who uphold, defend and propagate them.

---

[254] J.S. La Fontaine, *Initiation*. Manchester: Manchester University Press, 1986, p. 119.

[255] Bruce Lincoln, "Culture", in Willi Braun and Russell T. McCutcheon (eds.), *Guide to the Study of Religion*. London: Casell, 2000, p. 415.

Social control, therefore, does not consist of mere force but is rather an interlocking of strategies for the maintenance of the universe. These are constituent parts of a larger explanatory scheme or ethical predicate known as worldview: how communities view their world. The epistemological foundation of any culture is its worldview. Ninian Smart confesses that "The English language does not have a term to refer to both traditional religions and ideologies; the best expression is perhaps worldviews".[256] The term worldview as used here goes beyond Ninian Smart's to denote how people view their world, not simply at the level of religion, but at the level of life in general. Hans Penner comes closer when he describes it as,

> not a logical system of judgements but a configuration which integrates cognition, volition, and affection; it is a synthesis of facts, values and ends ... worldviews are products of history, not just inner life for they reflect the influence of cultural tradition, nationality and epoch.[257]

It is not a personal but a mental construct through which a society explains why things are the way they are, thereby giving coherence to otherwise disparate cultural facts. It encapsulates the value system of a community, and serves as a point of reference for societal values. The custodians of the moral foundations of community, especially in oral cultures, refer to the ingredients of the worldview as normative. They sacralise the worldview so as to lend credence to it and deal with the theory of obligation. This is why communal religious organisations and institutions serve as the custodians of a society's worldview and value system. They tend to be more conservative than the general society and exert influence through, *inter alia*, rituals, symbols, liturgies, and doctrines.

In spite of efforts to encrust them as inherited customs with sacred origins, the worldview is always under contestation, and the rituals, symbols and institutions, which operate them are often challenged. One obvious reason is that culture is dynamic. The sources of culture change may be internal or external. The environment itself is under constant change forcing internal readjustments, just as external contact could produce change. Discussing the factor of cultural change in Africa, Bronislaw Malinowski held the

---

[256] Ninian Smart, *Worldviews*. New York: Charles Scribner's Sons, 1983, pp. 1-2.

[257] Hans H. Penner, "Interpretation", in Willi Braun and Russell T. McCutcheon (eds.), *Guide to the Study of Religion*. London: Casell, 2000, p. 61.

view that, "The African world of contact and change consists of three distinct orders of cultural change: the African, the Western, and that of transition".[258]

Internal change may come, for instance, from the realisation that some norms do not serve the community well and should be changed or dropped. But the agents of change may also be external. Among these are colonialism, Christianity, education and the post-independence state. These are usually discussed under the rubric of modernity because colonialism and Christianity inserted Western value system into Africa. Islam does not feature in our discussion of change agents because it does not constitute a major factor in the area of our research, as the number of Muslims is negligible.

Change may be structural, meaning that it takes place at the level of the institutions of the community, in our case such institutions would include for instance *bukulo* (joking relationships), socio-political institutions like that of *bubakoki* (age-set mates) and the council of elders who played the role of assisting the *bakasa* (cultural chiefs) in their legislative and judiciary tasks.

Change may also be cultural, taking place at the level of the values, which the community holds dear. In our particular case the values that the Bamasaba held dear prior to their contact with the agents of change were socio-religious in nature. In a nutshell, their value was abundant life here on earth evidenced by wealth, health, children, and a long life; and ultimately life in the hereafter when they would be remembered by being named by their living kin. Magesa captures this point well when he writes that,

> the ancestors are directly interested in and concerned about the birth of a new baby into their community, their clan ... it is an ancestor's vital force that returns to earth in the person named ... Through remembrance in naming, the vital force of the ancestors is transmitted to the entire clan.[259]

---

[258] Bronislaw Malinowski, *The Dynamics of Culture Change: An Inquiry into Race Relations in Africa*. New Haven: Yale University Press, 1961, p. 64.

[259] Laurenti Magesa, *African Religion: The Moral Traditions of Abundant Life*. Maryknoll, New York: Orbis Books 1997, p. 91.

Change could be perceived as an aberration from the normal conditions prevailing at what Lucy Mair has termed "point zero" of culture change, for as Bronislaw Malinowski has pointed out, it "generally implies maladjustment, deterioration, social strain, and confusion in legal and moral principles".[260]

There is also a difference in the direction and pace of this change in terms of whether it is gradual (reformist), radical (striking at the roots) or revolutionary (violent) in nature. For instance, change tends to be gradual in the rural areas and rather more radical in urban ones. It has, therefore, affected novices from these different areas unevenly.

In the discussion of change, it is necessary to point to the source, nature, type, direction, pace and consequence of the said change. For purposes of clarity, the effort here is in three parts:

Firstly, we shall examine each of the seven phases of *imbalu* to see what changes have occurred to each of them. Change at this level of *imbalu* has to do with change in symbolism, and how society still identify with and subscribe to the symbols of *imbalu* or not. Therefore, this will be discussed in connection with symbolism.

Secondly, using the categories developed in the interpretation, we shall investigate how change has affected each of the remaining components of *imbalu's* **significance** among the Bamasaba in time-perspective. These are community and culture; identity; power and authority.

The third part will present the anatomy of the exterior change agents, namely, colonialism, Christianity, education, modernity and post-independence state, focusing more directly on their respective importance and impact in the changes that have occurred to *imbalu* over the years.

We should, however, not lose sight of the fact that in a multi-variable analysis of change, a particular change may be caused by more than one factor.

---

[260] Ibid., p. 27.

6.2. CHANGE IN THE PHASES OF *IMBALU*

Attempting to interpret religious symbols, Hans Penner gives some of their interpretative principles as follows,

> Religious symbols reveal a modality of the real that is not evidenced in immediate, empirical reality ... signify a unity, destiny and integrating function for human beings ... express the contradictory aspects, the *coincidentia oppositorum* of ultimate reality.[261]

Symbolism retains its significant role especially in religion where it helps to bridge the abyss between the human and the goal of his religion, namely transcendence. Symbolism then directs man to what his religion identifies as the subject of his faith, following paths posited by the vision of that religion.

There is no attraction without distraction, so whenever man embraces another religion whose vision is different, his earlier vision comes under contestation. And when man becomes secularised through the scientific vision of the universe, the religious vision comes under even more contestation, as the two have little in common.

Contact between the Bamasaba and the different agents of change have lasted about a century now. During this time they negotiated and re-negotiated many cultural aspects at the religious, socio-political, economic and cultural levels. This no doubt has left rifts and scars on the body politic of the Bamasaba in general, thus reshaping the ritual and symbols of *imbalu* in particular.

Over the years, especially since the onset of colonialism, which brought with it Christianity, education and modernity in its train, change has occurred to the structure of *imbalu*. We shall now examine each phase in turn to identify and evaluate the changes that may have taken place in each of them.

6.2.1. *Phase One,* Isonja *(Communal Dance)*

Of the seven phases of *imbalu*[262], *isonja* has been drastically affected to the point that it exists only in the most out-flung parts of the district,

---

[261] Penner, in *Study of Religion*, p. 62.
[262] For details of the phases refer to 4.6.1.

notably in Manjiya county. This has been due to a plethora of reasons, including formal education; land pressure; lack of *namyenya* (chief soloist cum composer); physical immaturity of novices; and scarcity of traditional dress items, among others. Let us examine them more closely.

Formal schooling

The system of formal education leaves the novices no time to engage in such a pastime as they are in school the whole day, five days a week. Those who may not be in school are themselves engaged in one or the other mode of economic wellbeing.

Land pressure

The population density has reached such proportions that there are no free fields where these dances could be held. Most land is under cultivation, either of perennial crops such as bananas and coffee, or seasonal ones such as millet, maize, beans, cotton, potatoes, groundnuts, cassava and others. Modern economy has turned traditional food crops into non-traditional cash crops, thereby fuelling the need to produce as much as possible for domestic use and leaving a surplus for marketing. Land has, therefore, become scarce to the point that even open fields where children used to play have disappeared, or have been fenced off.

Lack of namyenya *(chief soloists cum composers)*

The office of *namyenya*, who were the village historians and composers of didactic songs, was a voluntary one based on a worldview where communal good surpassed personal considerations. These were identified from the way they sang and danced during their own initiation. Their services were appreciated and rewarded by the initiates' parents with chunks of meat brought home by the novices. Land pressure has seen the community drop their pastoral element to focus on sedentary agriculture. Today fewer people own herds, so the slaughter of goats or cows for novices has become less common. In the monetary economy nobody has the time to compose songs and lead others in dance for no pay. Even at the level of individual novices, today there are less *namyenya* available for the job.

Physical immaturity of novices

In the past *imbalu* was allowed only to boys who were physically mature as evidenced by the mock-fight between the novice-to-be and his father (see 4.3). *Isonja* gave the novices physical fitness and acclimatised them to the wearing of *bitzentze* (metal thigh bells). Thumping the ground, jumping into the air and travelling long distances to visit distant relatives all required physical fitness on the part of the novices.

Today some of these factors do not apply, at least not in the same way as times have changed. Novices are mostly in their early teens, so they lack physical maturity. Many of them no longer travel long distances on foot as modernity has introduced public transport instead.

Scarcity of accoutrement

There is generally lack of the traditional accoutrement[263] that made *isonja* colourful, flamboyant and competitive. Most of the items traditionally worn are now non-existent. Items made from leopard and monkey skins are hard to come by as most of them have since got worn out due to wear and tear in the successive vigorous dancing sessions. There is no new supply of these items as the forests have shrunk and most of these animals have been hunted to near extinction in the district. The remaining animals are only found in the government gazetted forests where it is illegal to hunt them. The items, which have survived are listed below in order of their relative availability.

- *Bitzentze* (thigh bells) are the most common item of dress and are largely available, as they are easily made from scrap metal.
- *Bibyuma* (beads) are also fairly easily obtainable from shops.
- *Ikwena* (circlets) are locally made out of wood improvising for the original ivory ones.
- *Lilubisi* (head-gear), *likhalala* (skin belt), *kamakayi* (strips of hide) and *ikutusi* are few and hard to come by but one still sees a novice wearing one or the other of these items here and there. For the average initiate, it is hard to come by one or the other of these accoutrement.

---

263 For more details on traditional dress see 4.5.

6.2.2. *Phase Two,* Khuwentza *(searching for)* imbalu

The idea of visiting relatives in far away places has lost relevance especially for the school going group of novices who have limited time. Though many **nabyalo** (village based) initiates still do, this is done during the third and fourth phases, namely closer to the day of circumcision, instead. The idea of carrying **kumukheti** (long stick) to relatives' homes to solicit material assistance is no longer in practice, especially since **imbalu** is no longer a necessary prelude to marriage.

6.2.3. *Phase Three,* Khuukhupaka *(Thrashing of millet)*

This still exists especially with **nabyalo** (village based) novices. The **namasomero** (school based) ones whose attachment to traditional cultural practices is in comparatively lax at best, do not necessarily always go through this phase. For some of them, the main idea is to pay the "cultural debt" and have peace to continue with their studies. The formalities are, therefore, not of primary consideration to this group.

6.2.4. *Phase Four,* Khuukoya *(Brewing)*

This phase is still very popular with most people and generally all who actually dance **imbalu** brew beer. This may be due to the symbolism attached to brewing of beer, as resembling the maturation process that a novice has to undergo to become a man. Beer also has the added feature of being the main drink at parties and feasts. The initiation of a son is a celebration, even where some may not agree with some features of the ritual. Especially for the village-based novices for whom symbolism is largely intact and meaningful, this is the main phase, which marks the beginning of the climax of **imbalu**.

The feature of running to the stream for water is losing relevance to many especially since most streams have dried up as the water-catchment forests disappeared under cultivation and logging. For those who live in areas with boreholes or piped water, for instance in urban and peri-urban areas, this practice does not hold considerable importance any more.

The rite of **khuakha**[264] (smearing with yeast) still exists to a large extent, but the mode is changing. Because of the prevailing monetary culture, many people regard painting the novice with a lot of yeast as a waste. The trend now is towards markings on the forehead, chest, hands and feet instead.

The mode of **khukhwingila**[265] (physical cutting or circumcision) has remained more or less intact for those who undergo it at home. But some "modern" parents may now prefer to take their sons to the hospital where it is done under local anaesthesia.

6.2.5. Phase Five, Mwikombe (Convalescence)

This phase is a given, albeit with many modifications in the elaborate corpus of symbolism. To begin with the idea of **likombe** (convalescence hut) has undergone change. To begin with, depending on how strictly the family subscribes to culture, **bafulu** (the newly initiated) may sleep in any house including his father's or his own. Secondly, the requirement that he may not enter or live there after convalescence is losing relevance. Thirdly, the symbolism of going round before entering **likombe** is not strictly observed anymore. Fourthly, the elaborate and symbol-laden rite of **khuusaabisa** (purification), which used to be performed on the third day after circumcision, has had to undergo certain modification. For the progressive-minded educated families and the committed Christians, it is no longer of absolute necessity. For those who are circumcised in the hospital it does not apply since the surgeon may even be an uncircumcised non-Masaba! It is incongruent for one to give others what one does not have! Even if he were a Masaba and circumcised, he would not be **umukhebi** (traditional circumciser) in the strict sense of the word. He would, therefore, not fit the profile of **umukhebi** so as to fulfil this cultural requirement.

Where it is observed, however, it is nowadays performed on the same day and without some elements of the elaborate symbolism that used to accompany it. Many of the items that were traditionally ceremonially handed to the novice have since disappeared. For instance spears and

---

264 For details of the smearing with yeast, see 4.6.4.2.
265 For more details, please see 4.6.4.6.

shields which were traditional weapons kept by every man for defence, have been rendered obsolete by the Modern State. The traditional self help and a national army and police forces have replaced ad hoc armies. Traditional spears and shields have since remained only in the museums or as relics in homes of some old people. Drinking-straws were relevant in a culture where drinking beer was a socio-cultural forum. Men met to socialise, exchange news and views, and either made friends or consolidated existing ties especially among **babakoki** (age-set mates). Today's teenage novices are mostly in school. And even for those who are not, given their age, it is rather incongruous to find them carrying drinking tubes or drinking among elderly men. There is a big cultural gap here, and elders as drinking partners in the same pot reject these youth. The idea of equality comes into the picture, as equality is based on *iselukho* (generation). For the old generations beer drinking is a forum for social contact, and the "circumcised men" have nothing in common to share with these "circumcised boys"[266]. The inference here is that circumcision *per se* does not make men, as the factor of age too must come into play. It is evident that physical maturity has a bearing upon manhood, and that one can only be considered a social adult when one is physically an adult too. That means circumcision can lift a physically mature person to make him a social adult, but cannot lift a physically immature person to social maturity. It would not do for the circumciser to give the circumcised boys drinking-straws and commission them to go out and drink, more especially if they are still in school.

In the past physical maturity was a prerequisite for circumcision, so manhood was synonymous with adulthood, and preceded marriage. Today, due to the tender age at which novices are circumcised, there has developed a dichotomy between manhood and adulthood, as the two no longer coincide. Given the age bracket of the novices, the circumciser cannot urge them to get married soon as was the practice earlier! Therefore, the rite of purification has been modified and to some extent lost some of its covenantal dimension. In many cases, where it is performed it has mostly a purificatory aspect. It may have relevance mostly for the village-based novices who tend to be initiated in their late teens, as they have no reason

---

[266] Leo Wawomola and Ludwig Wamono, interviewed by author on 6th November 1999 in Butiru village.

for rushing to get circumcised. We can here see a clear instance of different paces of culture change: among the village novices on the one hand, and the school going group on the other.

6.2.6. Phase Six, Khukhwiyalula *(Hatching)*

The rite of **Khukhwiyalula** (hatching) or *lusantza* that characterises the incorporation of the novices into the community as full adult members of the community is popular mostly with the village-based initiates. It is losing currency with the schooling group because of their being away in school. And where it is still practised there are modifications too. To begin with, except for those who choose to religiously observe the traditions, novices no longer use **kamasantza** (dry banana leaves) for bedding. Consequently, there would no **kamasantza** (dry leaves) to burn during the would-be *lusantza* (banana leaves burning ceremony). But some school going and the many of the village-based novices who want to go through **imbalu** the prescribed way, observe this major rite. These also observe the consequent purificatory rite of going to wash in a brisk running river the following morning.

6.2.7. Phase Seven, Ineemba *(Convocation Dance)*

This has largely remained in place though owing to diminished enforcement capacity by cultural institutions, attendance may not be felt as obligatory by some **batembete** (newly initiated) as it was in the past. It is staged only in particular parts of the district, namely Buwagogo, Buwabwala and Bupoto in Bubulo County; Bududa, Bukigai, Bulucheke, Bubiita and Bukiga sub-counties in Manjiya County; as well as Busano and Wanaale in Bungokho County. Its festive values are still widely appreciated, and coming as it does during the dry months of the year when work is at its lowest, many people have time for leisure.

Having seen the change that has come about in each of the seven phases, we shall now proceed to look at how change has affected each of the component categories, namely community and culture; identity; power and authority; and indeed symbolism.

6.3. ASPECTS OF INTERNAL CHANGE

Internal changes have not been extensive in *imbalu*, especially because the customs have encrusted into the life of the people. People are normally averse to any form of probing to the point that even a casual questioning of any aspect of culture may be negatively construed as a challenge, hence deviance if not subversion. This is precisely because knowledge, real or assumed, lends power and with it authority to the bearers. That precludes any free discussion and exchange of it. Knowledge is for doing and not for exegesis. Society has tended to be protective of its knowledge and institutions by reacting thus defensively, often violently, against any perceived attack. It does so as a warning and deterrent to would-be saboteurs, that society would neither tolerate nor condone any challenge to their customs. They see any questioning, not as a genuinely well-intentioned observation by stakeholders, but rather as an attempt to undermine and subvert the authority of the community. This is quite understandable though, bearing in mind the fact that culture is the fabric of meaning in terms of which human beings interpret their experience and guide their actions. Preservation of the community and its cohesion[267] is important, so questions usually associated with the Western worldview may look like a challenge. These are perceived by the elders and others as an attempt on the part of social deviants to undermine culture. As Clifford Geertz has pointed out,

> sacred symbols function to synthesise a people's ethos...In religious belief and practice a group's ethos is rendered intellectually reasonable by being shown to represent a way of life ideally adapted to the actual state of affairs the worldview describes, while the worldview is rendered emotionally convincing by being presented as an image of an actual state of affairs peculiarly well-arranged to accommodate such a way of life.[268]

Culture sacralises its beliefs and values by invoking supernatural origins and sanction, making any attack on their culture a religious affront. But at

---

[267] Clifford Geertz, *The Interpretation of Cultures*. New York: Basic Books, 1973, p. 145.
[268]Ibid., pp. 90-91.

other times the negative reaction may be but a defence mechanism borne out of ignorance. Since aspects of culture are never explained many people may know what is done, where and when but hardly ever why. So even where the reasons and meanings behind certain aspects of ritual may have been lost, the people retain the actions or gestures, comfortably continuing to perform the ritual in that very manner. This does not mean that the ritual is meaningless as for instance Staal would claim, but that due to lack of cultural exegesis, some participants may not know the meaning. Purvis says that the Bamasaba "distinguish themselves as a race apart from others by the name basani, i.e. men, whilst all men of uncircumcised nations are called basinde, i.e. boys".[269] *Imbalu* constitutes the one practice that binds them together as a people and affords them an identity, their mark of superiority to their uncircumcised neighbours. To them *imbalu* like religion is sacrosanct and casting aspersions upon it is tantamount to sacrilege, an insult which is deeply resented and will be violently rebutted. Indeed, among them,

> the clan feeling is very strong, and each individual is intensely loyal to the call of the clan in time of need. An insult offered to the humblest individual is offered to, and will be resented by, the whole clan.[270]

It is interpreted as cowardice if the person questioning is not circumcised, and as subversion if he is. In the case of the former, they will proceed to circumcise him by force as a way of venting their anger.

The Bamasaba are immersed into *imbalu* at almost the exclusion of everything else. Rev. J. B. Purvis who served as a pastor in the district in the first decade of the last century remarks how in 1903 he and his wife got lost while walking towards the mission station. While being guided by local boys, the missionaries saw an umbrella in the distance, evidence of civilisation, and hurried with lighter hearts towards it. He cites their utter

---

[269] J. B. Purvis, *Through Uganda to Mount Elgon*. London: T. Fisher Unwin, 1909, p. 271.

[270] Ibid., p. 274.

disgust and disappointment to find that it covered an aspiring African escorted by a crowd of admirers, who were far more interested in this native parade than in the advent of two Europeans.[271]

They were disappointed that the parade of *imbalu* procession had captured the total attention of everybody to the point that they did not even notice the arrival of two white people, who at that time in history must have been quite rare.

Imbalu still generates so much interest that if the procession passes near a church during service, the attention of the congregation would be distracted and children would run out while the adults would restrain themselves but with more attention to *imbalu* than to the preacher. This is what disturbed a Roman Catholic priest ministering in Masabaland, to the point of writing thus,

> Circumcision rite is a platform for unity.... Christianity is for unity in its deepest sense. But why it is that many people are not attracted to attending catechumen classes? Why does *imbalu* attract such large crowds where Christianity fails? Why do people participate more actively and devotedly in the *imbalu* ceremony than in the celebration of Mass? These are questions, which require honest answers.[272]

6.4. CHANGE IN CULTURE AND COMMUNITY

The power and impact of change have been immensely felt by traditional cultures of Africa in the contact with external change agents. Social institutions that are the heartbeat of any culture have been forced to adjust to the enlargement of the social scale. New 'publics' have emerged, comprising the primal public, Westernised public, and an emergent public, which combines both but differs from either.

It has its own moral values and operates in the modern sector. It is the culture of urbanity and could be traced to the primal sector as urban values seep into rural areas. The intention here is, therefore, to show how the new value system and enlargement of scale are conspiring to disintegrate

---

[271] Ibid., pp. 297-298.

[272] L. Walakira, "Circumcision Ceremony Among the Bagisu", in *The Second National Theological Week* (August 1983), p. 165.

traditional institutions, values and meaning of core cultural forms such as *imbalu*.

Among the Bamasaba, *imbalu* is a very central and, therefore, crucial way in which "culture exercises control over the apprehension of experience, and causes the eye and ear to "half create" what they perceive".[273] The worldview upon which it was founded was certainly different from the one that is prevailing today. For instance the primal worldview was one where time consisted of events, as evidenced by the topical names of the age-sets in *imbalu,* which form a catalogue of events in the collective history of the Bamasaba as a community. The value system of this worldview places God and the community above individual interests and a person can only identify himself in terms of the community to which he belongs. In the biennual festival of *imbalu*, elders as representatives of the community, display their knowledge, power and authority as religious specialists. This is precisely because in it, the human and the spiritual coincide and interface. Society's beliefs, norms and values are held to be sacrosanct and the young are socialised to revere them as such. Prohibitions are religiously observed, as they are believed to have socio-religious authority and sanction, resulting in divine punishment upon the culprits if flouted. For instance, contravening the prohibition of marrying a daughter of one's age-set is socially unacceptable, and the parents of both parties would not assent to it. A marriage against the advice of the parents of both parties is unthinkable as society would ostracise them and refuse to sanction it anyway. But if the couple went ahead against the better advice of society or eloped to a distant place, it is believed that barrenness would occur, or if they have children they would not prosper.

This punishment is believed to be from the ancestors, therefore one with religious underpinnings. The threat of curses as punishment is the instrument used to elicit obedience and compliance with the customs of society. The elders are believed to have power to bring blessings or curses upon a novice, thereby influencing his life positively or negatively. Being close to the ancestors, the elders are believed to have powers to "invoke the ghosts of the recently dead, the *bamakombe*".[274] These punish any of their

---

[273] Aylward Shorter, *Songs and Symbols of Initiation*. Nairobi: CHIEA Press, 1987, p. 3.

[274] Suzette Heald, *Manhood and Morality*. London: Routledge, 1999, p. 83.

junior kinsmen and cause them to wander about aimlessly, unable to hold on to any meaningful enterprise in life, and unable to marry and bring up a family. It is especially at the time of initiation when the novices are at the threshold of manhood that curses are most feared. Malevolence is feared to be afoot at this time from people who are enemies of the initiate's father who may perceive the son as a strong prop to his father. Since a son is seen as a man's success, some of his kinsmen who may not be so successful may be jealous and maliciously want to cause misfortune to the family. So the boy needs the support and "knowledge" of his elder kinsmen for protection by warding off any such malevolence.

Among the Bamasaba, *khumanya* (knowledge or wisdom) has the connotation of understanding the inner workings of the elements in the universe, and the ability to harness their power to promote one's life force. This includes the ability to protect one's lifeforce by warding off harmful influences from nature and from man. If one is already married, a curse is believed to wreak havoc on the family, especially among his children. *Sitsubo* (a curse) is believed to be possible by any senior kin to a junior one, but not the vice versa. Even the mere fact of a senior relative being annoyed with his or her junior relative is tantamount to a curse and believed to bring about negative results in the life of the latter. Echoing this sentiment, La Fontaine points out that,

> the anger of certain relatives, if they are provoked by the impiety of a kinsman, may act like witchcraft and visit misfortune and even death on the offender. The relatives who have this power are senior ones: the father and his brothers, the father's sister and mother's brother. The anger of age-mates (who rank as brothers) may also operate in this way.[275]

The socio-political institutions of *bukulo* (joking relationship) and *bubakoki* (age-sets) help to maintain and perpetuate these restrictions by safeguarding the social status quo. *Bakulo* (joking relatives) who have the special privilege of jokingly mocking or insulting any of their counterparts while actually criticising their conduct are a medium through which community shows disapproval of an individual's conduct, and warns him to reform his ways. People fear to be ridiculed especially in public, and would

---

[275] J. S. La Fontaine, "Witchcraft in Bugisu", in J. Middleton et al (eds.), *Witchcraft in East Africa*. London: Routledge and Kegan Paul, 1978, p. 193.

do everything possible to avoid the embarrassment such a rebuke can cause them. The *babakoki* (age-set mates) on the other, hand help to police one another's conduct to ensure that their age-set is not brought in disrepute or ridicule. A *mukulo* (joking counterpart) will mock the age-set mates of the person whose conduct is perceived as unbecoming, thereby intimating that the entire age-set comprises social deviants. This way the weight of the age-set is called into play to discourage any errant member among them.

So the combined threat of a curse by the elders, social upbraiding and ridicule by both *bakulo* and *babakoki* act as deterrents against deviance, while blessings and social approbation act as inducements for socially approved conduct. Rewards by society consist in, for instance, being given the prestigious offices of *uwesanda* (bearer of the ritual gourd) used for blowing beer upon the novice, and *umuakhi* (smearing elder). Acknowledgement also comes from being charged with staging *imbalu* in one's home for the whole minimal lineage. Only people in whose goodness and ability society has faith would be entrusted with the future wellbeing of their sons at this most auspicious stage in their lives.

In the above religious cosmology, the elders closely control what the community believes (doctrine), how it is organised (polity), how it worships (liturgy) and how people are expected to behave (ethics). They use initiation as the instrumental forum of catching recalcitrant novices and bringing them to heel. During this time the novices are at the complete mercy of the community in general, and the elders in particular as they are in charge of the rituals. Socialisation, therefore, stresses subordination to authority and respect for kinship, and *Imbalu* is a central festival in the life of the community. As it affords them the opportunity to celebrate these values, *imbalu* encapsulates the ethic of community for it mobilises all and sundry, thereby affording it social cohesion and indeed identity.

Change has occurred to *imbalu* owing to the resultant change of worldview from the largely communitarian one of traditional life, to a new individualistic one propagated by Christianity largely through formal education. Christian eschatology is assaulting the idea of collective immortality posited by traditional Masaba world. It is fast replacing it with that of individual retribution by souls going to heaven or to hell. The ethic of community is premised on the word of elders, perceived as the 'voices of the ancestors'. Education creates both dislocation in physical space and

195

mental space in the young generations. It raises the spectre of the theory of obligation, namely, why should the elders be obeyed and societal norms observed? The slurs on traditional religion by the forces of external change have not helped matters. It seeks to demystify and deconstruct traditional myths and symbols of community. The balance of power and authority now rests on a tilting fulcrum that threatens to tip over, unless propped up.

6.5. CHANGE, AND THE BALANCE OF POWER AND AUTHORITY

It should be noted that power in itself is neutral, while authority is legitimised power. Power can be defined as coercive force, whether as the result of physical or economic pressure, while authority the recognised right to command, legitimised by appeal to principles which are part of the moral order.[276]

When that legitimisation is contested by some other power-source, the ability of the original power to express itself is distorted; therefore it diminishes, and often malfunctions. As argued in an earlier chapter, much of *imbalu* rests upon the coalition of various power dimensions, both physical and spiritual. In contemporary times, the meaning of *imbalu* has been eroded by changes in the balance of power and authority. Enlargement of scale as the community has grown and shifted, has reduced the coercive resources of the holders of cultural power.

In an environment where the community interests were supreme and individual interests subordinate to them, power and authority resided with the community, and was wielded by the elders, who conferred it upon younger generations upon fulfilment of certain cultural requirements. It was, therefore, relatively easy for the elders to elicit compliance and conformity from the community in general, and the novices in particular. The elders were revered because they were believed to be able to influence the lives of their younger kinsmen either positively or negatively. Their authority was founded upon that of the ancestors, the authors of *imbalu*, in whose name they spoke and acted. Initiation rituals, then, proceeded along certain grooves, and emphasis was focused on certain features of initiation

---

[276] La Fontaine, *Initiation*, p. 17.

namely, the authoritative, the instructive and the physical, which lent weight to the status quo.

The authoritative aspect

The rituals were always conducted and supervised by the elders, therefore they carried both the collective authority of the community and the authoritative weight of tradition. Being initiated thus meant entering into this network of authority as defined by the community, supported by a religious tradition, which legitimated the elders' authority. Only the ritual elders could smear the novices with yeast and chyme while invoking the blessings of the ancestors upon them. They alone were in charge of the burial groves where the ancestors were interred, and they alone bore the secrets of the clan. They alone had the authority to carry *isanda* (ceremonial gourd) and blow beer upon the novices and their escorts as a symbol of blessing. They were the only ones in charge of the sacred swamp where the novices were smeared with sacred mud.

Today, where some parents avoid these requirements by either taking their sons to the hospitals, or by privately inviting a circumciser to the home, the elders are denied this role. *Imbalu* is no longer an exclusively communal and public affair as people now have the option of carrying it out quietly in the privacy of their homes or in the hospitals. As the community is no longer the sole measure of what is good, the community's display of its power and authority over the individual has reduced.

The intensely instructive aspect

A process of instruction, indoctrination and covenanting using the myths, laws and customs of the community accompanied the dramatic symbolic activities. Invocations, libations, exhortations, blessings, and sacrifices were some of the socio-religious media of communicating their power and authority. The shared network of beliefs held by the community were inculcated into the initiate and was sealed by the shedding of blood. This acted as a covenant entered into with the community during the purification rite by the circumciser. The smearing with yeast and chyme were also sessions for pointing out the individual initiate's shortcomings and flaws of character. The elders took the advantage of these sessions to inculcate socio-religious beliefs, values and social norms into the novices. What was expected of them as men was not only a social but a religious requirement. The rite of **khusaabisa** (purification) by the circumciser was the climax of the instructions by the community. It was done in a formal covenantal formula, sealing the contract with the community and the ancestors. The novice formally accepted to identify with the community, to subscribe to its worldview, indeed to defend and propagate the community's beliefs, norms and values. Aylward Shorter refers to this by saying that

> The initiant had to become a tabula rasa on which society inscribed its thoughts...was taught to think with the community and to see the world as it saw it. he ...was given a cultural framework or 'grammar', a configuration of images and meanings, with which to confront experience.[277]

Urging them to de-identify with childish behaviour and instead identify with that of men did indoctrination of the socially approved beliefs and norms into the novices. As seen above, the age-set mates who did not want their collective identity besmirched further upheld this.

Today, as elders continue to cede their power and authority to modernity, in the same measure does **imbalu** continue to lose its power as an authoritative means of instruction to the young. Where the initiates do not go through all the prescribed phases of **imbalu**, this feature is by-passed. The instructive and indoctrinative features have been disabled precisely because the elders have lost some of their coercive ability. When some parents disregard the community by usurping its power of giving birth to social individuals, the novices too are likely to do the same. What is at stake, therefore, is the question of obligation, need to enforce the requirement of circumcision for all Bamasaba males. *Inter alia*, the phenomenon of the ad hoc militant groups forcefully circumcising defaulters has helped to restore this coercive factor.

The physical aspect

The rituals involved a physical test and ordeal culminating in circumcision, which acted as a visible mark of identification and bond with the community. Ordeal made the novice realise that though supported by the community, growth entailed experiences which he must undergo alone as

---

[277] Shorter, *Songs and Symbols*, p. 5.

an individual. Therefore growth meant both assimilation into the fabric of community, but also detachment as an individual, hence an individual member in a community. Like weaning, pain was a means of this detachment and growth as he alone could experience it, though among and supported by the community. As Lawrence Sullivan says, ordeals are not simply arbitrary infliction of pain but

> tests that stretch the limits of patience, skill, or strength and that aim at a revelation, the critical self-knowledge required for human maturity ... ordeals reveal what is essential and enduring about an individual character.[278]

Pain has a sobering and transformative effect upon the individual as it brings into focus the person's vulnerability as part of his character formation. The novice realises that life will call upon him to undergo pain which he ought as an adult to bear bravely and patiently as society can only play a supportive role in these moments. Symbolic death reminds him of physical death at the end of this physical life, but since it turns out to be but a gestation period from which he emerges as a better person, this makes physical death also seem like a time of gestation, a rite of passage to a higher life with the ancestors.

Like many other African communities, the Bamasaba lived in a world where the spiritual and the mundane were intertwined. In their religious cosmology, they attributed major misfortunes in life, for instance, barrenness, impotence, and successive deaths in a family, to some religious cause. These might be for instance broken prohibitions, curses, evil spirits acting at the behest of a witch or some other human agent, and witchcraft or sorcery. For this reason, medicine men acted as both psychologists and psychiatrists by first dealing with the religious dimension of the problem before turning to the medical. Medicine itself was a religious undertaking as the herbal knowledge was revealed to one while under possession by some spirit, thereby making a medicine man a religious personage. This view of life made sense only in a religious cosmology where the division between the human universe and its spirit counterpart overlapped without any contradiction. That is why healing was surrounded by so many religious observations that ensured ritual purity.

---

[278] Sullivan, *Icanchu's Drum*, p. 346.

Today, the phenomenon of ordeal is not necessarily present as hospitals use anaesthesia. Secondly, the extended ordeal experienced during convalescence is largely dispensed with as modern medication keeps the pain at bay. But as evidenced by the elaborate celebrations in its seven phases spanning the whole year, *imbalu* is infinitely much more than simply cutting off the fore skin. Nor is it simply a transitive ritual, as it ought to be transformative too. The physical is only one of its multi-dimensional natures. At stake are the other dimensions including the educational, social, religious, psychological, and relational.

The basic roles of religion consist in explanation, prediction and control of the space-time events. These were invested in the elders and other religious personages such as diviners, rainmakers, medicine-persons, and circumcisers. These enjoyed authority sanctioned by traditional religious beliefs and values, inculcated into the young by socialisation.

The various agents of change have continued to contest the power and authority, which these traditional religious institutions exercised over the community. Consequently, these personages have continued to cede some of their hold on society, and with it their coercive power and sanction enshrined in blessings and curses, which they exercised over the young. The role of these institutions has been rendered less authoritative, hence less efficient, as the traditional worldview continues to lose to modernity and the attendant secularisation. The ritual elders have lost their monopoly of knowledge, and worse still, their religious "knowledge" has been largely discounted by scientific knowledge.

Consequently, rainmakers who were revered for their power to bring or withhold rain have lost their power to the meteorologists. Diviners may be patronised by some especially in times of personal or family crisis but this is mostly as a last resort rather than the norm. The circumciser has lost his lustre and privilege as the efficient cause without whom novices would not become men, as the medical practitioner usurps his place.

6.6. CHANGE AND IDENTITY

Identity may be psychological, defining person-hood. *Imbalu* is about the individual's identity and covenant with the community to which he binds himself as a full member, implying internalisation of the community's worldview, and subscription to its beliefs, values and norms. The foregoing chapters make it evident that ancestor veneration has an important role in the ritual of *imbalu*, as the rites and sacrifices are replete with invocation and libation to them.

Imbalu was used in instilling the community's cultural values and ideals into the initiates, to adhere to, defend and propagate for life. These values were handed to the initiate within the community setting, and practised in a community, with the community and for the community. The initiate of *imbalu* manifested a marked transformation of attitude and behaviour, different from his earlier ones, because society helped him do this with examples, encouragement and sanctions. The conviction that the initiate had emancipated beyond certain childish, inferior and impure actions provided the impetus to live up to the society's expectations. This was a clear-cut, non-negotiable situation, a growth, and therefore irreversible. Society could not afford to allow contravention of its values, for good and evil had a communal aspect. An individual's actions either engendered life or endangered it as life was communal. The personal good was subordinate to the common good, and this explains why it was not optional, as the responsibility fell upon the community to see to it that no member contravened the social norms. It was incumbent upon them to ensure that every member of the community was helped to fulfil the social requirement.

The act of circumcision as public ceremony helped to drive home the point that the community had marked the individual as one of their own, what Mary Douglas refers to when she says, "What is being carved in human flesh is an image of society".[279] This mark also symbolised the new ethical obligations that were binding on the person who had become a new member, as the newly circumcised was expected to behave as a man. Manliness was so stressed that to be told that one was behaving in an unmanly manner was the epitome of ridicule. For instance bravery was a manly virtue while cowardice was unmanly. Fortitude, patience, forbearance, honesty, sociability, teamwork, ability to share what one had with others were all extolled as manly virtues, and their opposite condemned. The institutions of *babakoki* (age-set mates) and *bakulo*

---

[279] Mary Douglas, *Purity and Danger*. London: Routledge and Keegan Paul, 1966, p. 116.

(joking partners) safeguarded and enforced these requirements for the community.[280]

Where some parents take their children to hospitals, sometimes at the tender age of between birth and ten or there about, identity is reduced to the physical mark. The aspect of sharing and internalising the community's beliefs, myths and values is compromised. Without the instructive aspect, the value and power of community in their lives is also reduced. Yet the physical mark of circumcision was meant to be an external mark bearing witness to some internal reality. They miss out on the community's instructive power in character formation, not to mention the didactic teaching on the history, legends and folklore of the community. The coercive sanction of the community in enforcing their ethos by punishing those who flout them and rewarding those who uphold them are eroded. These children identify with the community in appearance but do not actually identify with it in actuality since Clifford Geertz makes a pertinent point when he says,

> religion by fusing ethos and worldview, gives to a set of social values what they perhaps most need to be coercive: an appearance of objectivity. In sacred rituals and myths values are portrayed not as subjective human preferences but as the imposed condition for life implicit in a world with a particular structure.[281]

They lack this inner identity in shared beliefs, worldview, norms and values that give the particular community its distinctive physiognomy and hence its identity.

Since *imbalu* no longer precedes marriage, the practice of visiting relatives far and wide that served the function of soliciting material support for the impending marriage has lost its appeal. The idea of kinship and community solidarity has been affected to the point that today some children do not know many of their parents' relatives. The fact that they are not in favour of dancing and travelling long distances makes it hard for them to see and meet their far away relatives. The relational aspect of *imbalu* where it was important for the novice to claim the relatives of his father as his own, has,

---

[280] For more details about the above typology, see David Chidester, *Patterns of Action: Religion and Ethics in a Comparative Perspective.* Belmont, California: Wadsworth Publishing Company, 1987, pp. 131-132.

[281] Geertz, Interpretation of Cultures, p. 131.

therefore, been weakened. Modernity, manifested especially in urbanisation, Western values, work ethic and cash economy, has negatively affected the value of kinship that used to bind the community neatly together. Modern education has drastically reduced the time at children's disposal, thereby impinging much upon the communal spirit. People spend long periods of time without visiting one another.

Another effect of modernity and its resultant hectic socio-economic regime on identity has been the removal of forums where the age-set members would meet. In the past there were many opportunities for the novices to meet and make acquaintances, which would be nurtured into life-long friendships. Some of these forums were *isonja* (communal dance), visiting relatives, long convalescence period, *ineemba* (convocation dance), and beer drinking parties where men met to exchange news and views. Today's hectic life has made such drinking parties less formal.

The novices also used to make acquaintanceships, which would be renewed during their intermittent visits to the relatives across the district. This would be sealed during the *ineemba* (convocation dance) where they would meet to congratulate one another. The newly initiated, therefore, had many opportunities of knowing who their age-set mates were and indeed of developing the comradeship which would be nurtured during drinking parties where men met to exchange news and views.

Age-set mates also met during their intermittent rounds to visit their respective relatives far and wide. They would stop to salute one another by dancing together briefly before parting to go their different ways. Today, these visits in dancing parties are few apart and do not cover much distance as modernity has solved the problem of visiting distant relatives by providing them with modern means of transport.

Modern medical facilities have made it possible for the newly initiated to go about their work fairly normally, and has also drastically reduced the time of convalescence from months to weeks. The pressures of modern life make it difficult for novices to have much spare time to leisurely move around in groups where they would meet their fellow newly initiated. The moral sanction, which the institution used in enforcing their demands of gifts from age-set mates who had initiated sons is fast disappearing, if it has not already done so. Apart from reciprocation, there was the threat of the age-set mate placing a curse upon the novice. Both Christianity and modernity have removed the sting from such a threat. Uttering such a threat might lead to litigation and a possible hefty fine. In a country where decades of military governments made guns accessible, such a threat of a curse might be countered, indeed cancelled out by a threat of violence.

Moreover, as the country moves from a simple technological society to a more diversified economy, social networks are shifting from age class to economic and other considerations. The institution of age-sets is fast losing its relevance and currency, and where it still exists it lacks the binding force it once enjoyed. In effect modernity has created multiple identities so that traditional age sets have lost cohesion and power.

6.7. ANATOMY OF CHANGE AGENTS

6.7.1. Colonialism as Agent of Change

Frederick Jackson visited Mount Elgon as early as 1889 and again in 1890 where he is said to have concentrated in collecting zoological specimens.[282] The MacDonald Expedition of 1896 did not do much in establishing any control, and attacks by the local inhabitants forced them to abandon the expedition camps and move to Nairobi in 1898. Otherwise as Michael Twaddle says,

> Gisu clans occupying the northerly and westerly slopes of this, the largest single mountain anywhere in the world at base level, remained independent of British colonial control...[283]

The advent of exposure to the external world came following the Uganda Agreement between the British represented by Sir Harry Johnston and the Buganda kingdom in 1900. Chief Semei Kakungulu was charged with pacifying and governing the then armophous eastern region known as Bukedi of present day Uganda for the British Empire.[284]

The Bamasaba were feared as a ferocious people and left alone, and it took Chief Semei Kakungulu from his stockade at Mpumudde (Nabumali), built at the end of 1900, many years to bring them under a semblance of control.

---

[282] Twaddle, *Kakungulu*, pp. 135.
[283] Ibid., p. 136.
[284] Ibid., p.137.

Even then, his presence in the district was resisted and sporadic fighting with his Baganda administration continued for some time. The Reverend J. B. Purvis comments that the former Commissioner of Uganda, Sir H. H. Johnston, once described the Bamasaba as "perhaps the wildest people to be found anywhere within the limits of the Uganda Protectorate".[285]

Two things happened that surprised and impressed the Bamasaba in their violent confrontation with the outside world represented by Kakungulu, thereby psychologically preparing them to be influenced by agents of external change. During their attack upon the stockade of Chief Semei Kakungulu and the battles that ensued, the Bamasaba warriors were armed with spears, sticks, shields and arrows, while their enemies carried guns. It was the first time they came in contact with guns, so they were deeply impressed by the "sticks, which vomited fire" which Kakungulu's army carried! During the indirect colonial rule that followed, they were also surprised and impressed by the fact that the Baganda administrators were able to communicate through "papers, which could speak".

Paradoxically, *imbalu* played a major role in resisting the intrusion of foreign influence in the district as the warriors were organised according to *imbalu* age-sets, for as Michael Twaddle observes,

> On the westerly slopes of Mount Elgon even more widespread resistance arose to Kakungulu's coming. There the military apparatus for co-ordinated attack against outsiders existed in the socio-religious shape of circumcision age-sets, which enabled disparate lineage groups to unite for common action as occasion demanded.[286]

At the beginning of the twentieth century the Bamasaba militarily resisted the intrusion of foreigners in their midst. Guns and literacy which most impressed them during and after this confrontation turned out to be precursors of a change that would completely and irreversibly transform Masaba landscape in all spheres of life: culturally, educationally, politically, socially and religiously. Colonialism affected the Bamasaba only by emasculating the traditional balance of power and authority. Prior to their contact with colonialism the distribution of social and political influence culturally operated through the executive represented by the *bakasa* (chiefs). The judiciary, that arm of the political organisation meant

---

[285] Purvis, *Through Uganda*, p. 268.
[286] Twaddle, *Kakungulu and the Creation of Uganda*, p. 149.

for settling disputes according to established rules and procedures, as well as the legislature meant to make laws, were held by the same *bakasa* assisted by their *bakasa bakekhe* (lower chiefs) and notable elders. There was thus no separation of political powers, just as there was no separation between political and moral-religious powers since these same elders were charged with guiding the community in religious and moral matters. That is why the elders in general, and the *bakasa* in particular officiated at the rites of *imbalu*.

Colonialism usurped the role of the above personages and as seen earlier, in 1956, the then Governor of Uganda, Sir Andrew Cohen, visited and officially inaugurated the circumcision year in the district. The dynamics of such an action was to, *inter alia*, indicate that the government was the over-seer of all spheres of life in the country including traditional activities. These fell under the laws of the country and were legally permitted, provided they were neither repugnant nor against public order. The colonial government was interested in public order and wanted to utilise the existing structures of cultural elders to enhance their indirect rule. The year was consequently given the name *Koheni* in honour of him. This role has been taken over by the post independence state, which does not unduly interfere in this traditional institution of initiation.

6.7.2. Christianity

The first missionary activity among the Bamasaba was in 1899 when Tucker of the Church Missionary Society set up a mission at Nabumali. A few years later, the Roman Catholic Mill Hill Missionaries established their own at Nyondo, a couple of kilometres away.[287]

William Anderson has described the advent of Christianity in East Africa in general, and Uganda in particular as a revolution, and he says that,

> The most characteristic element in this revolution was *kusoma* (reading). It was literacy. It was education. It was learning the ways of Europe. It was reading God's Word.[288]

But this does not mean that the pace of change among the Bamasaba was revolutionary. Change has been gradual especially in the rural areas where

---

[287] La Fontaine, *The Gisu of Uganda*, p. 12.
[288] Anderson, *The Church in East Africa*, p. 37.

the bulk of the people live. Christianity through its school-dispensary-church method opened up the district to external influence, but these were generally pockets of influence. The construction of roads speeded up the influence as coffee and cotton were introduced as cash crops, and traders set up shopping centres. But apart from these pockets of modernity, many of the more out-flung areas remained largely within the traditional context.

Christianity was spread through these school-dispensary-church pattern, a type of Christianity that Anderson defends as not being foreign but in many ways an African form, as he argues that,

> The pattern of school-dispensary-church was developed because it succeeded in Africa. The outposts, although supervised by missionaries, depended greatly on trained African Christians to run them .... East African Christians commonly used to say they go to Church *'kusoma'* (to read) rather than *'kusali'* (to pray), a reminder of the great literacy movements, which appeared in Buganda in the 1890s, and were repeated in so many other places.[289]

Christianity in Masabaland was but an extension of that in Buganda where the missionaries first arrived, and took the same pattern as described above, especially as the first catechists and teachers were Baganda. The missions became the centres of missionary activity and education, and many Bamasaba became Roman Catholics, Anglicans (Church of Uganda), Seventh Day Adventists or members of some other Christian denominations. The concentration of Muslims is around Mbale town as many of the early Baganda chiefs associated with Kakungulu were Muslims.

The early missionaries normally confused the alien with the evil, and perceived African culture as being largely, if not completely, heathen and demonic. The missionaries wanted to remove any traces of traditional religion, which was a stumbling block in their work, in order to plant Christianity. They perceived circumcision, which constitutes an ensemble of the religious beliefs of the Bamasaba as sexual mutilation, a barbaric custom, which should be discouraged and indeed abolished. As Malinowski points out, their prevailing view was that,

> The missionary is the initiator and centre of the religious revolution ... in Africa. ... As a matter of fact, his brief is to regard all the other

---

[289] Ibid., p. 111.

forms of religion as misguided, fit only for destruction, and to regard Christianity as entirely different, the only true religion to be implanted. Far from leaving other cults side by side in juxtaposition with the message of the Gospels, the missionary is actively engaged in superseding them.[290]

Militant fundamentalist denominations like the Seventh Day Adventists, the Jehovah's Witnesses, and the other *balokole* (born-again Christians) both foreign and indigenous tended to hold a radically negative attitude towards *imbalu*. The way the novices were covered with yeast and mud, the animal skins, which made them look wild, the permissive atmosphere that pervaded the vigils during the three days of the brewing phase, the gyrating of the waist and sexually explicit language were all seen as immoral. Also on their list were sacrifices as these go against Christian religious beliefs and the message of the Christian Gospel.

Missionary seminaries and boarding schools were averse to their boys undergoing circumcision. But the missionaries soon realised that if, especially their Bamasaba priests were not circumcised, they would be regarded as deviants and would not be accepted by their Bamasaba congregations! It was absolutely necessary for these boys to identify with the culture of their forefathers if they had to be recognised and accepted as men in society. They were also aware that if these priests lived within the district, there existed the danger of their relatives circumcising them by force to avert believed collective ritual guilt caused by their uncircumcised condition among them. Their children too would be regarded as social outcasts. They eventually, albeit reluctantly, allowed a modified version of it. Circumcisers were brought to the seminaries and boarding schools where the boys attended prayers before undergoing the ritual.[291] This modified form was calculated to give the priests some identity with the people they preached to.

Christianity presented itself as opposed to African culture in general, and Masaba *imbalu* in particular, and thus antagonised many from the very outset. The early converts were held with a mixture of suspicion, pity and disdain and regarded as sell-outs and deviants. This coupled with the hand-

---

[290] Malinowski, *The Dynamics of Culture Change*, p. 16.
[291] Leo Wawomola, interviewed by author on 6th November 1999 in Butiru village, said he himself underwent this form of modified initiation in Tororo College in 1954.

in-glove relationship that existed between the missionaries and the colonialists made many Bamasaba at first wary of it. But gradually the prospects of education for their children made many embrace it. No wonder Anderson argues that the church-school-dispensary system worked in East Africa.

Commenting on the irruption of Christianity into African community, Ogbu Kalu warns of the disruptive consequences thus,

> When Christianity comes into ... a community, sets up shop, offers a new covenant and essays to domesticate a new set of values, a hidden warfare below the obvious acts of persecution would ensue. A spectrum of reactions would emerge as individuals, families, and clans and village communities respond to the spiritual challenge.[292]

The introduction of Christianity has modified *imbalu* in several respects including the question of nudity or near nudity,[293] which was condemned as indecent, so today the novices dress in shorts. There has also been a change as far as the circumcision ritual is concerned as it is now done in *bisakati* (enclosures), started in 1934 as evidenced by the title name *Nabisakati*[294] (see *imbalu* topical names) given to the circumcision year. Christian influence has also brought about more consciousness in the language used during these festivities, with sexually explicit language and dancing largely discouraged and absent. This crusade was initiated mostly by the *balokole* (born again) Christians who always tend to be fundamentalist and more vocal about aspects of culture, which are incongruent to the Gospel message. They mostly subscribed to the maxim that Christianity was the measure and judge of all cultures.

6.7.3. Formal Education

Imbalu was traditionally a test of maturity and preceded marriage, so it took place between the ages of 18 to 24 or even higher for those who had exhibited fear and had postponed it for several years. Today it is no longer a test of maturity and does not necessarily precede marriage. Many boys and girls spend a long time in school and marry only later on. The age of *imbalu* has consequently come down to between 14 and about 18 years of

---

[292] Ogbu U. Kalu, *The Embattled Gods*. Lagos: Minaj Publishers, 1996, p. 49.
[293] Purvis, *Through Uganda*, p. 272.
[294] For more details see 4.5.7.2., where *imbalu* topical names are discussed.

age. With the introduction of formal education, most of the youth in this age bracket are either just finishing their primary education or have just joined secondary education.

One aspect that has been affected by the formal education system is that of *isonja* as novices do not have the time to invest in communal dancing. The decline of *isonja* has also affected the important role of *namyenya* (song-leaders cum composers) and their contribution to the cultural landscape in terms of didactic songs, folklore and legends. This has also in effect cut out this one phase of *imbalu* (see *imbalu* phases, 4.6. above) thus effectively reducing them to only six.

Before the introduction of formal schooling, circumcision took place in August after the main harvest when there was adequate supply of food for the novices and their parties. With the introduction of formal education, this time of the year is inconvenient for the school-going youth as they have only a short holiday. This is the time when many of them are preparing for the Primary Leaving Examinations, which come in November. It has, therefore, necessitated a change in the circumcision calendar by introducing a two-tier initiation season. Those novices who are not in school, locally known as *nabyalo* (villagers), follow the traditional circumcision calendar and are initiated in August. But the school going novices, known as *namasomelo* or "schoolers", are instead circumcised during the long holiday in December.

Modernity has influenced people's view towards *imbalu*, marriage, and fecundity. Though apart from those who may feel called to celibate life, everybody is expected to marry and bring up a family, there is more consciousness on the need of limiting children. Due to high child mortality in the past, polygamy was a cultural means of begetting many children so that even though some would die there would be sons to protect and perpetuate the father's line. Today many children are no longer a source of pride but a burden as the economy has shifted from subsistence to monetary. Education has become more appealing, and fees are high, so many children mean straining to take care of them.

The traditional system viewed women in terms of labour and child rearing. Women had no independent social or economic power besides that of the husband, for they owned neither land nor cows. Today many girls who have had education hold important posts in the public and private sectors and are a source of help to their parents and siblings. This has changed the public opinion about girls and led to their acceptance as almost equal to boys. Coupled with the awareness that life does not consist in naming as many ancestors as possible, many people who happen to have only daughters would not feel cheated in life. This relative relaxation of stress upon boys as being of vital importance in the home would be ascribed to several factors including:

- reduced parental and societal influence upon individuals,
- girls have proved to be as helpful, if not even more helpful to their parents than boys. They are capable of being bread earners too to supplement the husbands' income, thereby attaining some measure of social and economic independence. The dependence attitude that was expected of women in the past and put them in a subordinate position has been largely abandoned and replaced by one of marriage as partnership. More and more women, both single and married ones, are progressively to be found among the ranks of their male counterparts and are competing effectively in business, politics, education and other spheres of life.

6.7.4. Modernity as Agent of Change

It is not easy to delineate the changes brought about by Christianity and those brought about by modernity, as the two came in the same train. Western culture has impinged upon traditional Masaba lifestyle, and the clash and interplay of the two cultures have produced new things.[295] Masaba culture has continued to come under severe attack by people who think that the old-fashioned customs are difficult to perpetuate and are in fact a hindrance to decent etiquette. Still others contend that these customs are good and useful and that our African identity is anchored in them. But the middle ground might be that African cultures are characterised by both conservative and transformative tendencies as the changes are still going on at different paces in different places. But even in the same places, there is still a cultural gap both materially and mentally. In the words of one African scholar,

---

[295] Malinowski, *The Dynamics of Culture Change*, p. 25.

Culture renaissance is neither a blind return to the past, nor a blind leap into the future. The past is re-incarnated into the present, and owing to that re-incarnation, visions of the future are facilitated.[296]

Money economy has contributed to certain changes in the way *imbalu* is now conducted. Foodstuffs are now seen as non-traditional cash crops, so the surplus is sold for cash to finance the education of children and to pay for other domestic needs. The parties accompanying the novices are now seen as too expensive for the relative hosting the novice to entertain. Instead of the novice coming with a retinue of people, therefore, the practice is now for the relative to invite him informally with a handful of close relatives. Whatever gift he may have for him is either given to him then, or is pledged and delivered after the initiation ceremony. That way one avoids not only the monetary cost of entertaining many hangers-on, but also the socio-economic disruptions these large crowds carry. As society becomes more diversified, economic and social considerations make it difficult to uphold the old ways of doing old things. Instead people look for new ways of dealing with old issues without sacrificing too much of either.

Another aspect of *imbalu,* which has been adversely affected, is that of *bubakoki* (age-sets). The new economic order precludes the availability of cows to be slaughtered and meat distributed to age-set mates. The fact that identity has been adversely affected as members do not know one another anymore makes the matter worse. Festivals, music and dance have been identified as forces, which bind society together, as modes of relaxation and entertainment, laughter, solidarity and affirmation of roots with the ancestors. The drama, creativity and aesthetics contained in for instance *isonja* are example of the non-religious dimensions of African life.[297]

In some instances *imbalu* is threatened with moving from the public arena and becoming a private affair in a family. Increasing numbers of parents are opting to circumcise their sons privately in the home or in the hospitals. The modalities, especially where dancing parties have to be fed for at least the three days' vigil subsequent to the brewing of beer, is unwelcome proposition as it is too expensive. Secondly, these parties are very disruptive, as they comprise many loafers who have little discipline in word

---

[296] J. N. K. Mugambi, "The African Heritage: Change and Continuity", in J.B. Ojwang et al (eds.), *The S.M.Otieno Case*. Nairobi: Nairobi University Press, 1989, p. 165.
[297] Kalu, *The Embattled Gods*, p. 49.

and deed. Especially the rich and the educated members of society who would not like to invite all and sundry into their homes would like to avoid this inconvenience.

A mixture of religion, education, and modernity brought about laxity in the supervisory role of the community to ensure that all male Bamasaba paid the cultural debt. This was seen by certain Bamasaba as threatening the institution of initiation, leading to *ad hoc* militant groups to spring up to rid the district of the menace. Therefore in 1966 the practice of forcefully circumcising defaulters came into vogue, and since then there have been many instances of these groups hunting down and forcefully circumcising defaulters in towns as far away as neighbouring countries, leaving them no option but to come back and face the knife gracefully. This became a new mode of social control, for as Horwitz notes,

> At the heart of any social order are conceptions of right and wrong. People may sometimes sacrifice their lives, yet at other times remain quiescent ... people might seek vengeance for an inequity or settle with those they see as responsible; internalise their hostility or mobilise courts of law ... Whatever the response, the definition and defence of the moral order is a fundamental aspect of all social organisation. Social control is the aspect of society that protects the moral order of the group.[298]

Many of these instances have taken place in the capital city Kampala and its environs where many defaulters had taken refuge perhaps because the capital city offers them employment opportunities and more cover owing to its cosmopolitan nature. There is more privacy in a city and the defaulters could comfortably camouflage themselves by passing off as members of any of the tribes of Uganda. Many Bamasaba speak Luganda and could masquerade as Baganda since Luganda was introduced into the district by Kakungulu as the official language and was until recently taught as vernacular in schools. Many Bamasaba migrated to Buganda in the middle of the last century, some got married to local Baganda women. Many chose to adopt the customs of their Ganda hosts and so their children were socialised as Baganda, a non-circumcising community. To them, therefore, the idea of circumcision comes as a completely foreign idea that they have not been socialised to expect. Although Masaba culture demands that all

---

[298] Allan Horwitz, *The Logic of Social Control*. New York: Plenum Press, 1990, p. 1.

these sons of Masaba wherever they are ought to undergo initiation as a mark of cultural identity, in reality it becomes difficult to effect it.

A combination of education, modernity and religion are conspiring to make this difficult, if not virtually impossible. Many of these boys deny that they are Bamasaba in the first place since they may never have had any contact with the land of their forefathers. The only culture and language they know are those of their mothers, their fathers having all but abandoned their culture and adopted those of their in-laws. Unfortunately, many of these boys have embarrassingly and unceremoniously found themselves at the sharp end of the circumcision knife, their loud and stringent protests notwithstanding! According to the customs of their ancestors, and in the vocabulary of their Masaba uncles, whether they speak their language or not is not important. To all purposes and intents, they are Bamasaba, and fully bound by Masaba traditions, and that is all that there is to it. Doubtless, many have sought protection from the police to no avail. Civil law does not interfere with cultural practices unless they are proved to be repugnant and contrary to common decency. And that is a tall order. Others may not see what one member might perceive as repugnant from the same perspective. Usually the first question by the police is to establish whether the complainant belongs to the said tribe. Suffice it to illustrate this point with a dramatic instance, which has come to be known among the Bamasaba, no doubt amusingly, as the Kabala affair.

Kabala's father Mafaabi ran away as a young man and settled in Buganda where he married a local wife and brought up his children in their mother's customs. He never taught them his native Lumasaba (language of the Bamasaba), and never brought them to Masaba as he never came home. Then in 1972 he was forced to come home due to the war in Buganda, where for political reasons Bamasaba were being targeted and killed. Though he did not want to identify with his tribe, those among whom he had married and settled identified him with it. At the advanced age of sixty-five years he returned home where he was welcomed back, only to be pounced upon and publicly circumcised as is the practice with defaulters! Mafaabi's brother who had also defaulted had died before being circumcised and was, as custom requires, circumcised before burial! While a student at the university, his Bamasaba colleagues often threatened Kabala himself, a member of the Seventh Day Adventist denomination known for its radical views against cultural practices, with forceful circumcision. So in 1994 while on a trip to Canada he denounced his Masaba roots and registered his own tribe under the Canadian Provincial Law.[299] But of course this would not make any difference in the eyes of the Bamasaba who would see it as but another futile attempt to elude *imbalu*. The ad hoc task forces are believed to be still hunting for him to exact what they believe he owes the ancestors. He may end up being publicly embarrassed by being forcefully circumcised like his father, or after death like his uncle was. In the latter case his family will pay dearly for the operation to compensate the surgeon for the ritually defiling job, which will abruptly and permanently end his circumcising career. There is no rite that can purify a circumciser or his knife after circumcising a corpse! In either case he will have paid dearly for a custom he knows about but cares little if at all about.

But the negative result upon *imbalu* is that it is at the risk of losing its religious value and becoming gradually secularised, as the focus rests more on the physical and the social functions of the ritual.

6.7.5. Post Independence State

Since Independence in 1962, the feeling of nationhood has been advocated to supplant that of belonging to a tribe. The historical factors for tribal allegiance included hostile neighbours who needed green pastures for their cattle, especially in times of drought in the more arid plains to its west and south. Because of the forests, the ridges of Mount Elgon receive a higher rainfall than the drought prone savannah plains occupied by their pastoralist neighbours. During times of drought, therefore, these neighbours needed the lush green plains surrounding the mountains for grazing their herds and flocks. The geographical factors, which gave rise to the particular physiognomy of traditional Masaba culture as it was until several decades ago, have lost currency and no longer prevail.

Imbalu is, therefore, no longer a sign of maturity, as the spectre of tribal wars for which physical maturity and bravery were required has been shifted to the shoulders of the national army and police force, respectively. Similarly, the volcanic loam soils of the ridges of Mount Elgon are ideal

---

[299] *New Vision*, Kampala (2 January 1995).

for the cultivation of cash crops like Arabica coffee, tea, tobacco and cotton. They are also good for diverse food crops like bananas, maize, beans, sweet and Irish potatoes, simsim, cassava, millet, finger millet and others which today have come to be known as "non-traditional" cash crops. The Bamasaba are, therefore, relatively much wealthier than their neighbours, an economic advantage which they readily put to use in acquiring land from these neighbours.

So the protection of life and property including land, now falls on the shoulders of the disciplined forces, while acquisition of land has now shifted from military to economic might. As the pressure upon available land has intensified, more and more people have been buying land in neighbouring districts like Tororo, Pallisa, Kumi and Sebei, which happen to be sparsely populated, and settling there.

With the disappearance of the spectre of wars, today less stress is being placed upon the ordeal component of *imbalu*, which was earlier instrumental in toughening the young novices into formidable warriors. *Imbalu* was expected to prepare, test, confirm and reinforce the positive values cherished by the community. This is now being viewed as not altogether necessary, and focus is now being placed instead on the fact that *imbalu* consists in affording the novices a mark of membership and identity as Bamasaba. The customs whose origin and sanction were attributed to the ancestors run the risk of being unmasked and dethroned, exposing their human and social face.

Imbalu is to a large extent being de-mystified, as the myths that present the ancestors as its authors thereby giving it supernatural sanction are being contested and their credibility assaulted. This view could only hold sway in a given cultural worldview where life was held to be a collective journey towards collective immortality with the ancestors. Christianity and modernity have advanced a view of salvation, which is quite incongruent with this primal worldview, thereby directing a searchlight upon the traditional teaching and beliefs.

Social evolution brings about increasingly large groups, growing division of labour, more heterogeneity and more social stratification. Social control, therefore, shifts from status relationships to the creation of moral systems, which are applicable to and by culturally, socially and economically diverse groups.[300]

These powers have now shifted from the cultural set-up to the central government appointed chiefs, many of whom are not indigenous, and so these offices no longer hold cultural significance.

The initiation season is still organised along maximal lineages, which also coincide with the administrative units known as *tsigombolola* (sub-counties). Increase in population has made it necessary to have new sub-county boundaries, so the government has sub-divided the original sub-counties and created new ones. Beginning with Bungokho-Mutoto, believed to have been at the origin of *imbalu*, the circumcisers proceed strictly from one to the next lineage, only resting on Sundays till all are completed. This holds good for both the August and December rounds of initiations. The ritual sites at Bumutoto are situated where the government has since built an army barracks. Discussions are still going on between the district representatives and the central government to resolve this issue.

6.8. CONCLUSION

Ogbu Kalu points out that in African communities, the

> socialisation process or acculturative social control involves initiation into the communal gods, mores of the people and the spirit which gives the community members a special identity.[301]

Among the Bamasaba, *imbalu* performs this particular role as it initiates the novices into full members of the community, covenanting them to the ancestors who are the authors of the ritual. As demonstrated above, Christianity, modernity and the post-independence state have conspired to relax the bonds that hold the community together. As the elders continue to lose their authoritative supervisory role, other cultural institutions like *bukulo* (joking relationship), and *bubakoki* (age-sets) too continue to lose their community policing authority.

What has hitherto survived best and almost intact is the obligation of having all Bamasaba male youth circumcised as a mark of membership.

---

[300] Horwitz, *The Logic of Social Control*, p. 2.
[301] Kalu, *Embattled Gods,* pp. 47-48.

This enjoys popular support in the community and is sanctioned by the militancy of the *ad hoc* task force groups. ***Imbalu*** is what gives the Bamasaba that unique special identity as a community of circumcised men, and they are not about to give that up. The few who may object to it for whatever reason, valid or otherwise, are easily discounted as social misfits who are not man enough to undergo the pain of the mighty knife. If they are within reach, the **task force** will certainly perform their duty as happened with Mafaabi or if death strikes first, these will be subjects of social derision like Mafaabi's brother.[302] Their families will bear the brunt of it all, hence the need for them to co-operate with the task force to forestall such an eventuality.

But for especially the educated, the main focus of ***imbalu*** is gradually shifting to the physical operation as that is the aspect that the community can still effectively supervise and sanction. The danger is for the agents of change to succeed in separating ***imbalu*** from the venerated ancestors, mores of the people and the spirit, which gives the members the distinguishing mark of identity as a community of circumcised men.[303] If this is not checked, then for them the real inner meaning of ***imbalu*** would have been lost as the younger generations strive to retain a ritual experience sometimes bereft of the fundamental meaning of linking them with their roots. This is perhaps what Frits Staal would refer to as meaninglessness ritual.[304] But the fact remains that though many of these youth may retain only the physical aspect at the expense of the authoritative[305] and instructive[306] features, they still know the meaning of the ritual. And society knows what it means to them. It means they have transited from childhood to adulthood, and been transformed into Bamasaba men. Society will henceforth treat them differently and this gives them a certain psychological confidence. They may now do things they would not have been allowed to do before. It is not so much the individual persons who matter, but the community, for initiation is what society does to and with

---

[302] For details, please see 6.7.4 above.

[303] Purvis, *Through Uganda*, p. 271.

[304] Frits Staal, "The Meaninglessness of Ritual", in *Numen*, Vol. xxvi, Fasc.1 (1979), p. 4.

[305] See for instance 6.5. above.

[306] See 6.5. above.

individuals. As Catherine Bell affirms, "rituals are 'analogous to culturally produced texts' that can be systematically read to endow 'meaning upon experience'."[307]

---

[307] Catherine Bell, *Ritual Theory Ritual Practice*. Oxford: Oxford University Press, 1992, p. 15.

CHAPTER SEVEN: HALLMARK OF MASABA IDENTITY

7.1. INTRODUCTION

In modern Uganda the idea of the Gisu as a nation of circumcised men remains as strong as ever. The biennial circumcision ceremonies act as both a focus for such sentiment and as a dramatic display of its power ... At the centre are the novices, with the ordeal of circumcision acting not only to validate their own claim to status as adult men but also to demonstrate the values of the entire community. When a ritual has this significance for a people, it is important to inquire into what values are being affirmed and why a single ritual complex is so charged.[308]

The above observation sums up the fact that in spite of the massive impact of the change agents, which have modified it, *imbalu* has hitherto survived eradication. Its significance for the Bamasaba may have been bruised, but it still evokes a veritable sentiment in their breasts, and remains the single most effective symbol of tribal identity and mobilisation.

This work has shown that there are seven phases of *imbalu* and not four as claimed by La Fontaine[309] and Turner,[310] nor three as claimed by Heald.[311] It has brought to the fore the importance attached to it by the people by discussing the concepts of identity, culture, community, and symbolism, which under-gird the ritual. It has also discussed the role of male power and authority in connection with the role of women in this male dominated ritual.

The principal change agents responsible for the modification found in the circumcision ritual have been identified. Their respective roles in this ongoing phenomenon of the old and the new, change and continuity have been discussed. It has, thus, given the ritual a fuller description and interpretation than has hitherto been presented by earlier authors. The effort here is to bring to the fore some of the factors that have facilitated the survival of *imbalu*, making it difficult for the change agents discussed in

---

[308] Heald, "Mafias in Africa", *Africa* 52 (1), p. 15.
[309] La Fontaine, *The Gisu*, pp. 42-43.
[310] Turner, in *Man in Africa*, p. 237.
[311] See Heald, *Controlling Anger,* pp. 62-63.

the previous chapter to eradicate it. This will be achieved by placing the ritual of Masaba initiation in a larger frame of significance, both as a religious form and as a socio-political culture for the people who practise it. Several themes will be discussed to explain the phenomenon of its resilience, and these are:

- Psychological meaning of circumcision to the Bamasaba
- Cultural conservatism and the cult of Manhood
- Attachment to land and its acquisition, and
- Internal contradictions in the change agents themselves.

But before discussing these factors which enabled *imbalu* to survive eradication by the change agents, we shall briefly summarise the work of three principal early writers, namely La Fontaine, Victor Turner and Suzette Heald.

7.2. EARLIER WORKS ON *IMBALU*

Particular interests in their research approach to *imbalu* conditioned each of these earlier writers. For instance, Jean La Fontaine set out to study the Bamasaba as part of the wider picture of East Africa ethnographic survey, sponsored by the East African Institute of Social Research.[312] As such she did not set out to describe Masaba initiation in the fullest details, or interpret it. She treated the circumcision ritual as but one feature of the wider concept of life cycle in the community.[313] Thus, she unfortunately missed, or was not interested in the religious dimension of the ritual. One has to give credit to missionaries like John Roscoe, who identified the religious nature of cultural initiation and treated it as such.[314]

La Fontaine posits four phases up to the circumcision rite, namely *isonja* (communal dance), *khuwentza* (searching), *khukhupaka* (thrashing of millet) and *khukoya* (brewing). She states that, "The fourth phase consists of the final ritual preparations for the ceremony"[315], indicating that she clearly understood the brewing phase as the final one, a preparation for the

---

[312] La Fontaine, *The Gisu*, p. vi.
[313] Ibid., pp. 39-50.
[314] Roscoe, *The Northern Bantu*, pp. 179-188.
[315] La Fontaine, *The Gisu*, p. 43.

"final ritual"[316] of physical operation. She treats convalescence and *ineemba* (final dance) only in passing, saying precious little about the important rite of *khukhwiyalula* (hatching). As the first anthropological survey of the Bamasaba, her work has been a guide for subsequent researchers including Victor Turner and Suzette Heald.

Victor Turner relied upon La Fontaine's data,[317] for the purpose of comparing the concepts of symbolisation and patterning between Masaba *imbalu* and Ndembu *mukanda*. He neither intended to give a detailed description nor an interpretation of *imbalu* as such. He was indeed an expert on the ritual of *mukanda* where he "spent nearly two and a half years in the field among the Ndembu"[318], but not on *imbalu* where he spent but "only two and a half months among the Gisu..."[319]

As regards his comparative work, informed by and drawing comparisons with those of the Ndembu *mukanda*, he correctly identified the three symbolic elements prevalent in *imbalu*, namely sprouted millet yeast, chyme and mud. He is good on the question of symbolisation and has interpreted them as symbols of fermentation, fertility, maturation and virility.[320] But Turner had a limited research perspective and particular focus during his equally limited time.

The present work goes beyond his by asking for symbolic meaning of not only the above three elements, but the entire ritual from beginning to end: from *isonja* (initial first communal dance) to *ineemba* (convocation and commissioning dance). He does not cover religious symbolism, which is only understandable in the context of Masaba traditional religious beliefs. For instance, to understand the symbolism behind hanging the heart and lungs of the sacrificed animal upon *lukangu* (ritual pole)[321] needs knowledge of their relationship to *basambwa* (ancestors) and to *Wele* (God) in the first place.

Understanding the symbolic meaning behind actions also requires knowledge of the people's culture and myths of origin. For instance, to

---

[316] Ibid., p. 43.
[317] Turner, in *Man in Africa*, p. 229.
[318] Ibid., p. 229.
[319] Ibid., p. 229.
[320] Ibid., pp. 240-241.
[321] For a description of this see 4.5.4.3., and for its interpretation see 5.3.4. above.

appreciate why the *batembete* (newly circumcised) point their sticks to the north east at the end of each dance during *ineemba* (convocation dance)[322] needs knowledge of how Nabarwa is believed to have brought *imbalu* to the Bamasaba.

Turner's account of the shaving of the novice by the father's sister whose own head he says had been shaved by her brother's daughter[323] seems incongruent. Neither in La Fontaine's,[324] Heald's, nor in my own research is the aunt's head shaved, or shaved by her brother's daughter. It would be difficult to see the symbolism of such an act as it is the novice's boyhood which is being symbolically severed by the shaving of his hair, and not the aunt's.[325]

Suzette Heald's account of the three phases is more detailed than La Fontaine's and Turner's, but she chose to ignore the phase of *khuwentza* (searching), thus, remaining with only three, namely, *isonja* (initial dance), *khukhupaka* (thrashing of millet) and *khukoya* (brewing phase). She mentions the washing or purification rite after circumcision, but neither the important rites of *khukhwiyalula* (hatching) nor *ineemba* (convocation dance).

In summary, all the three concentrated on the phases (four for La Fontaine and Turner, and three for Heald) leading to the day of circumcision, which they regarded as the climax. But they all failed to see *imbalu* as a complex whole, a symphony which continues to play itself out long after the physical operation, which only marks the threshold.[326] Circumcision demarcates the beginning of the transition phase, where the initiate is clearly between Gennep's two borders,[327] or Victor Turner's "between and betwixt".[328] The present research goes beyond theirs, clearly demonstrating that in this complex ritual both the phases prior to circumcision and those after it are equally important. This work shows that Masaba initiation ritual

---

322 For a description of this see 4.5.7., and for its interpretation see 5.6. above.

323 Ibid., p. 239.

324 La Fontaine, *The Gisu*, p. 43.

325 For description of the shaving ceremony see 4.5.4.3., and for interpretation see 5.4.5. above.

326 van Gennep, *Rites of Passage*, p. 20.

327 Ibid., p. 21

328 Turner, *Ritual Process*, p. 95.

is a socio-cultural, socio-political and indeed religious phenomenon, and interprets it as such. Only the seven phases fulfil van Gennep's scheme of separation, transition, and incorporation.

With regard to her sociological interpretation of *imbalu*, Suzette Heald identifies *lirima* (anger) as being responsible for bravely enduring the ordeal. She associates violence with manhood and anger, arguing that,

> The ordeal of circumcision ... is crucial to understanding both Gisu perceptions and experience, for the qualities that a boy has to develop in order to undergo the ordeal courageously are the same which might later lead him to violence.[329]

She contends that anger is inculcated into the initiate for the purpose of bravely enduring *imbalu*, concluding that having no war to channel it into, this anger finds vent in social violence. According to her,

> The courage of men comes from their capacity to experience some emotions more strongly than women ... Women and children are believed to be capable only of the weaker form of emotional arousal as given in *libuba*, while men are subject to that of *lirima*. *Lirima* is pre-eminently a manly quality.[330]

Circumcision is certainly premised upon bravery, and encourages manliness of which bravery is a central notion. Especially when challenged, a man would tend to meet the challenge head on, and this leads to many brawls. Like Okonkwo who, dazed with fear, drew his machete and cut down Ikemefuna because he was afraid of being thought weak,[331] the Bamasaba perceive weakness as being unmanly.

However, it is our contention that anger plays no role in the ritual, and is not the key to bravely standing the ordeal. It is neither applied, controlled, nor is it conceptualised in the ritual. Instead, the operative word is *kamani* (strength), which is clearly conceptualised. As she herself notes, "The boy is continually exhorted: *samba imbalu ni kamani* – dance *imbalu* with strength – and *amba imbalu ni kamani* – hold on to *imbalu* with strength."[332] The above exhortation is instructive since *kamani* (strength) refers both to strength of mind and of body. It finds expression in the

---

[329] Heald, *Controlling Anger*, p. 5.
[330] Ibid., p. 58.
[331] Chinua Achebe, *Things Fall Apart*. London: Heinemann, 1983, p. 54.
[332] Ibid., p. 61.

determined and purposeful actions of the initiate, which in turn point to how he might stand the pain of the knife. Inner commitment is needed to endure the pain, and the initiate is continually urged to,

> breathe normally and let his stomach muscles relax; there must be no trembling, no give-away involuntary movements of his body which betoken fear. The commitment required of the boy is total, evidenced by his complete command of his body at the time of the operation.[333]

Manliness is identified with ability to control one's emotions including anger. But self-control is an aspect of maturity, even in non-circumcising communities. One would be more correct to argue that when the initiate is challenged to step down if he feels he is not ready, he reacts with defiant determination. In his literary work Wangusa depicts how a novice who is disparagingly told to lay down the dancing regalia and enter his mother's house reacts with defiant resolve. He resents being identified with children and women, and loathes the insults concomitant with boyhood. He reacts with resentment when he imagines continuing to put up with demeaning insults, and calls the bluff, motivated and determined to embrace the higher status of manhood. Insults may goad him into taking the plunge, but he needs inner strength of character to stand the pain. Indeed, as La Fontaine observes, "It requires, ...both strength of purpose to conquer fear and strength of body to maintain self-control"[334] under the ordeal.

We shall now examine some of the factors that explain why *imbalu* has survived the debilitating impact of the change agents.

7.3. PSYCHOLOGICAL MEANING OF *IMBALU* TO THE BAMASABA

Although the Bamasaba traditionally had no unifying political structure or ruler, they have always been acutely aware of their unique tribal identity. The internal divergences in dialect and even variations in ritual are explained as marks of related descendants of a common ancestor. They perceive themselves as a people speaking one language and sharing common cultural values epitomised by circumcision. These common

---

[333] Ibid., p. 61.
[334] La Fontaine, *Initiation*, p. 121.

cultural values make them an entity whose loyalty can be mobilised by appeal to these common symbols. *Imbalu* is still a mobilisation force generating much interest, as it is a dramatisation of their cultural identity and power. It is not so much about an initiate's transformation as it is about a community's cultural unity. As individuals, the initiates need to identify with something bigger than themselves, and through circumcision the individual feels himself part of the wider society.

Identification with a bigger group provides a certain sense of security to the individuals. Through *imbalu* they seek to integrate themselves into the community's inner life. Through the power of the spoken word, uttered especially during the rites of *khuuakha* (smearing with yeast and chyme) and during *khuusaabisa* (purification), society ensures that these values are deep-seated. I concur with the sentiment that,

> Gisu initiation thus defines unequivocally for any Gisu the widest group with which he can identify himself. This community can be described as 'we', as against its opposite, 'they', the non-initiate aliens. This common identification indicates the acceptance of common values and a common code of ethical norms ...[335]

The biennial ceremonies act as a continual renewal of their common identity, by recourse to myths and legends, which legitimise this cultural unity, determining who they are, as compared to outsiders. F. B. Welbourn echoes this sentiment when he says that,

> initiation was the means by which individuals became fully men, participants in every aspect of the life of the tribe. Their new identity set them apart from the uninitiated – from tribes which did not practise initiation ... Those rituals, myths and beliefs ... were part of their being as ... Gisu.[336]

Imbalu has, therefore, survived due to the value attached to it by the Bamasaba. It affords them a unique identity by setting them apart from all other men of non-circumcising communities who are considered as boys.

But apart from its social and religious aspects, *imbalu* has a psychological dimension. It serves to legitimate and affirm the cult of manliness and strength by successful completion of the ordeals. Manliness as a concept

---

[335] La Fontaine, *Tribalism*, p. 187.
[336] F. B. Welbourn, *Religion and Politics in Uganda, 1952-1962*. Nairobi: East African Publishing House, 1965, p. 52.

does not depend solely on whether one has been circumcised or not. More important are the questions whether one went through the ordeals, and how one fared under them. The ordeals make those who go through them successfully feel braver than other men. Certainly, there are men who, though circumcised, have not been seen to have undergone the ordeals and triumphed. Such persons have been "circumcised by an uncircumcised circumciser! Or even a woman ... A woman circumciser of womanly men".[337]

It would appear that circumcision qualifies one to be a Masaba man, but successful completion of the ordeals defines what type of man one is. While the ordeals may scare some to seek the less painful anaesthetised method of circumcision, social ridicule counterbalances it. Tribal identity has not been eradicated by political independence, and the need to identify with the community often leads to compliance and conformity. There are many variables feeding the question of cultural decline or renaissance. As Peter Probst has shown with *nyau* cultural performances, contrary to assumptions, which predicted decline, the reality was a revival instead.[338] The most we can safely say, which is the subject of this research, is that *imbalu* has survived this far. How it survives in future will be material for another inquiry altogether.

7.4. CULTURAL CONSERVATISM AND THE CULT OF MANHOOD

As shown in their profile, Bamasaba are a sedentary agricultural community, whose characteristics include the fertility of their volcanic soils, and inaccessibility due to the remoteness of their mountainous territory. The fertile soils ensure food security, while availability of cash crops such as coffee provide a flourishing economy that enables them to remain within the confines of their territory. But they also keep cattle, goats and sheep, used for obtaining wives.[339] This double image prompted some

---

[337] Ibid., p. 44.

[338] Peter Probst, "Ritual Space and the Dialectics of Tradition in Central Malawi", p. 3. (Unpublished manuscript).

[339] Roscoe, *The Northern Bantu,* p. 168. See also Turner, in *Man in Africa*, p. 231.

authors to refer to them as "pastoral".[340] Since they had both agricultural produce and animals, this precluded the need for barter trade with their neighbours. Such sufficiency gave them cultural pride and sustained their cultural conservatism. Coupled with the unfriendly terrain and the people's famed ferocity[341] these kept outsiders at bay, leaving the Bamasaba with little contact with other cultures. Even when contact was made, inaccessibility enabled them to resist change for a long time, as they often simply withdrew further up into the mountains. The invaders could not subdue them within this unfamiliar terrain. As one British agent once reported,

> The theatre of war consisted of broad terraces ... separated from each other by precipitous cliffs in which were situated numerous caves, used by the predatory natives as places of refuge.[342]

When colonialism finally irrupted upon them, it was through *imbalu* that the Bamasaba resisted the intrusion of colonialism. The age-set system enabled disparate lineage groups to unite for common action,[343] though they were finally defeated through the superior firing power of "the noise, the mystery and the almost supernatural power of the ... sticks which vomited fire."[344]

Cultural conservatism is usually at the basis of political conservatism. Although the Bamasaba were traditionally a chiefless society, organised in a pyramidal system of localised patrilineages,[345] after independence the community presented a common political front under the paramountcy of *umuinga* (the high one) as a rallying symbol.

Imbalu was, therefore, used as a tool to forge cultural unity among the different lineages. It also supplied political and military unity, producing hardened young men to fight any outsiders, believed to harbour hostile intentions. It acted as a weapon against outside threat to Masabaland. In the

---

[340] See Purvis, *Through Uganda*, p. 271.

[341] Roscoe, *Northern Bantu*, p. 161. See also Suzette Heald, *Controlling Anger*, pp. 22-23.

[342] Twaddle, *Kakungulu and the Creation of Uganda*, p. 136.

[343] Ibid., p. 149.

[344] Ibid., p. 150.

[345] La Fontaine, "Land and the Political Community in Bugisu", in William A. Shack and Percy S. Cohen (eds.), *Politics in Leadership*. Oxford: Clarendon Press, 1979, p. 98.

new era, however, Masaba's very survival as a cultural entity was threatened since *imbalu*, their most basic symbol of unity and identity was under attack by the agents of change! Therefore, *imbalu* and other cultural institutions had to be strengthened and defended. They also had to be strengthened to provide the necessary political unity and loyalty, with which their collective rights as Bamasaba could be defended.

7.5. ATTACHMENT TO LAND, ITS ACQUISITION AND PROTECTION

There is a correlation between the ancestors, people, *imbalu* and land. They all refer to Masaba the common ancestor, who bequeathed to them *imbalu*, which is their defining feature. He also bequeathed to them land as their ancestral heritage. Land and *imbalu* are important and connected features of Masaba identity. As a symbol of identity and unity *imbalu* was used in protecting land against outsiders. Land, then, is more than just an economic resource. As an ancestral inheritance where the bones of the ancestors lie, it has religious and sentimental significance for the people. Jomo Kenyatta asserts that,

> Communion with the ancestral spirits is perpetuated through contact with the soil in which the ancestors of the tribe lie buried ... Thus the earth is the most sacred thing...[346]

Echoing this sentiment, La Fontaine observes that,

> The traditional Gisu view of their material environment and human settlement in it is composed of three distinct concepts...place, land and territory ... The precise local immanence of ancestors during a ritual has significance ... for it links a lineage in a historical association with a particular place ...[347]

Territory is also a political entity for the different lineages. While an individual thinks of land in terms of where to build and farm, the collective lineage look upon land as their definitive political locus. *Imbalu* is a prerequisite for qualification to a piece of the ancestral land. Social approbation is anchored upon *imbalu*. Ancestral land is inherited only after

---

[346] Jomo Kenyatta, *Facing Mount Kenya*. Nairobi: Heinemann, 1985, p. 21.
[347] La Fontaine, *Land and the Political Community in Bugisu*, p. 98.

230

one has been initiated and not before. An uninitiated son, however old, cannot lay claim to any of the land his father possesses. A father can continue to enjoy all his land by postponing the initiation of his sons. Victor Turner associates the higher age of novices in the north with the higher intensity of land scarcity in the area.[348] Since the right to receive ancestral land is acquired only upon circumcision, a father can purposely postpone the circumcision of the sons in order to postpone their obligation of sharing his limited amount of land with them. As long as they remain uncircumcised, he can enjoy his land. Acquisition of land acts as a powerful incentive for circumcision.

Since the Bamasaba had to fight many battles, both in armed conflict and legally against their neighbours over land, *imbalu* has always provided them with political unity as Bamasaba, giving them unique identity. In the 1930s, the question of land, where the Bamasaba were grouped together with Bukedi and Sebei, caused serious agitation and unrest. The Bagisu Welfare Association spearheaded popular opposition to the authorities over this thorny issue. The myth that their common ancestor emerged from the crater on Mount Masaba strengthens their claim over it against their neighbours. The fact that a Land Commission was set up to look into this question[349] goes to show how important and sensitive the question of land is to them.

This was also the time when *Dini ya msambwa* (religion of the ancestors) mooted as a religio-political liberation movement to counter the destructive tendencies of colonialism and Christianity was spreading in the district. It advocated a resumption of cultural religious forms of expression as a means of stemming the tide of Western influences. It was a rejection of and protest against both colonialism and Christianity, seen as but one and the same. The colonialists in neighbouring Kenya had laid claim to the best land, displacing the indigenous population who became squatters on their own ancestral land. It was felt that the same might happen to Masabaland because of its fertility and ideal altitude. This indigenous religion had anti-colonial undertones, and was introduced as an alternative to Christianity. The latter was seen as a colonial tool for taming and blindfolding the

---

[348] La Fontaine, *Land and the Political Community in Bugisu*, pp. 99-100.
[349] Ibid., pp. 99-100.

Africans while colonialists grabbed their land. It was, however, quickly suppressed by the colonial administration because of its impact and socio-political implications.[350]

7.6. INTERNAL CONTRADICTIONS: COLONIALISM AND CHRISTIANITY

Colonialism and Christianity may have made an irruption upon Masaba culture in general, and *imbalu* in particular, but they did not conquer the spirit of fierce cultural nationalism. Ogbu Kalu points out that Africans "build up a covenantal relationship with spiritual forces in the air, land, water and ancestral world to aid the capability to cope and excel."[351] Disengagement from these covenantal relationships is not easy for fear that these spiritual powers may visit calamity upon them and theirs. The three themes at the centre of worship and prayer point to the issues at the heart of existence, namely health, wealth and re-incarnation as an ancestor. Aspiration to ancestor-hood presupposes belief in them, coupled with observances of ancestral traditions.

Colonialism and Christianity failed to eradicate *imbalu* because of internal contradictions in their cultural policies. While the former was more accommodating to indigenous cultures and religions, the latter was openly hostile to them. Due to the First World War (1914-1918), the Great Depression (1929-1933) and indeed the Second World War (1939-1945), the colonial powers were over-stretched in terms of personnel. They devised a strategy of using indirect rule where they utilised existing cultural forms of government to maintain order. In pursuit of order, and due to limited personnel in the colonies and protectorates, the colonial government tended to be more positive towards the cultural practices than the missionaries who saw them as superstitious and demonic, an impediment to the evangelisation project. The colonial government used the cultural organisation to maintain law and order to enable their indirect rule policy to succeed.[352]

---

[350] J. C. Usher-Wison, "Dini Ya Msambwa", in *Uganda Journal* vol. 6 no. 2 (1952), pp. 125- 129.

[351] Ogbu Kalu, *The Embattled Gods*. Lagos: Minaj Publishers, 1996, p. 46.

[352] For more on this issue refer to 6.7.1. above.

Christianity was especially identified as an enemy because of its opposition to and condemnation of circumcision and other cultural forms, which it demonised. As Kenyatta laments,

> They condemned customs and beliefs which they could not understand ... the missionaries insisted that the followers ... give up dances, ceremonies, and feasts which are fundamental principles of the African social structure.[353]

Such attacks on cultural forms in general, and *imbalu* in particular, only fuelled defensive counter opposition to Christianity.

F. B. Welbourn describes cultural initiation as being "integral to the life of the tribe. Therefore, an attack on one aspect of one ceremony appears to be an attack on the tribe itself".[354] Initiation was felt to be essential to the stability of the tribe, and Christianity was perceived as invading not only *imbalu* but also the community itself. There was, therefore, a felt need to strengthen the defences against it, in order to safeguard cultural forms and ward off imperialist influences out to destroy cultural identity and cohesion.

Though many embraced Christianity, religion in general has never been a serious contender for allegiance and identity, for it is not a serious signifier. Even today, members of the same family often do belong to different religious groupings but still live in harmony. They identify rather with their culture, epitomised by *imbalu*. All foreign religions in their different forms are regarded as religions of *basamba metzi* (foreigners). Instead, kinship is a very important factor, whose ties are periodically renewed through *imbalu*.

Christianity was not able to supplant circumcision because it was not allowed to get to the heart of the community. To many, Christianity became an extra form of security, juxtaposed against their cultural forms. But in times of crisis, they almost always fall back upon their time-tested cultural wisdom. As Emmanuel Milingo has exclaimed,

> The Africans have been communing with their dead ancestors from time beyond reckoning. It is the one thing which colonisation never succeeded in suppressing ... if the Church had been wise, it would have penetrated the funeral rituals, marriage ceremonies, naming

---

[353] Kenyatta, *Facing Mount Kenya*, p. 271.
[354] Welbourn, *East African Christian*, pp. 111-113.

rituals and so on. These are the areas where the Africans have still remained themselves, and thanks be to God that this has happened because otherwise we should have no identity.[355]

This assertion by Milingo, himself a Christian archbishop, partly answers Walakira's question why the Bamasaba are so actively involved in *imbalu* and not in the Christian service. They identify with *imbalu* and not with Christianity. The former is their culture signifier whereas the latter is foreign. *Imbalu* defines what the Bamasaba are, but Christianity does not. So far what seems to have happened has been a state of divided loyalty: to the cultural values inculcated especially through the instructive feature of *imbalu* on the one hand, and to the values espoused by Christianity on the other. Because Christianity demonised cultural forms and other religions, many adherents felt the two were incompatible, and either superimposed or juxtaposed them. This state of affairs has been well depicted when the writer laments thus,

> When an African Christian encounters a real deep crisis, when illness and misfortune occur, the temptation is great to use old means and ways, to ask the wise men and women for counsel. Many Africans are reluctant to speak about this, because fetishism and magic fit an image of paganism, which makes them primitives in the view of white people ... Why has the old Africa still so much power over hearts? Why does not the Christian message suffice in times of crisis?[356]

While the Masaba Christian holds to this dual identity, it has been difficult for Christianity to eradicate cultural values in general, and circumcision in particular.

This duality of loyalty has necessitated a search for a synthesis between the two traditions, to meet the implicit need of converts torn between their African identity and their Christian convictions.[357] This effort is commonly known as inculturation, which means,

> the honest and serious attempt to make Christ and his message of salvation evermore understood by peoples of every culture, locality

---

[355] Emmanuel Milingo, *The World in Between*. Maryknoll, New York: Orbis Books, 1984, p. 76.

[356] Göhler, Johannes, "Noah Dzobo's African Melagbe Theology: A German Approach to Understanding his Theology", in *The Reformed World* 40 (1989), p. 108.

[357] Francois Kabasele, "Sacramental Inculturation in Zaire", in *Lumen Vitae*, Bruxelles, Vol. 42, No. 2/3 (1987), p. 283.

and time ... the reformulation of Christian life and doctrines into the very thought patterns of each people.[358]

In the case of cultural circumcision, some writers have suggested a synthesis between the two initiations as a solution that would help converts torn between their Christian convictions and their African identity.[359] This might be regarded as possible because of resemblance between Christian and cultural initiation, such as fasting, retreats, special formulas, purification, offerings, and new understanding. There is also a commonality through their ultimate aim, namely union with the Beyond, the gods, and immortality.[360]

Modernity and secularism failed to do away with cultural forms like *imbalu* because of continued thirsting for religious expression that is meaningful to the people, "a place to feel at home".[361] Religious pluralism has led to a multiplicity of religious innovation, among them the need to return to the time-tested religious forms of the ancestors for solace.

Where *imbalu* was the traditional weapon for invoking loyalty to fight their enemies, this time the weapon itself was under threat. The change agents attacked both the structure and meaning of *imbalu*. Now it was feared that it might destroy the institution itself. Something had to be done, and done quickly. With the weapon under contestation, outsiders threatened their coveted land bequeathed to them by the ancestors. They were being forced to share their ancestral land with uncircumcised outsiders! As a weapon *imbalu* had to be extricated, protected and used for its traditional purpose of safeguarding Masabaland. There was need to get rid of both external and internal opposition to *imbalu*.

Where the power and authority of the community through the elders had always been sufficient to bring about conformity, the change agents had eroded some of it! There was, therefore, need for a different form of

---

[358] John Mary Waliggo, "Making a Church that is Truly African" in J. M. Waliggo et al (eds.), *Inculturation: Its Meaning and Urgency*. Kampala: St. Paul Publications, 1986, p. 12.

[359] See for instance Kabasele "Sacramental Inculturation", p. 283, and Sanon T. Anselme, "Jesus, Master of Initiation", in Robert J Schreiter (ed.), *Faces of Jesus in Africa*. Maryknoll: Orbis Books, 1991, pp. 93-94.

[360] Ibid., p. 282.

[361] F. B. Welbourn and B. A. Ogot, *A Place to Feel At Home*. London: Oxford University Press, 1965, pp. 133-145.

enforcement to be brought into play to ensure conformity. Hence the formation of *ad hoc* militant vigilante groups whose detail was to rid Masabaland of all internal opposition by circumcising all defaulters. Then they were to pursue and circumcise all those Bamasaba living outside the borders of the district.

Victor Turner observed that the initiation rituals acquired a militantly nationalistic character, especially since independence, serving as a marker of identity.[362] After independence, it was felt that the Bamasaba needed a political forum for agitating for Masaba demands, to avoid marginalisation by other communities who had cultural kings. They needed a leader who would espouse Masaba cultural unity to champion Masaba interests. Hence *umuinga* (the high one) was manufactured out of necessity, to provide a socio-cultural cum socio-political front.

As regards the modern state, it has posed no threat to *imbalu* as such. Since independence, there has been a tendency towards a revival of traditional cultural institutions, which give the different communities cultural diversity. Independence brought about a thirsting for African identity where, in the words of Desmond Tutu, Christianity had made us "ashamed of being ourselves because they ... so often tried to 'circumcise' us into Europeans before allowing us to become Christians."[363] Modernity and secularism have tended to make people want to go back to their roots to find identity and meaning. This partly explains why *imbalu* has continued to survive, albeit in a modified manner.

Indeed *imbalu* is about identity, power, and culture among the Bamasaba community. Through it the initiate is made to identify with his community. It begins and ends with his lineage that supports the individuals and assimilates him as one of their own. Victor Turner could not help but exclaim that,

> Gisu circumcision ... is the 'high spot' of their ritual system ... an index of pan-tribal solidarity ... has something of a harvest festival ... a life-crisis ritual indicating the status elevation of a male individual

[362] Turner, in *Man in Africa*, p. 234.

[363] Desmond Tutu in the preface to W. B. Anderson, *The Church in East Africa, 1840-1974*. Kampala: Centenary Publishing House, 1981.

both within the wider setting and also-and crucially-within the patrilineage.[364]

The individual is presented as a candidate of a particular patri-lineage, which has invested their future in him. Through the ritual of *imbalu* the community transforms and gives him a share in the collective power and authority.

Manhood is not only a right but also a duty to internalise and live by the community's beliefs, norms and values. The individual is expected to uphold, propagate and defend them as his own. Furthermore, one is expected to hand them on to subsequent generations who will continue the stream of ancestral life through the patri-lineage. Aided by his age-set mates, and in solidarity with the wider community with whom he identifies, the individual acquires security to live, to grow, to become an elder, and finally, an ancestor.

---

[364] Turner, *Man in Africa*, p. 236.

BIBLIOGRAPHY

PRIMARY SOURCES

Name	Age	Profession	Place	Date
Bukuna, John	50	Farmer	Buketera	28. 09. 99
Malemo, Judith	26	Student	Mbale	03. 10. 98
Matanda, Abdul	53	Teacher	Bukhaweka	01. 10. 99
Matanda, Antony	49	Farmer	Bumuki	11. 09. 99
Namonyo, Steven	48	Civil Servant	Bugema	21. 08. 98
Namonywe, Praxeda	56	Retired Teacher	Musiru	28. 08. 98
Namunyala, S.	40	Teacher	Buketera	28. 09. 99
Tsemale, Lawrence	80	Retd. Teacher	Bunamboko	11. 09. 99
Tumwa, Joseph	47	Civil Servant	Namatala	05. 11. 99
Wabuti, Lawrence	59	Bookkeeper	Mbale	22. 08. 98
Wakoli J. T.	49	Religious	Nairobi	30. 12. 98
Walukhaso, F. R.	40	Farmer	Musiru	28. 08. 98
Walwanda, Wakhasa	74	Retd. Circumciser	Bumukoya	26. 09. 98
Wamono, L.	53	Telecoms Officer	Bukhaweka	22. 08. 99
Wandende, A. M.	62	Retired Civil Servant	Nakaloke	26. 11. 98
Wandende, D.	82	Farmer	Musiru	01. 10. 99
Wawomola, L.W.	68	Retd. Civ. Servant	Butiru	06.11.99

SECONDARY SOURCES

ADOGAME, AFE U. *Celestial Church of Christ: The Politics of Cultural Identity in a West African Prophetic-Charismatic Movement.* Frankfurt am Main: Peter Lang, 1999.

AHANOTU, A. M. *Religion, State and Society in Contemporary Africa.* New York: Peter Lang, 1992.

AHLBÄCK, TORE (ed.). *The Problem of Ritual.* Aboensis: Scriptura Instituti Donneriani, 1993.

ALLPORT, G.W. *The Individual and His Religion.* New York: Macmillan, 1973.

ANDERSON, William B. *The Church in East Africa.* Nairobi: Uzima 1981.

ARENS, W. and KARP, I. (eds.). *Creativity of Power: Cosmology and Action in African Societies.* Washington: Smithsonian Institution Press, 1989.

------------ *The Man-Eating Myth.* Oxford: Oxford University Press, 1980.

AYMES, MARIA DE LA CRUZ et al. (eds.). *Effective Inculturation and Ethnic Identity.* Rome: Gregorian University, 1987.

BANTON, MICHAEL. *Anthropological Approaches to the Study of Religion.* London: Tavistock Publications, 1966.

BARGATZKY, THOMAS. "Embodied Ideas: An Essay on Ritual and Politics in Pre-Capitalist Society" in Claessen, H. J. M, and Oosten, J. G. (eds.). *Ideology and the Formation of Early States.* Leiden: E. J. Brill, 1996, pp. 298-320.

---------------*Einführung in die Ethnologie.* Hamburg: Buske, 1985.

---------------and KUSCHEL, ROLF (eds.). *The Invention of Nature.* Frankfurt am Main: Peter Lang, 1994.

BARRETT, D. B. (ed.). *African Initiatives in Religion.* Nairobi: East African Publishing House, 1971.

BARRETT, L. E. "The Use of Models in Anthropological Fieldwork" in *Journal of Anthropological Research* 32 No. 2, 1976, pp. 161-181.

BAUMANN, HERMANN et al. *Völkerkunde von Afrika*: Essen: Essener Verlagsanstalt, 1940.

BEATTIE, JOHN. *Other Cultures*. London: Routledge and Kegan Paul, 1977.

BEHREND, HEIKE. *Alice Lakwena and the Holy Spirits: War in Northern Uganda 1985-97*. Kampala: Fountain Publishers, 1999.

------------and LUIG, UTE (eds.). *Spirit Possession: Modernity and Power in Africa*. Kampala: Fountain Publishers, 1999.

BELL, CATHERINE. *Ritual Theory Ritual Practice*. New York: Oxford University Press, 1992.

------------*Ritual: Perspectives and Dimensions*. Oxford: Oxford University Press, 1997.

BENEDICT, RUTH. *Patterns of Culture*. London: Routledge and Kegan Paul, 1980.

BERNER, ULRICH. "Afrikanische Gottesvorstellungen: Methodische Probleme bei der Erforschung Afrikanischer Religionen", in Preißler, Holger und Seiwert, Hubert (eds.). *Gnosisforschung und Religionsgeschichte*. Marburg: Diagonal-Verlag, 1994, pp. 367-377.

------------"Polytheismus" in *Theologische Realenzyklopädie,* Bd. 27, Berlin/New York, 1996, pp. 35-39.

------------"Mircea Eliade 1907-1986" in Michaels, Axel (ed.), *Klassiker der Religionswissenschaft. Von Friedrich Schleiermacher bis Mircea Eliade*. München, 1997, pp. 343-353.

------------"Religionswissenschaft und Religionsphilosophie" in *Zeitschrift für Religionswissenschaft* 5 (1997), pp. 149-178.

------------"Reflections upon the Concept of New Religious Movement" in Geertz, Armin W. and McCutcheon, Russell T. (eds.). *Perspectives on Method and Theory in the Study of Religion*. Köln, 2000, pp. 267-276.

BETTELHEIM, B. *Symbolic Wounds*. Glencoe, Illinois: Free Press, 1954.

BIANCHI, UGO (ed.). *Transition Rites Cosmic, Social and Individual Order*. Rome: L'erma di Breitschneider, 1986.

BLOCH, M. and Parry J. (eds.). *Introduction to Death and the Regeneration of Life*. Cambridge: Cambridge University Press, 1982.

BOHANNAN, PAUL (ed.). *African Homicide and Suicide*. New York: Atheneum, 1967.

BOLE, KEES, W. "Myth" in Eliade, Mircea (ed.). *The Encyclopedia of Religion*, Vol. 10, 1987, pp. 261-273.

BOND, GEORGE et al (eds.). *African Christianity: Patterns of Religious Continuity*. London: Academic Press, 1979.

BOOTH, NEWELL S. Jr. (ed.). *African Religions*. New York: NOK Publishers, 1979.

BOURDILLON, M. *Religion and Society*. Harare: Mambo Press, 1990.

BREITINGER, ECKHARD (ed.). *Uganda: The Cultural Landscape*. Kampala: Fountain Publishers Ltd., 1999.

BUDD, SUSAN. *Sociologists and Religion*. London: Collier-Macmillan Publishers, 1973.

CARMODY, JOHN et al. *Interpreting the Religious Experience: A Worldview*. Englewood Cliffs: Prentice-Hall, 1987.

CHIDESTER, DAVID. *Patterns of Action: Religion and Ethics in Comparative Perspective*. Belmont, California: Wadsworth Publishing Company, 1987.

------------"Colonialism" in Braun, Willi and McCutcheon, Russell T. (eds.). *Guide to the Study of Religion*. London: Cassell, 2000, pp. 423-437.

COHEN, A. *The Politics of Elite Culture*. Berkeley and Los Angeles: University of California Press, 1981.

COHEN, Y. *The Transition From Childhood to Adolescence: Cross-Cultural Studies of Initiation Ceremonies, Legal Systems and Incest Taboos*. Chicago: Aldine Publishers, 1964.

COMAROFF, JEAN. *Body of Power Spirit of Resistance*. Chicago: University of Chicago Press, 1985.

COX, JAMES L. (ed.). *Rites of Passage in Contemporary Africa*. Cardiff: Cardiff Academic Press, 1998.

------------*Rational Ancestors: Scientific Rationality and African Indigenous Religions*. Cardiff: Cardiff Academic Press, 1998.

DE WOLF, JAN JACOB. "Circumcision and Initiation in Western Kenya and Eastern Uganda" in *Anthropos* Vol 78 (1983), pp. 369-410.

DORSON, RICHARD M. *Folklore in the Modern World*. The Hague: Mouton Publishers, 1978.

DOUGLAS, MARY and Kaberry, Phyllis M. (eds.). *Man in Africa*. London: Tavistock Publications, 1969.

DOUGLAS, MARY. *Implicit Meanings: Essays in Anthropology*. London: Routledge and Kegan Paul, 1975.

------------*Ritual, Tabu und Körpersymbolik*. Frankfurt am Main: Surkamp, 1981.

------------*Essays in the Sociology of Perception*. London: Routledge and Kegan Paul, 1982.

------------*In the Active Voice*. London: Routledge and Kegan Paul, 1982.

------------*Natural Symbols: Explorations in Cosmology*. New York: Pantheon Books, 1982.

------------*Constructive Drinking: Perspectives on Drinking from Anthropology*. Cambridge: Cambridge University Press, 1989.

------------*Risk Acceptability According to the Social Sciences*. London: Routledge, 1992.

------------*Purity and Danger: An Analysis of Concepts of Pollution and Taboo*. London: Routledge, 1994.

DURKHEIM, EMILE, and Marcel Mauss. *Primitive Classification*. London: Cohen and West, 1969.

------------*The Elementary Forms of the Religious Life*. London: George Allen and Unwin, 1976.

ELIADE, MIRCEA. *Die Religionen und das Heilige: Elemente der Religionsgeschichte*. Salzburg: Otto Müller Verlag, 1954.

------------*Rites and Symbols of Initiation: The Mysteries of Birth and Rebirth*. London: Harper and Row, 1958.

------------*The Sacred and the Profane: The Nature of Religion*. New York: Harcourt, Brace and World, Inc., 1959.

------------*Ordeal by Labyrinth*. Chicago: Chicago University Press, 1982.

EVANS-PRITCHARD. *The Position of Women in Primitive Societies and Other Essays in Social Anthropology*. London: Faber and Faber Ltd. 1965.

------------et al. *The Institutions of Primitive Society*. Oxford: Basil Blackwell, 1967.

------------*Witchcraft, Oracles, and Magic Among the Azande*. Oxford: Oxford University Press, 1976.

ELZEY, WAYNE. "Mircea Eliade and the Battle against Reductionism" in Idinopulos, T. A. and Yonan, E. A. (eds.). *Religion and Reductionism: Essays on Eliade, Segal, and the Challenge of the Social Sciences for the Study of Religion*. Leiden: E. J. Brill, 1994, pp. 83-94.

FASHOLE-LUKE, E., et al (eds.). *Christianity in Independent Africa*. Bloomington: Indiana University Press, 1978.

FERNANDEZ, JAMES W. *Bwiti: An Ethnography of the Religious Imagination in Africa*. Princeton: Princeton University Press, 1982.

FETTERMAN, DAVID M. *Ethnography*. London: Sage Publications, 1998.

FIEDLER, KLAUS. *Christianity and African Culture*. Leiden: E.J. Brill, 1996

FIRTH, RAYMOND. *Symbols, Public and Private*. London: Allen and Unwin, 1973.

------------(ed.). *Man and Culture*. London: Routledge and Kegan Paul, 1980.

FORTES, MEYER. *The Dynamics of Clanship Among the Tallensi*. London: Oxford University Press, 1945.

------------*The Web of Kinship Among the Tallensi*. London: Oxford University Press, 1949.

------------"Pietas in Ancestor Worship", in *Journal of the Royal Anthropological Institute* 91 (1961), pp. 166-191.

------------and Dieterlen, G. (eds.). *African Systems of Thought*. London: Oxford University Press, 1965.

------------*Kinship and the Social Order*. London: Routledge and Kegan Paul, 1969.

------------(ed.). *Marriage in Tribal Societies*. Cambridge: Cambridge University Press, 1982.

FRAZER, SIR J. G. *The Belief in Immortality and the Worship of the Dead*. London: Macmillan, 1913.

GEERTZ, CLIFFORD. *The Interpretation of Cultures*. New York: Basic Books, 1973.

------------*Local Knowledge*. New York: Basic Books, Inc., 1983.

GIFFORD, PAUL. *African Christianity: Its Public Role*. London: Hurst and Company, 1998.

GLUCKMAN, MAX. *Custom and Conflict in Africa*. Oxford: Basil Blackwell, 1956.

------------*Order and Rebellion in Tribal Africa*. London: Cohen, 1963.

------------(ed.). *The Allocation of Responsibility*. Manchester: Manchester University Press, 1972

GORT, JERALD et al (eds.). *Dialogue and Syncretism: An Interdisciplinary Approach*. Michigan: William B. Ferdmans Publishing Company, 1989.

GRAINGER, ROGER. *The Language of the Rite*. London: Longman and Todd, 1974.

GRAY, RICHARD. *Black Christians and White Missionaries*. London: Yale University Press, 1990.

GRIMES, RONALD L. *Beginnings in Ritual Studies*. London: University Press of America, 1982.

------------*Ritual Criticism*. Columbia: University of South Carolina Press, 1990.

------------"Ritual" in Braun, Willi and McCutcheon, Russell (eds.). *Guide to the Study of Religion*. London: Cassell, 2000, pp. 259-270.

GROTTANELLI, CRISTIANO and Bruce Lincoln, "A Brief Note on (Future) Research in the History of Religions" in *Method and Theory in the Study of Religion* 10 (1989), pp. 311-325.

GULLIVER, P. H. *Social Control in an African Society*. London: Routledge and Kegan Paul, 1968.

------------and Pamela Gulliver, *The Central Nilo-Himites*. London: London: International African Institute, 1968.

------------*Tradition and Transition in East Africa.* London: Routledge and Kegan Paul, 1972.

GUTHRIE, MALCOLM. *The Classification of the Bantu Languages.* London: Oxford University Press, 1948.

HALL, STUART, and Tony Jefferson (eds.). *Resistance Through Rituals.* London: Harper Collins Academic, 1991.

HALL, WILLIAM T. *Religion: An Introduction.* San Francisco: Harper and Row Publishers, 1985.

HAMMERSLEY, MARTYN. *Reading Ethnographic Research.* London: Longman Publishers, 1991.

HANSEN, H.B., et al (eds.). *Changing Uganda.* Kampala: Fountain Press, 1991.

HEALD, SUZETTE. "The Making of Men: The Relevance of Vernacular Psychology to the Interpretation of a Gisu Ritual" in *Africa* 52 (1982), pp. 15-36.

------------"Witches and Thieves: Deviant Motivations in Gisu Society" in *Man* ns. 21/1 (1986), pp. 65-78.

------------"Mafias in Africa: The Rise of Drinking Companies and Vigilante Groups in Bugisu District, Uganda" in *Africa* 56 (1986), pp. 446-467.

------------*Controlling Anger: The Sociology of Gisu Violence.* Manchester: Manchester University Press, 1989.

------------*Manhood and Morality: Sex, Violence and Ritual in Gisu Society.* London: Routledge, 1999.

HERDT, G. H. (ed.). *Rituals of Manhood: Male Initiation in Papua New Guinea.* Berkeley, Los Angeles and London: University of California Press, 1982.

HERRICK, ALLISON BUTLER et al. *Area Handbook for Uganda.* Washington D.C.: U.S. Government Printing Office, 1969.

HERSKOVITS, M. J. *Man and His Works: The Science of Cultural Anthropology.* New York: Knopf, 1948.

HERTZ, ROBERT. *Death and the Right Hand.* Glencoe, Illinois: The Free Press, 1960.

HICK, JOHN. *A Christian Theology of Religions*. Louisville, Kentucky: John Knox Press, 1995.

HORTON, ROBIN. "Judaeo Christian Spectacles: Boon or Bane to the Study of African Religions?" in *Cahiers d'Etudes Africaines* (1984), pp. 391-435.

HORWITZ, ALLAN, V. *The Logic of Social Control*. New York: Plenum Press, 1990.

HUNTINGFORD, G. W. B. *The Nandi of Kenya: Tribal Control in a Pastoral Society*. London: Routledge and Kegan Paul, 1982.

IDOWU, BOLAJI. *Towards an Indigenous Church*. London: Oxford University Press, 1965.

------------*African Traditional Religion: A Definition*. London: SCM Press, 1973.

IKENGA-METUH, E., *God and Man in African Religion*. London: Chapman, 1981.

------------(ed.). *The Gods in Retreat: Continuity and Change in African Religion*. Enugu: Fourth Dimension Publishers, 1985.

------------*African Religions in Western Conceptual Schemes: The Problem of Interpretation*. Jos: IMICO Press, 1991.

------------*African Inculturation Theology: Africanizing Christianity*. Onitsha: IMICO Books, 1996.

JAMES, WILLIAM. *The Varieties of Religious Experience*. London: Harvard University Press, 1985.

JANOWTZ, MORRIS. *On Social Organisation and Social Control*. Chicago. University of Chicago Press, 1991.

JULES-ROSETTE, BENNETTA (ed.). *The New Religions of Africa*. Norwood, New Jersey: Ablex Publishing Corporation, 1979.

KABASELE, FRANCOIS. "Sacramental Inculturation in Zaire" in *Lumen Vitae* Vol. 42, No. 2/3 (1987), pp. 281-290.

KALU, OGBU U. "Gods in Retreat: Models of Religious Change in Africa" in *Nigerian Journal of the Humanities*. University of Benin, No. 1 (1977), pp. 42-53.

------------(ed.). *Readings in African Humanities: African Cultural Development*. Enugu: Fourth Division Publishers, 1978.

------------*The Embattled Gods: Christianisation of Igboland 1841-1991*. Lagos: Minaj Publishers, 1996.

------------*Power, Poverty and Prayer*. Frankfurt am Main: Peter Lang, 2000.

KAYODE, J. O. *Understanding African Traditional Religion*. Ile-Ife, Nigeria: University of Ife Press, 1984.

KENYATTA, JOMO. *Facing Mount Kenya*. London: Heinemann, 1985.

KING, NOEL Q. *African Cosmos: An Introduction to Religion in Africa*. Belmont: Wadsworth Publishing Company, 1986.

KITAGAWA, JOSEPH M. (ed.). *The History of Religions: Retrospect and Prospect*. London: Collier Macmillan Publishers, 1985.

LA FONTAINE, Jean S. *The Gisu of Uganda*. London: InternationalAfrican Institute, 1959.

------------"Segmentary Societies in Uganda: The Gisu" in Richards, Audrey (ed.). *East African Chiefs*. London: Faber and Faber, 1960, pp. 260-277.

------------"Gisu Marriage and Affinal Relationships" in Fortes Meyer (ed.). *Marriage in Tribal Societies*. Cambridge: Cambridge University Press, 1962, pp. 88-120.

------------"Homicide and Suicide Among the Gisu" in Bohannan, Paul (ed.). *African Homicide and Suicide*. New York: Atheneum, 1967, pp. 94-129.

------------"Parricide in Bugisu: Study in Intergenerational Conflict" in *Man* Vol. 2 No. 2 (1967), pp. 249-259.

------------"Tribalism Among the Gisu" in Gulliver, P. H. (ed.). *Tradition and Transition in East Africa*. London: Routledge and Kegan Paul, 1972, pp. 177-192.

------------(ed.). *The interpretation of Ritual*. London: Tavistock, 1972.

------------"The Power of Rights" in *Man*. n.s. Vol. 12, No. 1 (1977), pp. 421-437.

------------"Witchcraft in Bugisu" in Middleton, John and Winter E. H. (eds.). *Witchcraft and Sorcery in East Africa.* London: Routledge and Kegan Paul, 1978, pp. 187-220.

------------"Land and the Political Community in Bugisu" in Shack, W. A. and Cohen, P. S. (eds.). *Politics in Leadership: A Comparative Perspective.* Oxford: Oxford University Press, 1979, pp. 95-114.

------------"The Domestication of the Savage Male" in *Man* n.s. Vol. 16 No. 2 (1981), pp. 333-349.

------------*Initiation.* Manchester: Manchester University Press, 1986.

LAITIN, DAVID D. *Hegemony and Culture.* Chicago: Univ. of Chicago Press, 1986.

LAMB, DAVID. *The Africans: Encounters From the Sudan to the Cape.* London: Methuen London Ltd., 1985.

LAWSON, E. THOMAS and McCauley, Robert N. *Rethinking Religion: Connecting Cognition and Culture.* Cambridge: Cambridge University Press, 1990.

------------*Religions of Africa. Traditions in Transformation.* San Francisco. Harper and Row, 1984.

LEACH, EDMUND. "Sermons By a Man on a Ladder" in *The New York Review* (October 20th 1966), pp. 28-31.

------------(ed.). *Dialectic in Practical Religion.* Cambridge: Cambridge University Press, 1968.

------------*Culture and Communication: The Logic by which Symbols are Connected.* Cambridge: Cambridge University Press, 1976.

------------(ed.). *The Structural Study of Myth and Totemism.* London: Tavistock Publications, 1988.

LEWIS, G. *Day of Shining Red: An Essay on Understanding Ritual.* Cambridge: Cambridge University Press, 1980.

LEWIS, I. M. *Ecstatic Religion.* Harmondsworth: Penguin Books, 1971.

LINCOLN, BRUCE. "Theses on Method" in *Method and Theory in the Study of Religion* 8-3 (1996), pp. 225-227.

------------"Culture" in Braun, Willi and McCutcheon, Russell T. (eds.). *Guide to the Study of Religion.* London: Cassell, 2000, pp. 409-422.

LITTLE, K. L. *The Mende of Sierra Leone: A West African People in Transition.* London: Routledge and Kegan Paul, 1951.

LUTAHOIRE, SEBASTIAN K. *The Human Life Cycle Among the Bantu.* Arusha: Makumira Publication, 1974.

LUTZBETAK, LOUIS J. *The Church and Cultures: An Applied Anthropology for the Religious Worker.* California: William Carey Library, 1970.

------------*The Church and Cultures.* South Pasadena: William Carey, 1977.

MACCORMACK, C. P. and M. Strathern (eds.). *Nature, Culture and Gender.* Cambridge: Cambridge University Press, 1980.

MAGESA, LAURENTI. "The Present and Future of Inculturation in East Africa" in *Jahrbuch für Kontextuelle Theologien.* Frankfurt am Main: 1994, pp. 129-146.

------------*African Religion: The Moral Traditions of Abundant Life.* Maryknoll, New York: Orbis Books, 1997.

MAIR, L. *Primitive Government.* London: Penguin Books, 1962.

MALINOWSKI, BRONISLAW. *Crime and Custom in Savage Society.* London: Kegan Paul, 1926.

------------*Magic, Science and Religion.* Glencoe, Illinois: The Free Press, 1945.

------------*The Dynamics of Culture Change.* New Haven: Yale University Press, 1961.

MARTEY, EMMANUEL. *African Theology: Inculturation and Liberation.* New York: Orbis Books, 1993.

MARTOS, JOSEPH. *Doors to the Sacred.* New York: Doubleday, 1981.

MBITI, J. S. *Concepts of God in Africa.* London: SPCK, 1971.

------------*New Testament Eschatology in an African Background: A Study of Encounter Between New Testament Theology and African Traditional Concepts.* London: Oxford University Press, 1971.

------------*The Prayers of African Religion.* Maryknoll, New York: Orbis Books, 1975.

------------*African Religions and Philosophy.* London: Heinemann, 1982.

-----------*Bible and Theology in African Christianity.* London: Oxford University Press, 1986.

McCUTCHEON, RUSSELL T. *Manufacturing Religion: The Discourse on Sui Generis Religion and the Politics of Nostalgia.* Oxford: Oxford University Press, 1997.

------------"Myth" in Braun, Willi and McCutcheon, Russell T. (eds.). *Guide to the Study of Religion.* London: Cassell, 2000, pp. 190-208.

MIDDLETON, J. *Lugbara Religion: Ritual and Authority among the East African People.* London: Oxford University Press, 1960.

------------and WINTER, E. H. *Witchcraft and Sorcery in East Africa.* London: Routledge and Kegan Paul, 1978.

MISZTAL, BRONISLAW and Anson Shupe. *Religion and Politics in Comparative Perspective.* London: Praeger, 1992.

MOL, HANS. *Identity and the Sacred: A Sketch for New Social-Scientific Theory of Religion.* New York: The Free Press, 1977.

NJUGUNA, GITAU SAMSON. *A Comparative Study of the Transmission, Actualization and Stabilization of Oral Traditions.* Boston: Boston University Press, 1994.

NTHAMBURI, ZABLON. *From Mission to Church.* Nairobi: Uzima Press, 1991.

------------*The African Church at the Crossroads: Strategy for Indigenization.* Nairobi: Uzima Press, 1991.

NYAMITI, CHARLES. *The Scope of African Theology.* Kampala: Gaba Publications, 1973.

------------*African Tradition and the Christian God.* Eldoret, Kenya: Gaba Publications, 1977.

------------*Christ as Our Ancestor.* Gweru: Mambo Press, 1984.

NYANG, SULAYMAN S. *Islam, Christianity, and African Identity.* Vermont: Amana Books, 1984.

O'DEA, THOMAS F. and Janet O'Dea Aviad. *The Sociology of Religion.* Englewood-Cliffs: Prentice-Hall, 1983.

O'DONOHUE, JOHN. *New Wine and Old Bottles.* Uppsala: Reprocentralen HSC, 1994.

ONWUBIKO, OLIVER A. *Theory and Practice of Inculturation*. Enugu: SNAAP Press, 1992.

OOSTHUIZEN, G. C. *Post-Christianity in Africa*. London: C. Hurst and Co., 1968.

------------et al (eds.). *Afro-Christianity at the Grassroots: Its Dynamics and Strategies*. Leiden: E. J. Brill, 1994.

ORTNER, S. and WHITEHEAD, H. (eds.). *Sexual Meanings*. New York: Oxford University Press, 1981.

OTTENBERG, SIMON. *Boyhood Rituals in an African Society: An Interpretation*. Seattle and London: University of Washington Press, 1989.

P'BITEK, OKOT. *Africa's Cultural Revolution*. Nairobi: Macmillan Books, 1973.

------------*African Religions in Western Scholarship*. *Kampala*: Uganda Literature Bureau, 1980.

PANIKKAR, R. *The Intra-Religious Dialogue*. New York: Paulist Press, 1978.

PARK, ROBERT E. *On Social Control and Collective Behaviour*. Chicago: The University of Chicago Press, 1967.

PARRATT, JOHN (ed.). *African Christian Theology*. London: SPCK, 1987.

PARRINDER, E. G. *African Traditional Religion*. London: Sheldon Press, 1976.

------------*African Mythology*. London: Hamlyn, 1982.

PENNER, HANS H. "Interpretation" in Braun, Willi and McCutcheon, Russell T. (eds.). *Guide to the Study of Religion*. London: Cassell, 2000, pp. 57-71.

PICKERING, W. S. F. *Durkheim on Religion*. London: Routledge and Kegan Paul, 1975.

PIROUET, LOUISE M. *Black Evangelists: The Spread of Christianity in Uganda 1891-1914*. London: Rex Collings, 1978.

PLATVOET, JAN (ed.). *The Study of Religions in Africa: Past, Present and Prospects*. Cambridge: Roots and Branches, 1996.

POBEE, JOHN, and Carl F. Hellencreutz (eds.). *Variations in Christian Theology in Africa.* Nairobi: Uzima Press, 1986.

PURVIS, J. B. *Through Uganda to Mount Elgon.* London: T. Fisher Unwin, 1909.

RADCLIFFE-BROWN, A. R. "On Joking Relationships" in *Africa* 13, (1940), pp. 195-210.

------------"A Further Note on Joking Relationships" in *Africa* 19 (1949), pp. 133-140.

------------*Structure and Function in Primitive Society.* Glenicoe, Illinois: The Free Press, 1952.

RAY, BENJAMIN C. *African Religions: Symbol, Ritual, and Community.* Englewood-Cliffs: Prentice-Hall, 1976.

RENNIE, BRYAN S. *Reconstructing Eliade: Making Sense of Religion.* New York: State University of New York Press, 1996.

------------(ed.). *Changing Religious Worlds: The Meaning and End of Mircea Eliade.* New York: State University of New York Press, 2000.

RICHARDS, A. I. "Social Mechanisms for the Transfer of Political Rights in Some African Tribes" in *Journal of the Royal Anthropological Institute* Vol. 9 (1960), pp. 175-190.

------------(ed.). *East African Chiefs.* London: Faber and Faber, 1960.

------------*Chisungu: A Girl's Initiation Ceremony Among the Bemba of Zambia.* London: Tavistock Publications, 1982.

RICKETTS, MAC LINSCOTT. "In Defence of Eliade: Toward Bridging the Communication Gap Between Anthropology and the History of Religions" in *Religion, Journal of Religion and Religions* 3 (1973), pp. 13-34.

RIESZ, JANOS, et al (eds.). *Approaches to African Identity.* Bayreuth: Universität Bayreuth, 1986.

ROBBINS, THOMAS. *Cults, Converts and Charisma: The Sociology of the New Religious Movements.* 1988.

ROSALDO, M. A. and Lamphere, L. *Woman, Culture and Society.* Stanford, California: Stanford University Press, 1974.

ROSBERG, C. G. and NOTTINGHAM, J. *The Myth of Mau-Mau Nationalism in Kenya*. Nairobi: East African Publishing House, 1966.

ROSCOE, JOHN. *The Baganda: An Account of Some of the Native Customs and Beliefs*. London: Macmillan and Company, 1911.

------------*The Bagesu and Other Tribes of the Uganda Protectorate*. Cambridge: Cambridge University Press, 1924.

------------*The Northern Bantu*. London: Frank Cass and Co. Ltd., 1966.

ROSMAN, ABRAHAM and Paul Rubel (eds.). *The Tapestry of Culture: Introduction to Cultural Anthropology*. Boston: McGraw Hill, 2001.

RUEL, MALCOLM. *Belief, Ritual and the Securing of Life*. Leiden: E. J. Brill, 1997.

SANDERSON, STEPHEN K. *Social Evolutionism: A Critical History*. Oxford: Basil Blackwell, 1990.

SCHINELLER, PETER. *Inculturation: A Handbook*. New York: Paulist Press, 1990.

SCHNEIDER, H. et al (eds.). *The Impact of Modern Culture on Traditional Religions*. Leiden: E. J. Brill, 1968.

SHACK, WILLIAM A. and Percy S. Cohen (eds.). *Politics in Leadership: A Comparative Perspective*. Oxford: Clarendon Press, 1979.

SHAPIRO, H. L. (ed.). *Man, Culture and Society*. New York: 1960.

SHAUGHNESSY, J. D., ed. *The Roots of Ritual*. Grand Rapids: W. B. Ferdmans Publications, 1973.

SHORTER, A., et al. *Towards African Christian Maturity*. Nairobi: St. Paul Publications, 1987.

------------*Songs and Symbols of Initiation: A Study from Africa in the Social Control of Perception*. Nairobi: CHIEA Press, 1987.

SKORUPSKI, J. *Symbol and Theory: A Philosophical Study of Theories of Religion*. Cambridge: Cambridge University Press, 1976.

SMART, NINIAN. *Worldviews: Cross-Cultural Explorations of Human Beliefs*. New York: Charles Scribner's Sons, 1983.

------------*Concept and Empathy*. Basingstoke: Macmillan, 1986.

------------*Religion and the Western Mind*. Basingstoke: Macmillan, 1987.

------------ *The Religious Experience*. New York: Macmillan, 1991.

------------*Buddhism and Christianity: Rivals and Allies.* Basingstoke: Macmillan, 1993.

------------*The World's Religions.* Cambridge: Cambridge University Press, 1998.

SMITH, EDWIN W. *African Symbolism.* London: Royal Anthropological Institute, 1952.

SMITH, WILFRED CANTWELL. *The Meaning and End of Religion.* San Francisco: Harper and Row, 1978.

SPENCER, P. *The Samburu: A Study of Gerontology in a Nomadic Tribe.* London: Routledge and Kegan Paul, 1965.

------------*Nomads in Alliance: Symbiosis and Growth Among the Rendille and Samburu of Kenya.* London: Oxford University Press, 1973.

SPERBER, DAN. *Rethinking Symbolism.* Transl. Morton, A. L. Cambridge: Cambridge University Press, 1975.

STAAL, FRITS. "The Meaninglessness of Ritual" in *Numen* Vol. xxvi Fasc. 1 (1979), pp. 2-22.

------------*Rules Without Meaning.* New York: Peter Lang, 1989.

STARK, RODNEY and BAINBRIDGE, WILLIAM SIMS. *The Future of Religion: Secularization, Revival and Cult Formation.* Berkeley: University of California Press, 1985.

STEWARD, J. H. *Theory of Culture Change.* Urbana: University of Illinois Press, 1963.

STEWART, CHARLES, and Shaw, Rosalind. *Syncretism/Anti-Syncretism: The Politics of Religious Synthesis.* London: Routledge, 1994.

STRAYER, ROBERT W. *The Making of Mission Communities in East Africa.* London: Heinemann, 1978.

SULLIVAN, LAWRENCE. *Icanchu's Drum.* London: Collier Macmillan Publishers, 1988.

SUNDERMEIER; THEO. *The Individual and Community in African Traditional Religions.* Hamburg: LIT Verlag, 1998.

SUNDKLER, BEGT. *The Christian Ministry in Africa.* Uppsala: Almquist and Wiksells, 1960.

TAMBIAH, STANLEY JEYARAJA. *Culture, Thought, and Social Action: An Anthropological Perspective.* Cambridge: Harvard University Press, 1985.

------------*Magic, Science, Religion, and the Scope of Rationality.* Cambridge: Cambridge University Press, 1990.

TEMPELS, PLACIDE. *Bantu Philosophie.* Paris: E.T., 1959.

TIBERONDWA, ADO K. *Missionary Teachers as Agents of Colonialism.* Lusaka: Associated Press, 1989.

TURNER, VICTOR W. "Symbolisation and Patterning in the Circumcision Rites of Two Bantu-speaking Societies" in Douglas, M. and Kaberry, P. (eds.). *Man in Africa.* London: Tavistock Publications, 1969, pp. 229-244.

------------"Symbols in Ndembu Ritual" in Emmet, Dorothy and MacIntyre, Alasdair (eds.). *Sociological Theory and Philosophical Analysis.* London: Macmillan, 1970, pp. 150-182.

------------ *The Forest of Symbols: Aspects of Ndembu Ritual.* London: Cornell University Press, 1973.

------------"Metaphors of Anti-Structure in Religious Culture" in Eister, Allan W. (ed.). *Changing Perspectives in the Scientific Study of Religion.* New York: Wiley, 1974, pp. 63-84.

------------"Three Symbols of Passage in Ndembu Circumcision Ritual: An Interpretation" in Gluckman, Max (ed.). *Essays on the Ritual of Social Relations.* Manchester: Manchester University Press, 1975, pp. 124-173.

------------*The Ritual Process: Structure and Anti-Structure.* New York: Aldine Publishing Company, 1979.

------------"Myth and Symbol", in Sills, D. (ed.). *The International Encyclopedia of the Social Sciences.* New York: Macmillan Publishers, 1979, pp. 576-582.

------------*The Drums of Affliction: A Study of Religious Processes Among the Ndembu of Zambia.* London: International African Institute, 1981.

------------*On the Edge of the Bush.* Tucson, Arizona: University of Arizona Press, 1985.

TWADDLE, MICHAEL. *Kakungulu and the Creation of Uganda.* Kampala: Fountain Publishers, 1993.

TWESIGYE, EMMANUEL K. *Common Ground: Christianity, African Religion and Philosophy.* New York: Peter Lang, 1987.

UDOH, ENYI BEN. *Guest Christology: An Interpretative View of the Christological Problem in Africa.* Frankfurt am Main: Peter Lang, 1988.

UKA, E. M. (ed.). *Readings in African Traditional Religion: Structure, Meaning, Relevance, Future.* Frankfurt a. M.: Peter Lang, 1991.

UKPONG, JUSTIN S. *Sacrifice African and Biblical.* Rome: Urbaniana University Press, 1987.

VAN BAAREN; TH. P. and H.J.W. Drijvers (eds.). *Religion, Culture and Methodology.* The Hague: Mouton, 1973.

VAN GENNEP, ARNOLD. *The Rites of Passage.* Chicago: University of Chicago Press, 1960.

WALAKIRA, Lawrence. "Circumcision Ceremony Among the Bagisu", in *The Second National Theological Week* (August 1983), pp. 161-167.

WALLIS, ROY (ed.). *Sectarianism: Analyses of Religious and Non-Religious Sects.* New York: Halsted Press, 1975.

WANGUSA, TIMOTHY. *Upon This Mountain.* London: Heinemann, 1989.

-------------*A Pattern of Dust.* Kampala: Fountain Publishers, 1994.

WELBOURN, F. B. *East African Christian.* Nairobi: Oxford University Press, 1965.

------------*Religion and Politics in Uganda 1952-1962.* Nairobi: East African Publishing House, 1965.

------------and OGOT, B. A. *A Place to Feel at Home.* Nairobi: Oxford University Press, 1966.

WERBNER, RICHARD P. *Ritual Passage, Sacred Journey.* Manchester: Manchester University Press, 1989.

WIEBE, DONALD. "Modernism" in Braun, Willi and McCutcheon, Russell T. (eds.). *Guide to the Study of Religion.* London: Cassell, 2000, pp. 351-379.

WILSON, M. *Rituals of Kinship Among the Nyakyusa*. London: Oxford University Press, 1957.

------------*Communal Rituals Among the Nyakyusa*. London: Oxford University Press, 1959.

WINTER, J. C. *Bruno Gutmann: A German Approach to Social Anthropology*. Oxford: Clarendon Press, 1979.

WIPPER, AUDREY. *Rural Rebels: A Study of Two Protest Movements in Kenya*. Nairobi: Oxford University Press, 1977.

ZUESSE, EVAN M. *Ritual Cosmos: The Sanctification of Life in African Religions*. Ohio: Ohio Univ. Press, 1979.

INDEX

259

Bayreuth African Studies

ECKHARD BREITINGER
New and forthcoming titles
2004

BASS 60
Onookome Okome: (ed) *Writing the Homeland:The Poetry and Politics of Tanure Ojaide*, 285 pp; ISBN 3-927510-67-X, EUR 22.95;

BASS 63
Bode Omojola: *Studies in African Pianism* 125 pp; ISBN 3-927510-76-9; EUR 10.95;

BASS 64
Bode Omojola *Three Yoruba Sacred Choral Works*, pp 84, ISBN 3-927510-77-7; EUR 10.95

BASS 65
Renè Philombe: *Bedi-Ngula, L'Ancien Maquisard* – *Un Roman*, pp 315, ISBN 3-927510-78-5; EUR 22.95

BASS 66
Wole Ogundele: *Omoluabi Ulli Beier, Yoruba Society and Culture*, 288 pp. ISBN 3-927510-79-3; EUR 22.95;

BASS 67
Ambroise Kom (ed): *Remember Mongo Beti*, pp 285, ISBN 3-927510-80-7; EUR 24.95;

BASS 68
Wotsuna Khamalwa: *Identity, Power, and Culture: Imbalu Initiantion among the Bamasaba in Uganda*, ca. 280 pp, ISBN 3-927510-81-5; ca EUR 22.99; (February 2004)

BASS 69
Alexi Tcheuyap (ed.): *Cinema and Social Discourse in Cameroon*, ca pp 220, ISBN 3-927510-82-3 EUR 22.59; (May 2004)

BASS 70
Haike Frank: *Role-Play in South African Theatre*, ca 325 pp; ISBN 3-927510-83-1 ca. EUR 24.95; (February 2004)

BASS 71
Akintune Akinyemi: *Yoruba Royal Poetry*, ca 410pp ISBN 3-927510-84-X, ca EUR 30.95 (April 2004)

Derek Wright *The Novels of Nuruddin Farah* now available in a revised, updated, enlarged edition with new chapters on *Secrets* and Farah's Non-fiction book. (ISBN 3-927510-85-8,EUR 18.95). When it first appeared, this study was praised as „a landmark" in criticism of postcolonial writers.
Revised, enlarged edition of Eckhard Breitinger (ed.)*Theatre and Performance in Africa* (236 pp, ISBN 3-927510-73-4, EUR 23.95) with new article on Soyinka's *Area Boy*. „ An important source for African Theatre" – Martin Banham

---

orders to Bayreuth African Studies / Eckhard Breitinger
eckhard.breitinger@uni-bayreuth.de or
Fax: 49-921- 55 3627 or 49-921-30728.
University of Bayreuth D 95440 BAYREUTH
www.breitinger.org

e-mail: eckhard.breitinger@uni-bayreuth.de

What the critics say....

„Bayreuth African Studies produces a stream of texts on African cultural issues that few British or American publishers appear able to rival... I wish to applaud the result of the endeavour"
Jane Plastow in *African Theatre Playwrights and Politics*

„une collection riche en publications de grande qualité" Abdourahman Waberi in *Hommes & Migration*

On BASS 30: Anglophone Cameroon Writing
„an important landmark in the critical discourse of Cameroon literature as a whole"
Teddy Ako in *Cameroon Post*

ON BASS 31: Breitinger: Theatre and Performance in Africa
„presents an excellent array of texts, good to pass on to students and colleagues"
Gaurav Desai in *Research in African Literature* (USA)
„an important resource for all concerned with African Theatre"
Martin Banham in *TheatreResearch International* (UK)

On BASS 32 Derek Wright: *The Novels of Nuruddin Farah.*
"a landmark in the criticism of the African novel"
Jaqueline Bardolph in *Research in African Literature* (USA*)*
„an admirable first book on Farah and indispensable reading"
Journal of Commonwealth Literature (UK)
„a most reliable critic, a rigourous scholar and yet a clearly a fan of the author"
Stewart Brown in *African Affairs* (UK)
„ an insightful introduction to Farah's work.   Chris Dunton in *West Africa* (UK)
„Readers of Farah are in Wright's debt for his research"
R.W. Dasenbrock in *World Literature Today* (USA)
„un rapporto attivo ed intelligente..con pregio di nuovi stimolanti interrogativi"
Maria Guarducci in *Africa* (Italy)

On BASS 39 Breitinger. Uganda: The Cultural Landscape
„Breitinger has done Isis work..gathered and remembered the scattered fragments – a rediscovered Rosetta stone"   Peter Nazareth in *World Literature Today* (USA)

On BASS 40 Obafemi: Contemporary Nigerian Theatre
„Obafemi knows his subject very well and his passion for theatre is in no doubt"
Osita Okagube in *African Theatre* (UK*)*

On BASS 42 Wright: Contemporary African Fiction
„Wright's distinguished scholarship guarantees that the contributions are so various, engaging and scholarly"   Anne Collet in *New Literature Review* (Australia)
„the articles demonstrate the complexity with which African writers relate to changing national landscapes and offer enlightening close reading"   Cecilia Moretti in *Review Journal* (Australia)

On BASS 43 Kerr: Dance, Media Entertainment & Popular Theatre
„Kerr is writing provocative and thoughtful good sense"
Jane Plastow in *African Theatre:Writers and Politics* (UK*)*

On BASS 48 Arndt: African Women's Literature
On BASS 49 Rohmer: Theatre and Performance in Zimbabwe
„another welcome nail in the coffin of library based criticism of African theatre"
Jane Plastow in *African Theatre*: (UK)

On BASS 55 Simatei: The Novel and the Politics of Nation Building
„a brilliant book"   Peter Nazareth in *World Literature Today* (USA)